RELIGION, TRUTH AND LANGUAGE-GAMES

LIBRARY OF PHILOSOPHY AND RELIGION

General Editor: John Hick, H. G. Wood Professor of
Theology,
University of Birmingham

This new series of books will explore contemporary religious understandings of man and the universe. The books will be contributions to various aspects of the continuing dialogues between religion and philosophy, between scepticism and faith, and between the different religions and ideologies. The authors will represent a correspondingly wide range of viewpoints. Some of the books in the series will be written for the general educated public and others for a more specialised philosophical or theological readership.

Already published

Further titles in preparation

RELIGION, TRUTH AND LANGUAGE-GAMES

Patrick Sherry

First published 1977 by
THE MACMILLAN PRESS LTD
London and Basingstoke
Associated companies in New York
Dublin Melbourne Johannesburg and Madras

ISBN 0 333 19710 0

Printed in Great Britain by
Billings & Sons Limited
Guildford, London
and Worcester

Contents

Preface

The later work of Ludwig Wittgenstein is of such importance that it impinges on nearly all the main areas of philosophy. Yet it is difficult to assess its relevance and value for the philosophy of religion. The work done so far in this direction is, I believe, disappointing, largely because it has either side-stepped the questions of religious truth and the rationality of religious belief, or else it has adopted a relativist standpoint on these issues. My aim now is to advance the discussion by suggesting a different way in which the work of Wittgenstein and some of his followers might be developed. This book should be viewed as an exploration, rather than a book about Wittgenstein. Since he wrote comparatively little about religion, I think that it would be a mistake to try to develop a Wittgensteinian philosophy of religion as such (whatever that might be). Rather, we should explore the issues of religious language, ways of life, truth and understanding which naturally arise from a consideration of religion in the light of Wittgenstein's philosophy. It will be found that his philosophical ideas have interesting and important implications for religious questions. I shall therefore consider whether there are indeed religious 'language-games' and 'forms of life' and, if so, what their nature would be and what sort of reasoning would be appropriate within them. I shall also discuss the importance of Wittgenstein's work for many specific issues, e.g. that of spirituality. I shall take particular account of the question of religious truth, and will try to show that one can both derive benefit from Wittgenstein and do justice to a propositional conception of religious truth.

Since this book is exploratory, its function is not to argue a case. But I believe that a view about the nature of religious belief will emerge: religion is essentially a response to experience, like art, science and many other spheres of life. It is a form of human behaviour, but one which depends on certain external facts, involves special responses (e.g. worship) and concepts, and has its own ends, especially the spiritual renewal of man. Clearly this account leaves us with the problem of where religious doctrines fit in (particularly metaphysical ones) and of the nature of their truth. I will suggest that the role of many religious doctrines is to describe and explain the possibilities of spiritual transformation which are available to men if they respond to the world in certain ways.

This work owes a lot to John Clayton, Steve Katz, and Barry Richards who have seen and discussed chapters of an earlier draft; and to Christopher and Elizabeth Hookway who have given me unfailing encouragement over the years, and have reminded me of what it is to practise a religion (as opposed to just writing about it). I would also like to thank the editors of *Philosophy*, *Theology*, the *American Philosophical Quarterly* and the *Heythrop Journal* for letting me use material published in their journals. I am grateful, too, to Mrs Geraldine Towers for her excellent typing. But my greatest debt of gratitude is reserved for Professor D. M. MacKinnon. It would be impossible to estimate how much I have gained from the numerous discussions which I have had with him, and from the unstinting way in which he devoted his time to my problems and shared his profound insights into them with me. Moreover, his vast range of learning has been immensely helpful in suggesting new lines of thought and areas of research. It has been a privilege, as well as a pleasure, to work with him.

P.S.

University of Lancaster

References and Abbreviations

To reduce the number of footnotes in this work, I have adopted the practice of putting abbreviated references in the text and giving fuller details in the bibliography. Such references are indicated by the author's name and, where I cite more than one work by the same author, a number in parentheses. For example, consultation of the bibliography will show that Holmer (6) p. 358 is an abbreviation for

Holmer, Paul, 'Theology and Belief', *Theology Today* (Oct 1965) p. 358.

In addition, I have used a number of other abbreviations in the text, of which these are the most important:

Aquinas, St Thomas

S.T. Summa Theologiae

C.G. Summa contra Gentiles

Barth, Karl

C.D. Church Dogmatics (English translation)

Newman, John Henry, Cardinal

U.S. University Sermons

G. A. An Essay in aid of a Grammar of Assent

Wittgenstein, Ludwig

T. Tractatus Logico-Philosophicus

P.R. Philosophical Remarks (references by section number)

P.G. Philosophical Grammar (references by section number)

B.B. Blue and Brown Books

L. & C. Lectures and Conversations on Aesthetics, Psychology and Religious Belief

R.F.M. Remarks on the Foundations of Mathematics (references by part and section, e.g. *R.F.M.* V. 15)

P.I. Philosophical Investigations (references to Part I are by section numbers, e.g. *P.I.* 34, and to Part II by page numbers, e.g. *P.I.* p. 209)

Z. Zettel

O.C. On Certainty

Moore/Lectures 'Wittgenstein's Lectures in 1930—33', in G. E. Moore, *Philosophical Papers* pp. 252—324.

On Frazer 'Bemerkungen über Frazer's *"Golden Bough"* ', *Synthese* (1967) pp. 233—53.

L.P.E. 'Notes for Lectures on Private Experience and Sense Data', *Philosophical Review* (1968) 271—320.

Biblical quotations are taken from the Revised Standard Version.

I Wittgenstein, Meaning and Religious Truth

INTRODUCTION

During the late 1920s and early 1930s Ludwig Wittgenstein met with some members of the Vienna Circle to discuss philosophical issues. A few of these discussions touched on religious questions. Moritz Schlick took the view that religion belonged to a childhood phase of humanity and would eventually disappear. Wittgenstein rejected this view, but he agreed with Schlick that religious doctrines have no theoretical content (Carnap (1) p. 26). Waismann records him as making the following remarks in December, 1930:

> Is speech essential for religion? I can quite well imagine a religion in which there are no doctrines and hence nothing is said. Obviously the essence of religion can have nothing to do with the fact that speech occurs — or rather: if speech does occur this itself is a component of religious behaviour and not a theory. Therefore nothing turns on whether the words are true, false, or nonsensical. (trans. Max Black, *Philosophical Review* (1965) 16)

These remarks were made at a transitional phase of Wittgenstein's philosophical development. But they suggest a line of thought later developed in his *Lectures on Religious Belief*, and they raise two important topics around which the discussions in this book will polarise, namely the nature of religious truth and the relevance of Wittgenstein's later philosophy to religious issues. As they stand, they will disappoint most religious believers, because Wittgenstein seems to be giving with one hand and taking away with the other. The kind of religion which he has in mind seems to be a mere skeleton when compared with the major religions of the world. Moreover, most believers do attach importance to the creeds and doctrines of their religion and certainly regard them as true. It is, of course, difficult to say what such truth consists in and how we reach it, and these difficulties are felt particularly by contemporary philosophers of religion; but Wittgenstein's approach does seem to amount to cutting the Gordian knot.

Still, Wittgenstein at least allows that religion makes sense, and that it is worthy of serious consideration. In this attitude he was at variance with most of the other members of the Vienna Circle, and eventually he would only meet with Schlick and Waismann. Carnap later accused him of having an indifferent, and even negative, attitude to science and mathematics, and of opposing 'enlightened' ideas (Carnap (1) pp. 26, 68–9). Wittgenstein's disagreement with the Positivists was, of course, eventually much more fundamental, as became apparent later on with the publication of his *Philosophical Investigations* in which, among other things, he criticised their theory of meaning. This theory had insisted that any meaningful statement must be either analytic or else verifiable through sense experience. Now it seems that religious, metaphysical and ethical statements will not fit into either of these categories, so the Postivists were content to dismiss them as nonsense, or at any rate as not cognitively meaningful.

It is Wittgenstein's attack on Positivism that has made many people regard him as an ally of religion. Of course, many theologians had attacked Positivism long before the publication of any of Wittgenstein's later work, arguing, for example, that no satisfactory version of the Verification Principle had been formulated. But the *Philosophical Investigations* seemed to provide an alternative theory of meaning, and one which was more tolerant of religious language than that of the Positivists. Wittgenstein argued that we must 'make a radical break with the idea that language always functions in one way, always serves the same purpose: to convey thoughts — which may be about houses, pains, good and evil, or anything you please' (*P.I.* 304; this statement, of course, is as much an attack on Wittgenstein's own previous views, in the *Tractatus*, as on other philosophers').

Instead, Wittgenstein maintained that 'For a *large* class of cases — though not for all — in which we employ the word "meaning" it can be defined thus: the meaning of a word is its use in the language' (*P.I.* 43).

Such 'uses' are multifarious: earlier on Wittgenstein had noted that there are countless kinds of sentences and uses of words, e.g. giving or obeying orders, reporting events, making up stories, guessing riddles, reporting dreams, translating, asking, thanking, cursing, greeting and praying (*P.I.* 23). He calls these 'language-games', and says that this term 'is meant to bring into prominence the fact that the speaking of language is part of an activity, or a form of life'. The concept of a 'form of life' is, as we shall see, a difficult one, but one of the points which Wittgenstein is making is that language always occurs in a certain human context: 'Only in the stream of thought and life do words have meaning' (*Z.* 173). We must not look for the meaning of language by always seeking out some objects which correspond to words or some particular mental activities, but by considering such contexts (*P.I.* 40, 693). We must get away, too, from 'the idea that using a sentence involves imagining something for every word' (*P.I.* 449). Wittgenstein constantly gives the analogy of chess: 'We only understand the statement "This is the king" if we know the rules of chess and thereby understand the context or surroundings which give the terms their meaning' (*P.I.* 31, 337).

WITTGENSTEIN, MEANING AND RELIGION

These remarks about meaning have an obvious application to religion. In general, we might say that religion involves many uses of language: prayers, parables, commandments, sermons, creeds and so on. We learn the meaning of such language by looking at its use, i.e. by paying attention to its contexts and to the purpose it serves. The theologian's role is to describe the situations in life in which religious responses and language-games occur, to teach people how to use religious terms, and to explain their historical and biblical background. If religious language seems meaningless to people today, this may be because they have lost sight of the practices and the contexts with which the language is associated. The remedy would be to return to the way of life in which the linguistic practices were born, to learn to be contrite, forgiving, long-suffering, hopeful and so forth. Of course, this 'learning how' may take a life-time, for its object is man's spiritual transformation and the understanding involved depends on a participation in religious 'forms of life'.[1]

I will discuss the concept of a religious language-game or form of life in the next chapter, since it is a development of his followers rather than something found in Wittgenstein himself. But Wittgenstein's own views on meaning have other important applications to religious questions, more specific than that already mentioned. These applications can be drawn out by considering his views on naming, mental processes and private language.

Names, Essences and Family Resemblances

Many religious writers treat 'faith' as if it was a particular faculty of the mind or kind of mental act. The assumption behind this seems to be 'the prejudice that there is one proper meaning of the word or that some one phenomenon in human existence represents the "real" meaning of "faith" ' (H. Richard Niebuhr in Hook, p. 94). Now one of the cardinal points of Wittgenstein's later views on meaning is that grammatical substantives do not necessarily denote a single thing or essence. The most famous *locus* for this principle is *P.I.* 66–7, where Wittgenstein argues that there is nothing common to all 'games', but that there is rather a complicated network of similarities which is best characterised as 'family resemblances'. Wittgenstein goes on there to apply his principle to the concept of 'number', but in general his most important applications are in the philosophy of mind. For example, he criticises Socrates for assuming that there must be a common element in all applications of the term 'knowledge', and points out that a term like 'expecting' may cover a variety of situations with no single common feature; rather, these cases form a family with many overlapping features (*B.B.* p. 20).

These remarks are clearly relevant to many terms used in theology: not just to the example of 'faith', but ones like 'grace', 'spirit', 'conscience' and perhaps 'reason'. Wittgenstein's work should deter us from assuming that they denote particular mental acts, faculties or dispositions. When a contrast is made, for instance, between 'faith' and 'reason', we may need to look at the context to see which of a possible family of distinctions is meant.[2]

Similarly with the concept of 'revelation'. Some recent writers have suggested that, because of the difficulties which it raises, the term should be abandoned or used only in a restricted context (cf. Downing (1)). Certainly it is misused and hence gives rise to much misunderstanding; but, again, may not the remedy be to gain a deeper understanding of the different features and distinctions which the word is trying to describe and to cease looking for a single model on which to construe the word? I am suggesting, perhaps, the need for a kind of Kittel's *Wörterbuch* in which the logical connections within and between theological concepts are carefully mapped.

Wittgenstein's point also has epistemological relevance: He points out that there are many different usages of the word 'proof', and that some philosophising mathematicians are not aware of this; likewise, there are many different meanings of the word 'discovery', e.g. discovering the South Pole, or discovering the construction of the pentagon (*B.B.* pp. 28–9). Now we might well ask ourselves here what kind of proofs and discoveries are in place in theology.[3]

Inner Processes and Surroundings

Wittgenstein is obviously combatting his own earlier view that 'A name means an object. The object is its meaning' (*T.* 3.203; *P.I.* 40 rebuts this). But in the philosophy of mind his target is a more specific one: it is the view that terms like 'belief', 'joy', 'expect', 'intend' and 'understand' denote unobservable private processes. Wittgenstein maintains that these terms stand for a complex of feelings, thoughts, behaviour and utterances occurring in certain situations. Such complexes often, though not always, include private processes or events (Wittgenstein is not a Behaviourist, as *P.I.* 306–8 make abundantly clear), but the point is that there is no *one* private process or event which *must* occur in every case and which is what the words really denote; rather, there are a number of things which can constitute appropriate conditions for their application. 'Understanding', for example, is not merely a private process, for we can say that a person understands nuclear physics when he is asleep or occupied with something

...se (likewise with 'believing' or 'intending'). Moreover, we expect understanding to be manifested in behaviour and so regard the latter as a criterion: for instance, being able to apply an algebraic formula is a criterion of our understanding it (*P.I.* 146); similarly, with map-reading (*Z.* 245). Of course, there may be a single process which occurs in all these cases of understanding. But why, asks Wittgenstein, should *it* be the understanding? If understanding is a hidden process, then how do I know what I have to look for and how can I say 'Now I understand'? (*P.I.* 153; cf. *P.G.* 41). This seems to be a case where 'Only God sees the most secret thoughts. But why should these be all that important? Some are important, not all' (*Z.* 560). Those who pick on the inner process as constituting the essence of understanding are looking for too simple a model. But in fact the criteria for 'understanding' are 'much more complicated than might appear at first sight . . . here we must be on our guard against thinking that there is some *totality* of conditions corresponding to the nature of each case . . .' (*P.I.* 182–3).

How, then, do we tell when people understand, expect and so forth? Wittgenstein's answer is that we consider the appropriate criteria for applying these concepts, and also look at the circumstances. Wittgenstein developed the term 'criterion' in his own special way, linking it with questions of meaning as well as with those of evidence (cf. Lycan), but part of what he has in mind is the commonsense point that we look at a variety of factors to judge people's beliefs and intentions, including their past history, present behaviour and general character, as well as their present utterances. Similarly, we do not just accept people's word that they understand or are able to do something but we devise tests to ascertain this. Sometimes the context or situation helps to define the proper application of concepts, particularly psychological ones[4]: coming to understand something may involve a special experience, 'but for us it is *the circumstances* under which he had such an experience that justify him in saying in such a case that he understands, that he knows how to go on' (*P.I.* 155). This also applies to concepts like love and hope (*P.I.* 583) or acting voluntarily: 'What is voluntary is certain movements with their normal *surroundings* of intention, learning, trying, acting' (*Z.* 577). We could not teach a dog to simulate pain because 'the surroundings which are necessary for this behaviour to be real simulation are missing' (*P.I.* 250). Again, he uses his favourite parallel of chess: '. . . a move in chess doesn't consist simply in moving a piece in such-and-such a way on the board — nor yet in one's thoughts and feelings as one makes the move: but in the circumstances that we call "playing a game of chess", "solving a chess problem" and so on' (*P.I.* 33). Similarly, he points out that the institution of money requires certain surroundings for its existence (*P.I.* 584; Z. 143).

These remarks about psychological concepts are a particular case of the point considered generally under (i) and they have a similar relevance to theology. During the last 300 years or so theologians, perhaps because they have been much influenced by Descartes and his successors, have tended to think that words like 'faith', 'conversion' or 'grace' refer to private mental events, and that a holy or spiritual life is mainly a matter of man's 'inwardness'. Certainly the inner life is a reality and one of great importance, but Wittgenstein's comment that 'an "inner process" stands in need of outward criteria' (*P.I.* 580) may help to remind us that holiness is recognised by its fruits! Thus, although certain inner processes may characterise 'sin', 'faith', 'grace' and 'prayer', we also need to take into account certain behavioural criteria, as well as a certain context or situation in life which is presupposed. To understand the full meaning of these terms we need to know the logical and conceptual links between them and to study the surroundings of their application. It might be the case, too, that we should construe expressions like 'encountering God' or 'finding God' at least partly in terms of such contexts or situations, rather than in terms of private mental events (of course, traditional theologians always regarded the context and the effect on a person's life as tests of the genuineness of a religious experience, but in recent times greater stress has been placed on the inner aspect[5]). This would mean that all the familiar arguments about the nature and validity of 'religious experience' would have to be restated and evauated. I realise, naturally, that these expressions raise questions about the existence of God, questions which go beyond Wittgenstein's discussions on psychological concepts and criteria. But then many of the other concepts which I have mentioned, e.g. 'grace', also raise specifically theological issues besides those of meaning and philosophical psychology.

Private Language

Wittgenstein's views on meaning, inner processes, criteria and surroundings form the background of his famous attack on the idea of a private language. This argument is difficult to grasp and often misrepresented. He certainly never denied that people can describe their own feelings or that they can use language in order to make things clear to themselves as well as to communicate with others (see *Z.* 329). Obviously, too, people can use private codes (though it is worth noting that they copy the form of an already existing public language). Wittgenstein's central point is that if the word 'red', for example, referred merely to a private sensation, it would not function as a word in a common language. In the first place, it might, for all we know, refer to something different in every case (*P.I.* 272, 274). Moreover, there would be no criterion for deciding whether people described their sensations correctly when they recurred (*P.I.* 258–65). Secondly, something does not become a symbol or a name simply in virtue of being associated with an image: it must also communicate something, and this entails that it be part of a system. In any case, the practice of naming is one which we learn from our use of the public language – it presupposes 'a great deal of stage-setting' (*P.I.* 257) and it gets its point from its function in communication between people.

Again, Wittgenstein's thought here disposes of the view that religious terms merely denote private experiences, and so helps us to discern false accounts of 'inwardness' in religion. Religious language is formulated against the background of the practices and beliefs of a religious community. The practice of private prayer is learnt through such a community, and it involves the language of a common tradition. God may, of course, speak to individual saints and prophets, but His message depends for its sense on a religious tradition – even a religious revolutionary starts from within some community and uses its terminology. It is also arguable that individual revelations depend on a community for their authenticity, though here the relationship is difficult to specify. But at any rate there must be some general tests for the validity of a religious revelation, even if the majority of contemporary witnesses apply these incorrectly in particular cases.[6]

QUESTIONS OF TRUTH

My discussion so far has centred mainly around the topic of meaning. Now this may well suggest a number of objections. In the first place, is not my discussion obsolete, since no one today does in fact dismiss religious statements as meaningless, as they did in the 1930s? Discussion today centres on particular religious concepts, particularly that of God. But one of the difficulties in applying Wittgenstein's philosophy in this area is that there is much dispute about the application of religious terms. We all agree about what constitutes pain, expecting, intention and so forth — the use of these terms is established. But religious traditions vary in their views of what constitutes salvation, divine revelation and so on, and indeed about the nature of God (Jews and Muslims, for example, feel that their concept of God precludes their recognising a man as divine). Hence we are faced with the question of conflicts between criteria — something which Wittgenstein hardly discusses (see Hacker, p. 302). Moreover, many religious terms seem to bring with them a controversial ontology: terms like 'grace' and 'divine presence' involve reference to God. Now someone might recognise that there are indeed criteria for their application, and yet doubt the existence of God. An obvious parallel is that of witchcraft: one may admit that men of the seventeenth century employed certain criteria for judging whether someone was a witch, and yet reject belief in the Devil. It seems, therefore, that religious concepts and their criteria raise very special problems.

One may evade these difficulties by simply analysing the concepts of a particular religion and showing their logical properties and relations. But such an evasion naturally raises a second objection: does not Wittgenstein fail to touch on the really important issue of theology today, which is that of deciding on what kind of truth religious statements have and on how we reach it? The natural conclusion which might be drawn at this stage is that his later philosophy has little of importance to offer on this issue. And indeed it seems to have become part of the 'conventional wisdom' (to use Galbraith's phrase) of contemporary philosophical theology to say something like this: 'Of course Wittgenstein's work is tremendously important for showing that religious language has a use, but this doesn't show that any of it is true, nor even how we should go about establishing truth in religion.'[7]

I believe that this conclusion is misguided, since many of the topics which Wittgenstein discusses, e.g. criteria and the relation between language and reality, have epistemological implications. But it is not surprising that it should have been drawn. The objections I have raised do reflect the feeling of many people that analysing the uses of religious language is of limited value: one may well admit that this language has a use, and yet be baffled by the question of truth. After all, Wittgenstein included 'reporting' and 'giving information' amongst his language-games (*P.I.* p. 190; *Z.* 160), and these functions do involve considerations of truth and falsity. Of course, the question of truth does not arise in the case of prayers, litanies or commandments, since these are not grammatically indicative statements; nor does it arise in the case of many 'performative utterances' (to use J. L. Austin's phrase[8]) such as 'I absolve you from your sins' or 'I acknowledge Christ as my Saviour'. But it does arise in the case of creeds, sermons and formulations of doctrine. The fact that the latter often have a performative element, in that their utterance involves the acknowledgement of a certain relationship to God or membership of a religious community, does not mean that we can ignore the issue of their truth value, since (as Evans (1) p. 31 points out) the 'that' clauses which follow 'constatives' like 'state', 'guess' and 'warn' can be evaluated for their truth or falsity, accuracy or inaccuracy, and correctness or incorrectness.

Perhaps the most famous *locus* in recent writings of the question 'How do we know whether religious doctrines are true or not?' is Anthony Flew's essay 'Theology and Falsification'. There he discusses statements like 'God has a plan', 'God created the world' and 'God loves us as a father loves his children', and remarks that they seem to be vacuous because they are compatible with any and every possible state of affairs in the world. However great the amount of suffering which he sees, the religious believer will never abandon his belief in God's love, nor will he admit under what circumstances he would do so. Flew does not ask that such doctrines be verified, presumably because he accepts Popper's claim that a statement may be scientifically acceptable even though it is not conclusively verifiable. Instead, he demands that religious beliefs be at least open to the possibility of falsification: he asks 'What would have to occur or to have occurred to constitute for you a disproof of the love of, or of the existence of God?' (Flew and Macintyre, p. 99).

Flew's challenge was crudely put, so that one might reply by refusing his demand, noting that Popper's criterion of falsifiability was originally proposed as a solution to the problems of demarcation, i.e. of distinguishing science from metaphysics, mathematics and other fields. Since noone is claiming that religious doctrines are 'scientific' in the modern sense of the word, the problem of verification or falsification does not arise. But this is to forget that our understanding of a statement involves some knowledge of what would have to be the case for it to be true and what kind of evidence counts towards its truth or falsity. As Wittgenstein said, 'Asking whether and how a proposition can be verified is only a particular way of asking "How d'you mean?" The answer is a contribution to the grammar of the proposition' (*P.I.* 353; cf. *T.* 4.024). Propositions which seem to be compatible with any state of affairs are naturally suspected of vacuity. Of course, it can be objected that Flew confuses truth-conditions with verification-conditions: putative factual assertions must indeed entail some things and be incompatible with others, but these conditions need not be states of affairs available for empirical checking here and now. But, again, this does not get to the heart of the matter. It can be claimed that both Flew and the Logical Positivists were giving philosophical form to the ordinary man's demand that religious doctrines should be supported by reasons and that they should have some 'cash value' in terms of his own experience or of facts about the world and human history. Particular philosophical formulations may be faulted, but this underlying demand remains.

Much of the philosophical theology published during the last thirty years or so has attempted to answer Flew's challenge or the Positivists' demand for verification. In general, there are two possible approaches: one may either try to show that at least *some* religious doctrines (perhaps in their traditional formulations, perhaps in some modern reformulation) are in principle verifiable or falsifiable, or else one can duck the issue by arguing that although religious language is meaningful, it is not 'fact-stating', and therefore the question of truth or falsity does not arise. R. B. Braithwaite, for example, took the view that religious assertions are primarily used to announce allegiance to a set of moral principles or rather an 'agapeistic way of life', with sets of stories as a backing. Similarly, other philosophers have argued that a religion may be an ideology, in which doctrines are really 'pseudo-factual statements' with disguised normative force (Nielsen (3) p. 118); or that 'the distinctive purpose of religious discourse is to articulate, rouse, sustain, and modify attitudes' and to 'give the human self an orientation' (Kennick, pp. 66, 63).

Now all these contributions point to different aspects of religious language and all of them are correct as far as they go, but they really seem to get us little further than the remarks quoted from Wittgenstein at the beginning of the chapter. They either ignore the question of religious truth or else they deny that there can be such a thing. Thus they seem to be no more than philosophically improved versions of nineteenth century attempts to reduce religion to feeling or to poetry, e.g. the claim that 'You may speak of the truth of a philosophy, of a theory, of a proposition, but not of a religion, which is a condition of the feelings' (Seeley, pp. 212 f.).

Hence other philosophers have attempted to grapple more directly with the problem, arguing, for instance, that some of the traditional proofs for the existence of God are valid, or that we have direct experience or 'intuitions' of God's existence and attributes, or that doctrines making predictions about life after death may be verified (though not falsified!) when the time comes. Others have favoured what I shall call 'Reductionism': they admit that religious doctrines are truth claims, but seek to avoid the difficulties involved in verifying or falsifying claims about transcendent beings by arguing that the doctrines should be viewed as statements about self-understanding or personal relations or perhaps political revolution. Paul van Buren, for example, interprets Christ's resurrection in terms of 'a new perspective upon life' (p. 132) opened up for the Apostles and for modern man, rather than as a physical rising from the dead which is a sign of Christ's divinity and a pledge of man's future resurrection. Such reinterpretations may or may not make Christian doctrines more palatable to people today, but they are certainly far removed from the intentions of the Fathers of the Church who originally formulated the doctrines.

WITTGENSTEIN AND RELIGIOUS TRUTH

It is impossible to say how Wittgenstein would have answered Flew's challenge, though it is interesting to speculate on the matter. Although he was sympathetic towards religious people, in his own life he apparently did not accept any particular creed (Malcolm (1) p. 72; Fann (1) p. 53); he remarked of two of his pupils who became Roman Catholics, 'I could not possibly bring myself to believe all the things that they believe'. Quite clearly he was opposed to all attempts to shore up religion with rational arguments, just as he was opposed to all those who dismissed it as unscientific. Malcolm records that he was impatient with 'proofs' for the existence of God. When Malcolm quoted to him a remark of Kierkegaard's to this effect: 'How can it be that Christ does not exist, since I know that He has saved me?' Wittgenstein exclaimed: 'You see! It isn't a question of *proving* anything!'[9] He attacked Frazer for viewing rituals as a kind of primitive and erroneous science, and argued that we are not dealing here with opinions which can be true or false (*On Frazer*, p. 240). It seems likely, therefore, that he would not have answered Flew by trying to verify or falsify religious doctrines.

What, then, is the role of religious doctrines for Wittgenstein? The remarks which he made to Schlick and Waismann, quoted at the beginning of this chapter, suggest that he did not regard them as cognitive statements. Later on, in his *Lectures on Religious Belief* he argued that the importance of religious beliefs does not lie in the proofs or reasoning which support them, but in the way they regulate our lives. For instance, if I believe in a Last Judgement, this is not a question of expecting a future event like a war, but of living with a certain picture before me and using this to influence my conduct. The question of evidence is irrelevant: '. . . if there were evidence, this would in fact destroy the whole business . . . We don't talk about hypothesis or about high probability. Nor about knowing' (pp. 56–7). Wittgenstein admits that Christianity is founded on historical facts, but says that these are not ordinary historical facts, subject to doubt and empirical test: 'They base enormous things on this evidence' (p. 58). Of course, some people claim to have evidence for their belief in God's existence: but what would it be for the evidence to be unsatisfactory or insufficient? And why is it regarded as bad not to believe in God, when 'Normally if I did not believe in the existence of something no one would think there was anything wrong in this' (p. 59)?

Quite clearly Wittgenstein is at least playing down, if not dismissing, the issue of rationality and truth in religion. Does this mean, then, that religious doctrines are necessarily unreasonable? He replies (p. 58):

'unreasonable' implies, with everyone, rebuke.
I want to say: they don't treat this as a matter of reasonability.
Anyone who reads the Epistles will find it said: not only that it is unreasonable, but that it is folly.
Not only is it not reasonable, but it doesn't pretend to be.

What then is the difference between a religious believer and a sceptic, if it is not a matter of rationality, proofs and arguments? Wittgenstein claims that it is a matter of living with different pictures before them, of different ways of life. Thus, to give another example, some people regard illness as a punishment sent by God, while others, including Wittgenstein himself, do not. Yet he does not regard himself as *disagreeing* with these people (p. 55): '... you can call it believing the opposite but it is entirely different from what we normally call believing the opposite. I think differently, in a different way. I say different things to myself. I have different pictures.'

It follows from this that there is no ordinary contradiction between the believer and the sceptic and indeed Wittgenstein draws this conclusion (p. 55). But if that is so, then it seems that the truth claimed for religious doctrines cannot be the ordinary truth of propositions, according to which we say that ' "p" is true if and only if p', and regard 'p and -p' as a contradiction. Hence some of his followers, influenced by the passages which I have just discussed, along with some other writings of Wittgenstein about the nature of language-games, have claimed that religious language-games have their own kind of truth and rationality. I shall explain my disagreement with them in the next chapter. For the moment I shall confine myself to Wittgenstein's own work and say that he does full justice to the sense in which religious doctrines are admitted by their adherents to be foolish in the eyes of the world and unreasonable. St Paul did indeed say that belief in Christ is folly to the man of the world, in that it does not pay off in worldly terms and requires wisdom and the understanding of spiritual things, rather than philosophical learning, for its comprehension. But he still regarded his beliefs as true and as justifiable in a certain fashion. Wittgenstein does not explain the nature of the truth that is claimed and the peculiarity of the reasoning on which it is based. Moreover, I think that he distorts the particular examples which he discusses. Many people *would* regard the Last Judgement as a future 'event', albeit one of a highly unusual kind, and would certainly regard their conduct in this life as having a determining influence on their fate after death. Wittgenstein does not do justice to Christian eschatological beliefs, nor does he explain the real fear which such beliefs can arouse, fear which would not be caused by a mere picture.[10] As regards the question of regarding illness as a divine punishment, Wittgenstein fails to reckon with the fact that this *can* be irrational. What if I were to recover speedily from my illness without repenting, and then continue happily in my sins? Bernard Williams discusses a similar case, that of attributing failures in crops to God's punishment of a people's wickedness, and notes that:

> the statement seems also to be in a crude sense falsifiable. For when the agriculturalists arrive, the irrigation is improved, the crops never fail, and the people riot in wickedness in the midst of plenty, the man who said that the crops failed because of the people's wickedness notoriously falls into discredit ... This is the familiar phenomenon of the elimination of religious language from a context. (Flew & MacIntyre, pp. 200–1)

DOCTRINES AND DESCRIPTIONS

Wittgenstein's *Lectures*, though his most substantial contribution to the philosophy of religion, are not necessarily his last word. Unfortunately, however, his later works offer us no more than hints about how his philosophical views might be applied to religious issues. Some of what he says suggests the kind of relativism to be considered in the next chapter. But I think that a different and more correct view of the nature of religious truth may be developed by paying attention to his general discussions about the relationship between language and reality. We have seen that Wittgenstein replaced both his own earlier theory of meaning and the Positivists' Verification Theory with the one which we have briefly considered. But he also came to modify his earlier views on such notions as 'picturing' or 'describing'. It is not just a matter of saying that language has many uses, and that only one of these uses is to convey thoughts or describe the world. The point is that even such apparently simply notions as 'describing', 'conveying thoughts' and 'stating the facts' raise many problems. Let us say that descriptions are word pictures of the facts; but there are many kinds of descriptions (*P.I.* 24) and many kinds of pictures besides those which hang on our walls, machine drawings, for example (*P.I.* 291). And even the pictures on our walls are of many different kinds: a portrait is an exact copy, whereas a *genre* picture has no such claims; yet the latter ' "tells" me something, even though I don't believe (imagine) for a moment that the people I see in it really exist, or that there have really been people in that situation' (*P.I.* 522). A picture may be quite 'correct' even though it is not a 'picture by similarity' or a 'copy': Wittgenstein gives the example of a plane projection of one hemisphere of our terrestrial globe (*B.B.* p. 37). He uses the phrase 'method of projection' more generally for the relationship between signs and objects, and for the way in which images or pictures are compared with reality (*B.B.* p. 53; *P.G.* 50–1 and Appendix 4, p. 213).[11] He also speaks of a form or method or representation: this term is not defined in the later work but it seems to be roughly equivalent to a 'conceptual system' (Hacker, p. 48). Wittgenstein says that it controls the way we look at things, and in one place he equates it with 'language-game' (*P.I.* 50, 122).

Wittgenstein's point about our variety of pictures was already foreshadowed in the *Tractatus* (4.011, 4.014, 4.0141). But in his later work we have also to reckon with a fundamental change in his views about the connection between language and reality. In the *Tractatus* Wittgenstein analysed propositions ultimately into combinations of names, each of which corresponds to an object (4.0311, 4.221); whereas in his later work he does not think that there is a *single* way in which language relates to the world, e.g. naming or picturing. There is a great variety of language besides names and logical constants, and we learn the connections between it and reality when we learn language (*P.G.* 55). Hence Wittgenstein prefers to approach the question by investigating, for instance, the relationship between wishes or expectations and their fulfilment, orders and their execution, and curses and their victims (it is in the context of such a discussion that he makes the cryptic remark: 'Like everything metaphysical the harmony between thought and reality is to be found in the grammar of the language' (*P.G.* 112; cf. *Z.* 55)). He thinks that we understand all these connections simply in virtue of our mastery of language, of knowing what it is to wish, expect, order and curse: 'Suppose it were asked "Do I know what I long for before I get it?" If I have learned to talk, then I do know' (*P.I.* 441; cf. 438 ff; 680; *P.G.* 112 ff.). Such a knowledge involves a grasp of the relevant criteria, for we do not know the meaning of the terms unless we know what constitute the conditions of their applicability (*P.I.* 572, p. 181; *Z.* 571). He also discusses the application of mathematics to reality, e.g. whether calculating uncovers facts: he asks '. . . why should not mathematics, instead of "teaching us facts", create the form of what we call facts?' (*R.F.M.* v. 15). Geometry seems a simpler case, perhaps, but even here 'Euclidean geometry too corresponds to experience only in some way that is not at all easy to understand, not merely as something more exact to its less exact counterpart' (*Z.* 572).

There is much that is difficult to understand in this account, but the central points are clear: there are many kinds of so-called 'descriptive' or 'fact-stating' language, and these relate to the world in different ways. Engineers' specifications, reports on experiments, musical scores, geometrical theorems, expressions of one's thoughts or feelings, and appreciations of pictures or dramatic performances all differ from each other markedly. Three factors account for such differences: the nature of the subject-matter (a machine is a different kind of object from a landscape, while thoughts, pains, symphonies and mathematical theorems are not material objects of any kind), the variety of 'methods of projection' used, and the 'grammar'[12] of the relevant terminology. Is it not possible, therefore, that religion has its own distinctive mode of representation? For instance, it seeks to map out possibilities of spiritual renewal: such possibilities are of a different realm of reality, though not in the sense that, say, the moon is. Thus Wittgenstein's insight into the variety of descriptions may contain the seeds of an alternative view of the nature of religious truth to that found in his *Lectures*. I am suggesting that there were at least three stages in Wittgenstein's thinking about the notion of 'picturing':

(1) The *Tractatus* view.
(2) The *Lectures*: pictures can be used in various ways, hence one needs to know 'the technique of using this picture' (*L. & C.* p. 63); in the case of religious belief the pictures essentially regulate one's life.
(3) The view just considered.

Wittgenstein himself did not apply the last of these to religious questions; but his remark (with reference to the difficulty of reconciling the Synoptics with St John's Gospel) that 'if you can accept the miracle that God became man all these difficulties are as nothing, for then I couldn't possibly say what form the record of such an event would take' (Drury, p. xiii) suggests that there could be descriptions which depict a religious reality without being 'copies' and yet which are not merely regulative.

Let us then ask ourselves what pictures and concepts are used in religion and theology: we want to know how doctrines are related to the world — what is their subject-matter and what kind of description are they trying to provide? Now it is unlikely that we will be able to reach a simple answer to such questions, because so-called 'religious language' is of many different kinds. I do not mean here that it includes many types of linguistic uses or speech acts, e.g. prayers, commandments, promises, creeds and so on — we have discussed that point already. Rather, I am drawing attention to the fact that even putatively 'descriptive' or 'fact-stating' uses of religious language are of many types. The Gospels and the creeds contain accounts of actions and events which are intended to be read as historical descriptions, even if they are of miracles or events having great theological significance. But they also contain mythological, eschatological, metaphysical, cosmological and allegorical uses of language, to mention only the main varieties. If we include the Old Testament the range of uses is wider, since it embraces a greater number of literary *genres*; and if we include the Epistles, we have some complex theological arguments to consider.

To see something of this variety, let us take the Nicene creed as an example. The words 'He was crucified also for us: suffered under Pontius Pilate and was buried' are, except for 'for us', a simple historical description. But how about 'He . . . ascended into Heaven, and is seated at the right hand of the Father'? Not to mention the earlier words 'born of the Father before all ages'. How are we to take these statements? Quite clearly the formulators of the creed intended them to be descriptive, i.e. 'corresponding to the facts', 'describing reality', 'saying how things are', or however one likes to put it. But it is unclear what is being claimed here. We cannot see if the statements quoted are true until we see what they mean; and we cannot see what they mean unless we understand them. But our understanding here seems to be limited by our failure to grasp the relevant technique of 'representation' and 'projection'. We may say that they are mythological or symbolic, but are we clear about the kind of contrast which these terms are trying to draw?

These considerations have led some contemporary philosophers of religion to speak of different 'strata' or 'logical strands' in religious doctrines (e.g. Smart (1) pp. 14–16). Much valuable work has been done in distinguishing the various kinds of religious statement. But we are still left with the problem of deciding how they are related to one another and to the relevant facts about the world. For example, what is the relationship between doctrines about a transcendent being and his actions on the one hand, and statements about the life of Christ or some situation in the world on the other? Could we compare the former to propositions using 'theoretical terms' in scientific explanations, as has been suggested by Ninian Smart (ibid. p. 8)?

One possible way of tackling these problems might be to follow up Wittgenstein's cryptic phrase 'Theology as grammar' (*P.I.* 373) by considering the different kinds of concepts used in doctrines and the ways in which they have been formed: for much of the difficulty consists in the fact that religion introduces special concepts like 'God', 'grace' and 'heaven', as well as using ordinary ones like 'father' or 'love' in an extended sense. Again, there is great variety here. For example, terms like 'Resurrection', 'Virgin Birth' and 'Crucifixion' are used to refer to certain alleged historical events, albeit ones of a unique kind with a special theological significance. 'Redemption' and 'Atonement' are more difficult to analyse, since they are seeking to explain the implications of these events for our own lives. Similarly, 'Providence', 'Creation', 'God's love' and 'grace' are seeking to establish a more general link between God's action and human life. Most of these concepts are derived by analogy from non-religious ones and have a long history of development; they are also causal concepts in that they are used to describe and explain facts about the world or historical events in terms of divine activity. 'Last Judgement' and 'eternal punishment' are also regarded as analogical concepts, in that they are examples of the extension of ordinary human concepts, but here the reference is not to this world but to eschatological events. Concepts like 'Guardian angel', 'Devil' and 'Transubstantiation' are hard to classify, whilst ones like 'God', 'Holy Trinity' and 'Incarnation' are the most complex, since they are the keystones, as it were, of the system of concepts used in Christian doctrines.

When he discussed mathematics Wittgenstein said that its proofs introduce new concepts and practices: 'a proof changes the grammar of our language . . . makes new connexions, and it creates the concept of these connexions' (*R.F.M.* II. 31; cf. V. 49). Clearly we cannot understand mathematics unless we grasp the concepts which it uses and their application. So may it not be the case that we cannot grasp theology, let alone assess its truth, until we have grasped the point of its concepts, the way they have been formed and their application? The variety of concepts and 'forms of representation' used in religion is one factor contributing towards the situation that it seems so difficult to *understand* many religious doctrines, never mind decide upon their truth. This suggests that the first task of the contemporary theologian is to recover the necessary understanding, and that the main value of Wittgenstein's philosophy for him will lie in whatever assistance it can provide to this end. This is the task to which the rest of this book will be devoted. But first of all I want to turn my attention to some of Wittgenstein's followers.

2 Some Followers of Wittgenstein

FORMS OF LIFE AND LANGUAGE-GAMES

During the last few years a number of writers have applied Wittgenstein's concepts of 'form of life' and 'language-game' to religion. If they were just saying that religion involves certain activities and that it plays a particular role in human life, this would be uncontroversial — though none the less true and important. But their main purpose has been to attack what they regard as misguided demands for a justification of religious belief. They have gone beyond Wittgenstein both in applying his ideas generally to religion and in their treatment of the issues of religious truth and justification. In this chapter I shall examine their work and subject it to some criticism. But I think that we shall thereby clarify the relationship between religion and language-games, and also gain some insight into the kind of justification which may legitimately be sought for religious beliefs.

In his review of the *Philosophical Investigations* Norman Malcolm said that one could hardly place too much stress on the importance of the notion of a 'form of life' in Wittgenstein's thought (Pitcher (3) p. 91). Later on he applied this concept to religion in his *Memoir* of Wittgenstein (p. 72) and especially in his article on St Anselm's Ontological Arguments. In the latter he said that he suspected that the argument could be thoroughly understood only by someone who had a view from the inside of that 'form of life' which gives rise to the idea of an infinitely great being and who therefore had some inclination to partake in that religious form of life (Malcolm (2) p. 62).

Similarly, D. Z. Phillips criticises many philosophers for failing to examine the contexts from which religious concepts derive their meaning, e.g. when they assume that they can settle the question of whether there is a God or not without trying to understand the form of life of which belief in God is a fundamental part (Phillips (3) p. 14). Wittgenstein himself, as far as I know, never described religion as a form of life, but he came very close to so doing when he asked in his *Lectures on Religious Belief* (p. 58) 'Why shouldn't one form of life culminate in an utterance of belief in a Last Judgement?'

It is quite clear that Malcolm and Phillips have an axe to grind here, and that they are not merely repeating the familiar apologetical point that religion is a way of life and not just a body of doctrines. For they have also applied the notion of a 'language-game' to religion,[1] attempting to establish the following two points:

(1) Religion is 'given' or basic, so that it need not be justified, and indeed cannot be.
(2) Its concepts are in order as they are, for '*this language-game is played*' (*P.I.* 654).

The first of these points follows from Wittgenstein's assertion that forms of life and language-games are simply *there*: 'What has to be accepted, the given, is — so one could say — *forms of life*' (*P.I.* p. 226, a text appealed to in Phillips (1) p. 27). For instance, Wittgenstein says that he would like to regard having a 'comfortable certainty' as a form of life: 'But that means I want to conceive it as something that lies beyond being justified or unjustified; as it were, as something animal' (*O.C.* 359).

It is difficult to say exactly what Wittgenstein meant by a 'form of life', because he gave so few examples. P. M. S. Hacker defines it thus: 'Agreement in language, possession of common concepts is what Wittgenstein here [*P.I.* 240—1] calls a "form of life", a common way of conceptualising experience together with the accompanying kinds of behaviour' (Hacker, p. 220). On the other hand, it is possible that the term denotes something on a smaller scale, e.g. measuring, hoping or pitying. Elsewhere (Sherry (2) pp. 161—3) I have favoured the latter interpretation and suggested that it is incorrect to label religion as a form of life; rather, it includes several forms of life, e.g.

worshipping, hoping and forgiving. If I am right, this is an important point, because it affects some of Malcolm's and Phillip's arguments about the illegitimacy of trying to justify religious beliefs. Of course, they would still be right in maintaining the absurdity of asking for a justification of something like hoping in general. But it is perfectly sensible to ask for a justification of *particular* hopes, for instance the Christian's hope for forgiveness of sins and future resurrection. Furthermore, even a specifically religious practice like 'worship' is not immune to demands for justification: we can rightly ask whether the object of worship actually exists and is indeed worthy of worship. In any case, even if religion as a whole can be described as a 'form of life', it is incorrect to suppose that anyone ever does want to justify it. Apologists and missionaries are always concerned to justify their own particular religions, rather than 'religion' in general. The latter is merely an abstraction.

Similar questions arise if we speak of religion as a 'language-game'. Richard Bell, for instance, objects to such a way of speaking, arguing that Wittgenstein's language-games are not complete types of discourse like legal, religious or scientific ones, but rather units of linguistic behaviour occurring in certain human contexts, e.g. greeting people. He thinks that the concept of 'religious language' used by so many contemporary philosophers is misleading, since although religion does have its own special terminology, it mostly uses terms drawn from ordinary non-religious contexts. He concludes that religion will include several language-games, like giving orders, reporting events of sacred history, making up stories (e.g. parables) and prophesying (see R. H. Bell (2) pp. 5–6, 12–14).

I believe that Bell's general conclusion about religious language is correct; and it is true that an application of, say, *P.I.* 23 would suggest the variety of language-games which Bell mentions. But I think that it must be pointed out that Wittgenstein's use of the term 'language-game' is more variegated than he realises. He does speak of mathematics being a whole language-game (*R.F.M.* v.15), and also of special technical systems like descriptive geometry and chemical symbolism as language-games (*B.B.* p. 81). This suggests that academic theology, at any rate, might be described as a 'language-game'. Moreover, Wittgenstein's description of everyday talk about material objects as a 'language-game' (*P.I.* p. 200) suggests that the ordinary believer's talk about God's nature and actions might also be described as such. But Bell would still be correct in saying that a religion like Christianity comprises several language-games. The difficulty is caused by the fact that Wittgenstein's use of the term is so wide as to cover both conceptual systems like geometry, chemistry or talk about physical objects, and 'speech acts' like asking questions or giving orders. This variety seems to preclude any single definition of the concept (whereas, in the case of the concept 'form of life', it is the paucity of examples which makes any definition a matter of conjecture) — though it is worth noting that in most cases Wittgenstein is using the term to emphasise the point that language plays a role in human life and activities: in his *Lectures on Aesthetics* he had said that the main mistake made by Moore and most contemporary philosophers was to look at language merely as a form of words, and not at the use made of them: 'Language is a characteristic part of a large group of activities — talking, writing, travelling on a bus, meeting a man, etc.' (p. 2; cf. *L.P.E.* p. 300).

I shall evade these difficulties by using the plural and speaking of 'religious language-games' (as indeed Phillips (3) p. 75 does). The most important issues here are those concerned with justification.

THE QUESTION OF JUSTIFICATION

Wittgenstein maintained that language-games, like forms of life, cannot and need not be justified. He argued, for instance, that the primitive language-game which speaks of material objects must simply be accepted: '. . . attempts at justification need to be rejected' (*P.I.* p. 200). Such language-games are simply 'given': '. . . the language-game is . . . something unpredictable. I mean: it is not based on grounds. It is not reasonable (or unreasonable). It is there — like our life' (*O.C.* 559). There comes a point when we must stop looking for justification and instead simply accept certain basic human reactions and modes of behaviour: 'If I have exhausted the justifications I have reached bedrock, and my spade is turned. Then I am inclined to say: "This is simply what I do" . . . Our mistake is to look for an explanation where we ought to look at what happens as a "proto-phenomenon". That is where we ought to have said *"this language-game is played"* ' (*P.I.* 217, 654).

The refrain 'This is what I [or we] do' is one frequently encountered in Wittgenstein's later philosophy. Usually it is introduced, as in the passage quoted above, to counter what he regards as a misguided hankering after justification. Wittgenstein insists that explanation must at some point give way to description (*P.I.* 109) and that it is sometimes silly to ask for reasons for things: 'Do we live because it is practical to live?' (*R.F.M.* V.14). 'Does man think, then, because he has found that thinking pays . . . Does he bring up his children because he has found it pays?' (*P.I.* 467).[2] No, for sometimes we must just say 'such is human life' (*On Frazer*, p. 236). Giving grounds comes to an end some time, but 'the end is not an unfounded presupposition: it is an ungrounded way of acting . . . it is our *acting* which lies at the bottom of the language-game' (*O.C.* 110, 204). This brings us to bedrock: 'The limits of Empiricism are not assumptions unguaranteed or intuitively known to be correct: They are ways in which we make comparisons and in which we act' (*R.F.M.* V.18). Sometimes Wittgenstein speaks in a similar way about 'The common behaviour of mankind' (*P.I.* 206), 'natural history' (*P.I.* 25, 415), 'customs' and 'institutions' (*P.I.* 199); these are all concepts which belong to the same family as 'form of life', constituting for him the fundamental given facts from which philosophy must start.

The applications of this line of thought are varied. Predictably, Wittgenstein attacks those who look for an explanation of religious practices like confession or customs such as burning effigies and kissing a loved one's picture (*On Frazer*, p. 236). More striking is his treatment of mathematics. He constantly stresses that this discipline has practical applications and must be related to human behaviour and purposes, e.g. when he says that 'The technique of calculation is part of the technique of house-building' (*R.F.M.* I.142). Measuring, weighing and costing are procedures of human behaviour, and going through mathematical proofs and accepting their results is 'simply what we *do*: this is use and custom among us, or a fact of our natural history' (*R.F.M.* I.63; cf. 146).[3] Hence he describes mathematics as an 'activity' (*P.I.* p. 227) or an 'anthropological phenomenon' (*R.F.M.* V.26), and therefore as something not requiring justification: 'The danger here, I believe, is one of giving a justification of our procedure where there is no such thing as a justification and we ought simply to have said: *"That's how we do it"* ' (*R.F.M.* II.74).[4] Both in mathematics and in other spheres he attacks those who misguidedly hanker after foundations and justifications:

> What does mathematics need a foundation for? It no more needs one, I believe, than propositions about material objects — or about sense impressions — need an *analysis*. What mathematical propositions do stand in need of is a clarification of their grammar, just as do those other propositions (*R.F.M.* V.13).

In some other cases we do need a justification, but often this is plain for all to see. Wittgenstein has a short way with sceptics about induction, for example: 'If anyone said that information about the past could not convince him that something would happen in the future, I should not understand him . . . If *these* are not grounds, then what are grounds?' (*P.I.* 481).

It is not surprising that this strand of Wittgenstein's thought should have proved attractive to philosophers of religion. Norman Malcolm, for example, quotes *P.I.* 654, *'this language-game is played'* in his article on St Anselm's Ontological Arguments. He is considering the view that God's existence cannot be described as 'necessary', since all existential propositions are contingent and logical necessity merely reflects linguistic conventions. Malcolm's reply is that we must *'look at the use of words and not manufacture a priori theses about it'*; now in the 'language-games' of the Jewish and Christian religions God has the status of a necessary being, so that 'we may rightly take the existence of those religious systems of thought in which God figures as a necessary being to be a disproof of the dogma, affirmed by Hume and others, that no existential proposition can be necessary' (Malcolm (2) pp. 55–6).[5]

I take it that Malcolm's move amounts to an assertion that the logical propriety of a concept is guaranteed by its being used in an established language-game. Such a claim will have to be investigated on its own merits, but it is doubtful whether it follows from *P.I.* 654 since the context suggests the Wittgenstein was concerned here mainly with certain psychological concepts. Nor, I think, would it follow from the remark that 'every sentence in our language "is in order as it is" ' (*P.I.* 98; cf. 124) since there Wittgenstein was attacking the quest for an ideal formalised language rather than the modern Humeans whom Malcolm has in mind.

D. Z. Phillips likewise attacks those philosophers who believe that their task is normative, to impose a criterion of good reasoning on theologians, using 'ordinary language' as a norm. He claims that the philosopher's task is not to advocate or criticise religious views, but to understand them: 'This fact distinguishes philosophy from apologetics. It is not the task of the philosopher to decide whether there is a God or not, but to ask what it means to affirm or deny the existence of God' ((1) p. 10). He does not deny that mistakes and confusions can occur in religious discourse, but insists that they can only be recognised from *within* religion because '... the criteria of meaningfulness cannot be found *outside* religion' ((3) p. 4). Philosophers who talk of proving or disproving the existence of God must not forget that words like 'existence', 'love' and 'will' are not used in the same way of God as they are of human beings or objects ((1) p. 8). Similarly the meaning of terms like 'real', 'unreal', 'rationality' and 'corresponding to reality' differs from context to context. Hence 'A necessary prolegomenon to the philosophy of religion, then, is to show the diversity of criteria of rationality' ((3) p. 17: cf. p. 84).

The view that religious concepts are *sui generis* and that consequently criteria of intelligibility and rationality are to be found only within the language-games has been christened 'the autonomist position' by John Hick (Hick (1) p. 237). It does seem to be in accordance with *some* of the things, which Wittgenstein says. We have already seen that he thinks that one can only justify statements *within* language-games, but not the language-games themselves. The relationship between them is somewhat like that between a system of measurement and the measurements themselves; and, of course, only the latter can be described as 'correct' or 'incorrect' (*R.F.M.* I.155). What counts as a reason or as evidence, therefore, depends on the context: all testing occurs within a system, so that it is idle to look for any *general* account of what constitute good grounds (*O.C.* 5, 82, 105, 203; *P.G.* 55; Bogen, pp. 131–40, 206). Hence he himself is much more concerned with the conditions of assertability for concepts like 'pain' or 'material object' than with any general theory of truth. But quite apart from this question, there is a strong strain of relativism in the later Wittgenstein: he often likes to imagine tribes with completely different concepts and practices from our own. For instance, he envisages a people who give what money they please for goods and get back what the merchant pleases; this seems entirely pointless to us, but then rituals like the coronation of a king are pointless too (*R.F.M.* I.152). He thinks that there is little that one could say to people who think they go to the moon and back in their dreams by a special route, who think that kings can make rain, and who refuse to rely on calculations (*O.C.* 106, 132, 212–17). When discussing the question of whether people who consulted oracles instead of a physicist, would be wrong, he asks 'If we call this "wrong" aren't we using our language-game as a base to combat theirs?' (*O.C.* 609).

Some of Wittgenstein's examples do seem rather dubious: his question about the oracle is silly as it stands — it would depend on why people consulted oracles and whether they were satisfied with the results, e.g. with regard to prediction of the future. There is, in any case, another side to Wittgenstein's philosophy in which he does not acquiesce in cultural relativism but instead roots our concepts and behaviour in facts about human life and the world. In Chapters 3 and 4 I shall give examples of language-games which, even if they are in some sense 'autonomous', are conditioned by certain facts.

Clearly writers like Phillips favour the relativistic aspects of Wittgenstein's thought, and perhaps much of what they say can be construed as being consistent with it. But I wonder whether he would have approved of some of the uses which they have made of his thought: in general I feel that they and many other 'Wittgensteinians' constantly miss the tentative and dialectical character of their master's thought and that their own work lacks the feeling of puzzlement and struggle which he thought essential for good philosophy.

In particular, I doubt whether Wittgenstein would have approved of the use of the 'this language-game is played' move as part of a religious apologetic. Let us look more closely at what Phillips says, and compare it with Wittgenstein's text.

Phillips starts *The Concept of Prayer* by quoting *P.I.* 124:

'Philosophy may in no way interfere with the actual use of language; it can in the end only describe it. For it cannot give it any foundation either. It leaves everything as it is.' He comments that what Wittgenstein 'is saying is that if the philosopher wants to give an account of religion, he must pay attention to what religious believers do and say' ((1) p. 1). This seems harmless enough, but he goes on to say that Wittgenstein's remarks also mean that philosophers can only describe religious language and must not try to justify it; it is nonsensical to talk of religion requiring a foundation or justification, for we can only justify particular religious assertions, using criteria of meaning and truth found *within* religion (pp. 8 ff., 27). He criticises believers like Mitchell and Crombie for trying to provide an apologetic which succeeds only in anthropomorphising God (pp. 88—94); but he also attacks sceptics like Flew and Hepburn for having 'paid too much attention to the surface grammar of religious statements' (p. 8). This has led them to look for a criterion of reality which is independent of context. But knowing God is not like knowing a person or a thing: 'to know how to use this [common] religious language is to know God' (p. 50). This is a matter of 'grammar' (in Wittgenstein's sense) for 'The philosopher is guilty of a deep misunderstanding if he thinks that his task in discussing prayer is to try to determine whether contact is made with God; to understand prayer *is* to understand what it means to talk to God' (p. 38). The task of philosophy is not 'to settle the question of whether a man is talking to God or not, but to ask what it means to affirm or deny that a man is talking to God' (p. 37), i.e. not to justify but to understand.

Whatever one may think of all these claims made by Phillips, it is surely doubtful whether they follow from the remarks of Wittgenstein which he quotes. Wittgenstein's views here should be seen, partly at least, as an attack on the search for an ideal language: he asks whether the language of every day is 'somehow too coarse and material for what we want to say? *Then how is another one to be constructed*?' (*P.I.* 120). But he is also discussing the scope of philosophy and the source of its problems: part of our failure to understand 'is that we do not *command a clear view* of the use of our words — our grammar is lacking in this sort of perspicuity' (122). Philosophical problems arise from the lack of understanding which would enable us to see connections (122–3), and the role of philosophy is simply to put everything before us and to 'assemble reminders for a particular purpose' (126–7).

None of these lines of thought, which form the context of *P.I.* 124, by themselves entail the ambitious conclusions which Phillips derives from them. Wittgenstein's thesis is about meaning and concepts, whereas Phillips goes on to talk about 'criteria of truth and falsity' ((1) p. 27). In any case, surely it is a mistake to equate the defence of religion or religious language with that of ordinary language? As a matter of fact, as I have already suggested, no one ever does try to defend 'religion' as such: apologists are always concerned to defend their own particular religion. Even philosophers who attempt to defend 'religious language' are nearly always concerned with the vindication of the metaphysical strand of Christianity against the attacks of those who claim that metaphysics or theism are unverifiable or unfalsifiable.

The remarks which I have just made serve also to show up the inappropriateness of two other parallels which Phillips gives: he argues that those who ask for a general justification of religious utterances are like those who ask for a general justification of science, whom Wittgenstein compared to the ancients who posited Atlas as a support for the world ((3) p. 124)[6]; and he compares questions about the reality of God to ones about the reality of the physical world ((1) pp. 21–3). Phillips himself realises that the first parallel breaks down at a crucial point: different religions often conflict with each other ((3) pp. 8–9). But this breakdown is a consequence of the more general objection that whilst it may be silly to ask for a *general* justification of religion or science, we can certainly discuss *particular* ones, e.g. Christianity or astrology (incidentally, although the question 'Is science true?' is absurd, the question 'Why pursue science?' is not).

The second parallel, that of 'reality', is used to make the point that the question 'Is the physical world real or not?' could not be answered by any empirical investigation, since the reality of the world is a presupposition of any such investigation. Similarly with the existence of God: 'the question of the reality of God is a question of the possibility of sense and nonsense, truth and falsity in religion' ((3) p. 3). Again, I must point out that different religions have varying concepts of God. Moreover, many people doubt the existence of God, whereas hardly anyone questions the reality of the physical world. Phillips replies to the latter point by saying that it is not really correct to say that we all agree about the reality of the physical world, for what would it be like to disagree? This is rather an odd reply, since Phillips is virtually admitting that his parallel does not hold (see (3) pp. 70—1); one could pursue the objection by pointing out that in the case of belief in the reality of the external world there is nothing corresponding to conversion and loss of faith.

FAIRIES, WITCHES AND THE PASSING AWAY OF LANGUAGE-GAMES

Phillips' argument is open to a further obvious and familiar objection: is he not committed to defending the legitimacy of talk about fairies and witches? I think that this kind of objection was first made by Sir A. J. Ayer in his inaugural lecture at Oxford, when he remarked that in a society which believed in witchcraft it might be perfectly correct to describe a person as 'bewitched' if he showed the commonly accepted marks of demonic possession, but that this would not entail that there actually were demons at work (Ayer (2) p. 18). Ayer was making the general point that we must not base too much on mere facts of usage. He did not apply his argument to religious belief, but Kai Nielsen has done so, remarking that once magic, witchcraft and belief in fairies were 'ongoing practices in our stream of life', but that they have been rejected as incoherent by people working from the inside (Nielsen (3) pp. 206, 208. Hudson (1) p. 68 makes a similar objection, using the parallel of belief in Santa Claus).

This objection, though frequently made, needs handling very carefully. Nielsen's charge about incoherence raises difficult questions about alternative conceptual schemes and the rationality of primitive societies which are a matter of debate among philosophers and anthropologists. Of course, he is right to point out that in magic and witchcraft we have examples of forms of life and language-games which were once current in the Western world but have now declined. But in primitive cultures magic and witchcraft may be one of the principal foundations of the whole social life of a people, so that they are not comparable to magical rites and beliefs which might be found in our own culture. It is this consideration which led Peter Winch (whom Nielsen is attacking, amongst others) to suggest that some systems of magic, e.g. that of the Azande, may constitute a coherent universe of discourse like science (Winch (3) p. 14). As regards the kind of witchcraft which was prevalent in Europe in earlier centuries, surely this was false rather than 'incoherent'? There is nothing incoherent or formally inconsistent in the belief that old women can kill or harm people with spells or potions. It is just that there does not seem to be enough evidence to make this belief generally acceptable today. Similarly with belief in astrology, ghosts, magic and so forth.

Nielsen seems to be on firmer ground when he points out that religious scepticism has a long and honourable ancestry (ibid. pp. 196, 205). Even when religious beliefs have been more widely accepted than they are today, there have usually been individuals who have come to wonder to whom or to what they were praying and who have contracted out of the religious language-games. But there is no similar parallel for contracting out of talk about material objects or out of ordinary arithmetical operations.

Phillips allows for such scepticism and apostasy. In his earlier writings he was at pains to insist that a man may simply fail to understand religious beliefs, or may understand them and yet find them unattractive ((1) p. 28; (3) p. 30). And in his most recent book he draws heavily on Wittgenstein's *Lectures on Religious Belief* in explaining how people come to lose their faith: in reply to Nielsen he argues that a religious picture loses its hold not because it is shown to be mistaken but because it is supplanted by a rival picture; e.g. after some tragic event ((4) pp. 74—5). But this account still fails to meet the point that there is a strain in the equation of religion with language-games, since most of the examples of language-games given by Wittgenstein are universal forms of human behaviour. Moreover, besides discussing individual conversion and loss of faith, Phillips needs to give some explanation of the ebb and flow in general religious interest from one era to another.

It might be replied that Wittgenstein does not regard all his language-games and forms of life as universal standard human behaviour, since he allows that new ones may come into existence while 'others become obsolete and get forgotten' (*P.I.* 23). In his *Lectures on Aesthetics* he comments that 'cultured taste' is a game which is played only in certain ages (p. 8). He also notes that language-games change with time (*O.C.* 256; cf. *P.I.* 132; these references, incidentally, constitute an adequate refutation of the widespread view that Wittgenstein did not allow for the possibility of linguistic change or growth — see Pole, pp. 53—7, 92—7, for an example). Presumably Wittgenstein's own example of cursing is one such language-game that is in danger of becoming obsolete, at least in its original religious form; one might instance the practice of doing word associations for psychoanalysis as an example of a new language-game coming into existence.

This reply is to the point, but it raises another and more serious difficulty for the view that philosophy should confine itself to description; for may not religion be one of those language-games which become obsolete and get forgotten? Malcolm's reply 'This language-game is played' invites the natural reply 'What if people stop playing it?' (cf. *Z.* 371: 'What then of a society that never played many of our customary language-games?'). Nielsen's comments about the decline of magic and witchcraft are obviously relevant here.

AUTONOMY AND JUSTIFICATION

Nothing of what I have said so far entails that religion is not a language-game or, better, a set of language-games, customs and so forth, and indeed I do not wish to deny this. My point is rather that such a claim, like the view that religion is a form of life, is of limited value taken by itself, and that it must not be used in order to evade some of the philosophical problems raised by religious beliefs. We have found the following difficulties:

(1) Language-games may pass away because people's interests and customs change, or because they reject certain beliefs, e.g. in magic.
(2) Religious belief differs from most other language-games in being a minority interest at present and in having phenomena like conversion, scepticism and loss of faith

associated with it.

But a gnawing doubt remains: what would it be like for all the claims of a religion to turn out to be false? By what standard would we judge them to be false? Nielsen says that 'gradually, as we reflected on the criteria we actually use for determining whether various entities, including persons, are or are not part of the spatio-temporal world of experience, we came to give up believing in fairies and witches' (p. 208). Now could not Phillips reply to this by saying that it is really just another case of the error for which he criticised Flew, Hepburn and others, namely that of treating the reality of God like that of objects and human beings? The whole point is that God's reality is the presupposition of the language-games of religion. A language-game is not so much a set of propositions as a linguistic context together with the rules which give our utterances their force and intelligibility, i.e. it is not what is said but rather the conditions of speaking meaningfully (see Phillips (3) p. 126, and Specht p. 171); hence, although a particular judgement within a language-game may turn out to be false or incoherent, it makes no sense to suppose that the language-game as a whole may be such, for by what standard can we judge it? A blunder can only be a blunder within a particular system; now in which language-game is religion supposed to be a blunder? Language-games have their own autonomy, hence they can neither be justified nor proscribed.

This answer, which is based on Phillips' reply to Hick and Palmer (see (3) ch. IV) and which I imagine that he, Winch and Malcolm would give to the objections which I have raised, does not, in my view, remove the force of these objections. In particular, it continues to speak, unrealistically, in terms of justifying religion as a whole: for instance, Phillips asks: if religion as a whole is a mistake, what sort of mistake is it? If religion is a delusion, why is it that religious believers are usually sane and normal people, quite unlike patients in mental hospitals who suffer from delusions? (see (1) p. 19; (3) p. 153). But these are silly questions as they stand, and can be answered simply by recalling that there are many different religions and that even a single religion is a family of many language-games. Thus we need to proceed gradually, case by case. Believers who put forward proofs of God's existence, as some do, may be making the mistake of putting forward invalid metaphysical arguments. In the case of historical religions, they may be making historical claims based on inadequate evidence. If they claim that God is a loving father who makes all events turn out for the best, it is apparent what kind of mistake they *could* be making — have those who use the 'but what kind of mistake/delusion?' gambit never read Freud?

But the answer does raise a few new questions and suggests that we must pursue the matter at a deeper level by investigating two positions, one of which John Hick has called the 'autonomist' position, the other of which I shall call the 'no justification' position, and by discussing Phillips' account of religious truth.

Phillips counters the objection that the practice of praying presupposes that we have proved that God exists by asking how we would establish this. He points out that establishing that I have a speck in my eye is different from establishing that I have a picture in my mind or a one in six chance of getting a job. Moreover, we have to decide what sort of an entity God is supposed to be, for the meaning of terms like 'fact', 'exist' and 'real' is dependent on the context ((1), pp. 13 f.); and so, *a fortiori*, is the meaning of 'corresponding to reality' ((3) p. 63). It will not do to reply that you will try to establish whether or not God exists by rational argument, for there are diverse criteria of rationality and intelligibility ((3) pp. 17, 133). Phillips quotes with approval Winch's view that: 'criteria of logic are not a direct gift of God, but arise out of and are only intelligible in the context of, ways of living or modes of social life. It follows that one cannot apply criteria of logic to modes of social life as such. For instance, science is one such mode and religion another; and each has criteria of intelligibility peculiar to itself.' Winch goes on to make the familiar points that it is only within their fields that actions can be assessed as logical or not, and that fields as a whole cannot be similarly assessed; that philosophy must remain uncommitted here; and that 'intelligibility takes many and varied forms' (Winch (1) pp. 100–2. In his essay 'Understanding a Primitive Society' he applies this line of thought to magic and witchcraft, arguing that there is no one context-free definition of 'reality' or 'rationality' which we can use to condemn them).

One may well wonder what 'criteria of logic' and of

intelligibility or rationality are, and how one 'applies' them. Still, the lines of the argument are clear: each department of our life must be judged by its own standards, hence we can only judge religious beliefs by the standards of religion. From this the convenient conclusion follows that it is nonsensical to talk of religion requiring justification, since we can only be asked to justify particular religious assertions, using the criteria which are to be found within our religious tradition: 'What I am urging is that the intelligibility of the family of language-games covered by the term "religion" is not assessed by wider criteria of meaningfulness' (Phillips (3) p. 71).

This is not to say that Phillips and Winch think that anything goes, for criteria and traditions are essentially public things: the religious community provides the standard of orthodoxy for judging the truth of religious doctrines and the common language that is necessary for prayers and liturgy. Prophets and reformers may introduce new elements into a religion and theologians may develop doctrines, but such changes can only occur against the background of a common language and tradition. Heretics and outsiders may be right and the churches and religious communities of the time wrong, but the former are still logically dependent on public traditions. People may disagree with their community about what the will of God is, but they cannot claim that absolutely anything is His will because the criteria here cannot be private; communal concepts determine at least the broad limits of what the will of God could be (Phillips (1) pp. 134 ff., pp. 153–6. This line of argument derives from Wittgenstein's attack on the possibility of a private language).

The 'autonomist' and 'no justification' positions which I have just outlined raise so many problems and appear so paradoxical that it is difficult to know where to start one's criticism. But I think that one's suspicions are aroused by the fact that, granted certain assumptions, the positions are invulnerable and irrefutable; and, if this is so, they may well be vacuous. Moreover one wonders, too, what the role of preaching and apologetics is supposed to be here. Certainly Phillips is correct to oppose any crude pattern of justification of religious beliefs (though his own approach often savours of an apologetic, albeit a purely defensive one); likewise, he is right to point out that terms like 'exists' and 'real' are not simply univocal, and that sceptics may have failed to understand the 'depth grammar' of concepts like trust in God and love of God. But these merits are offset by many difficulties.

The most serious objections are concerned with religious truth. How can we be sure that the standards of truth or validity which are accepted by our religious community are the right ones? Obviously Phillips will dismiss such an objection as missing the point, since the relevant criteria can only be found *within* the religious tradition and there is no independent standard by which we can grade different religions ((3) pp. 4, 246). Each one regards its own scriptures, traditions, etc. as the touchstone of truth.

Phillips' strategy here reminds one of those philosophers who counter sceptical objections about memory, induction and so on with arguments like this: 'Our remembering something is a good ground for thinking that it happened. This is what we mean by "good grounds". It is, therefore, absurd to ask if memory can give us knowledge of the past.' But such arguments run the risk of committing the Naturalistic Fallacy.[7] Thus, to give another example, in his book *An Examination of the Place of Reason in Ethics* Stephen Toulmin was in danger of defining 'good reasons' in ethics in terms of accepted moral standards, and so preventing moral reformers from asking the perfectly sensible question 'are these reasons really good reasons?'[8] Similarly, if we define religious truth in terms of a particular tradition, we preclude ourselves from asking whether this tradition really embodies the truth.

Such a criticism is not merely captious or academic, because religious communities do change their beliefs over the centuries and different communities often hold mutually contradictory views. What are the conditions of legitimate change? And how do we arbitrate in disputes between religions or churches? The first of these questions is easier to answer, since changes are rarely sudden or drastic, and can usually be related to some process of natural development or internal consistency. Phillips is right to point out that concepts like 'the will of God' must have public criteria of application, so that not anything at all can be claimed as being in accordance with it and any development must be gradual. He is, however, less satisfactory in explaining how and why the criteria of application of such concepts may change over a period of time, largely because his discussion eschews detailed examples. Perhaps one could shed light on this topic only by taking particular concepts like 'redemption', 'grace' and 'salvation' and showing how they have gradually acquired new shades of meaning in the course of their long history, both in the Old Testament and in Christian theology. Such changes often go hand in hand with doctrinal development — another topic which Phillips discusses only very summarily and generally, although it is very important for his enterprise for it raises interesting and difficult philosophical problems about conceptual change and the nature of religious doctrines. Compare, for example, the way in which the mediaevals used Aristotle's terminology to formulate the doctrine of transubstantiation, or the attempts of some modern writers to reformulate the doctrine of original sin in Freudian or Marxist ('alienation') terms.

The second question, that of doctrinal disputes, is much more difficult to answer, and here Phillips is extremely unsatisfactory. He is quite correct to point out that different religions are not necessarily 'competing claimants for the same throne' ((1) p. 25; cf. (3) p. 11) since they may be talking about different things. Moreover we might add that many disputes between religions and churches are with reference to a common tradition, e.g. the Reformation controversies about justification and grace, or disputes about the Real Presence, so that they are perhaps in principle resoluble by appeal to a common scripture or tradition; it is not *inconceivable* that one day all Christians will come to accept a common interpretation of scripture and a common doctrine. The really difficult cases, however, are those in which two different religions disagree over an issue: for example, the views of a Muslim or a Jew about the nature of Christ are surely incompatible with those of a Christian; and the Hindu belief in the reincarnation of the soul is not accepted by Christians. In these cases there does not seem to be any common standard or authority to which the different parties can appeal, as Catholics and Protestants can appeal to scripture. Yet both sides cannot be right, for their positions contradict each other.

Phillips realises that there are such disputes, and admits that his treatment may stress religious meaning at the expense of religious truth; but he asks why we should suppose that philosophy can indicate which religion is true: 'As a philosopher it is not my task to decide on anyone's behalf who the true God is' ((1) p. 149; cf. (3) p. 11). He remarks that, 'To say that the criteria of truth and falsity in religion are to be found within religious traditions is to say nothing of the truth and falsity of the religion in question', and warns his readers against confusing his epistemological thesis with an absurd religious doctrine ((1) p. 27; cf. (3) p. 12).

At first sight all this reads like a gross confusion amounting to little more than the observation that different religions claim different 'truths' and the logical comment that they cannot all be really true. One is tempted to retort that no one is asking Phillips to arbitrate between different religions. The whole point at issue is that if the truth claims of different religions conflict and there seems to be no way in principle of resolving such disagreements (unlike scientific ones), then the whole status of religious 'truth' or 'knowledge' is called into question. Phillips seems to be admitting the difficulty and yet saying limply 'Well, it's none of my business', apparently failing to realise that it drives a coach and horses right through his whole argument. No wonder that one critic accused him of confusing the question of what is truly religious with that of what is religious truth (see A. G. N. Flew in *Mind* 1967, p. 295).

I think that some sense can be made of Phillips' position by ignoring his lapses into talk about 'criteria of truth and falsity' and simply regarding it as a thesis about meaning. He is arguing that the 'grammar' of religious language controls what can be said within a community. Most Christians, for instance, would accept St Anselm's definition of God as a being such that no greater can be conceived, and so dismiss other conceptions of God as idolatrous. But another religious community might have an entirely different definition of God, yet we could not accuse them of misusing the term, for it might be the correct usage within that community. After all, Britons and Americans use terms like 'hood' and 'wash up' with different meanings, but it does not make sense to ask whose definition is the 'correct' one: it depends on where you are living. Philosophy cannot arbitrate in such cases; nor can it arbitrate in cases where people are using the same religious 'grammar', but disagree about their conclusions, for such disagreements can only be resolved (if at all) by theological argument.

Such a reply, however, is not entirely faithful to what Phillips actually says and it does not dispose of all the difficulties. For the interesting thing about theological differences is that they have often originated in disputes *within the same community* about the grammar of certain terms. For instance, the Jews of the first century could not admit that Jesus was God, because, among other reasons, their concept of God could not allow them to admit that a man could be God. Similarly, a lot of Reformation controversies hinged on the meaning of terms like 'grace' and 'justification'. It seems, therefore, that in theology questions of meaning and truth are often inextricably mixed and that people may appeal to certain facts as a justification for changing the grammar of religious terms (I am not saying that *all* theological disputes are of this nature, nor that such a problem is confined to theology: many scientific disputes are conceptual in nature, e.g. with regard to terms like 'mass').

Now the problem today is that there are often several different conceptions of God to be found within a single country. How is someone who has not been brought up within a particular sect going to make up his own mind on religious questions? Is there really no single truth to be found here?

TRUTH AND RATIONALITY

I think that most of the difficulties which I have uncovered in this chapter stem from a single factor: Wittgenstein's followers wish to claim that religion has its own standards of truth and rationality, and yet at the same time to avoid what Winch calls a 'Protagorean Relativism'. There is no point in claiming that God has His own kind of reality or religion its own kind of truth unless there is at least some similarity between these and other kinds of reality or truth; otherwise, like Humpty-Dumpty, we are merely using the words to mean whatever we choose to mean by them.

I think that, despite his disclaimers about relativism, Winch is in danger of making this mistake. He says that there are many different standards of rationality and kinds of intelligibility and that it is difficult to see what it means to say that the Zande conception of reality is incorrect or mistaken. Unfortunately there seems to be a contradiction in the Zande theory of witchcraft which he has been examining: they, however, do not press their theory to its logical conclusion, nor do they reject it as obsolete when the contradiction is pointed out to them. Winch notes this, but questions whether they are being irrational, since their notions of witchcraft do not constitute 'a theoretical system in terms of which Azande try to gain a quasi-scientific understanding of the world' (Winch (3) pp. 22–4). But I wonder whether we can stretch the term 'rational' to this extent? Just how far can 'criteria of logic' go?

It is perhaps a little unfair to seize on Winch's unfortunate phrase 'criteria of logic' since he introduced this in the context of a critical discussion of Pareto, in which he was trying to make the point that 'intelligibility takes many and varied forms', and that Pareto was wrong to set up science as the norm for intelligibility in general ((1) pp. 100–2). Winch argues that the artist, the philosopher and the scientist are all making the world intelligible in different ways, that they use different kinds of rules and explanation, and that their work requires varying kinds of understanding. Now these points are more acceptable, but none of them amounts exactly to a proof that there are different kinds of rationality, since artists, philosophers and scientists presumably all seek to avoid incoherence, contradiction, prejudice and so on. Of course, the facts, concepts and arguments which they consider differ according to their field, and I take it that it is this consideration which Winch has particularly in mind here. But the correct conclusion seems to be that 'reason' may be employed in many ways, rather than that there are different standards of rationality.

There is more to Winch's position than I have mentioned here, but even if we could accept his thesis, it seems a rather back-handed defence of religion. Even if there are different standards of rationality (a view requiring more explanation and justification than Winch or Phillips have offered), it remains to be shown that one person can manage to operate with several standards at the same time. Maybe magic and witchcraft make some sense for Azande, but can they really seem intelligible to a contemporary educated European? It is not unknown, of course, for people to divide up their lives into several different compartments which they keep separate, but it seems a drastic measure to need recourse to such cultural schizophrenia in order to defend religious belief. In fact many religious people are quite at home with modern techniques of scientific and

technical thinking and yet they consider these to be compatible
with their religious beliefs. Are such people really using
different standards of rationality in their religious life? And if
so, exactly how does this reasoning differ from their other
reasoning?

Similar strictures apply, I believe, to D. Z. Phillips' treatment
of religious truth. He wants to insist that there are standards of
truth in the language-games of religion and thus to counter the
objections to his position made by Hick, Nielsen and others.
Yet the kind of truth which he envisages is far removed both
from our ordinary everyday sense of truth and from the
understanding of traditional theologians. Let us look more
closely at what Phillips says, paying special attention to his
more recent work in which he does advance beyond the
apparent confusions which I have already discussed — though I
think that he provides only suggestions rather than a fully
worked out theory.

(1) In his paper 'Philosophy and Religious Education' Phillips
suggests that in the phrase 'religious truth' the word 'truth' is
used in a way akin to that in which it is used when we say
'There's a lot of truth in that', or the way in which it was used
when Jesus said, 'I am the way, the truth, and the life' ((3) p.
158). Unfortunately Phillips does not analyse these examples
any further, beyond saying that in neither case is there any
question of an external check. But the first example is unclear
as it stands and the second one has been the subject of much
comment: it needs to be related to other remarks in St John's
Gospel about truth and knowledge, e.g. that no one has ever
seen God and that it is His only son who has made him known
(1.18). In particular, we should note that St John says that
Jesus is the *logos* of God made flesh (1.14) and that God's *logos*
is truth (17.17), thus giving us a connection between Jesus and
truth.[9]

Phillips gives a third example, 'I have come to see the truth of
the saying, that it is better to give than to receive' ((3) p. 158)
where the speaker has come to realise the worth of generosity.
But I think that this remark can be construed as asserting that
one's own experience has confirmed the saying, so, in a sense,
there is an 'external check', for there is here a correspondence
between language and experience.

(2) In his paper 'On the Christian Concept of Love' Phillips

remarks that we cannot say that Christianity is a *better* religion, for this assumes an 'objective religious norm'. All we can do is to reject some religious beliefs or concepts as false, e.g. morally inadequate conceptions of God ((3) pp. 246–8; cf. (1) pp. 159–60).

(3) In *Death and Immortality* Phillips discusses the belief that the spirit of a dead man may return to his family home, and other such beliefs. He notes that we are not dealing here with would-be empirical propositions and cautions us against asking literal-minded questions: 'To ask someone whether he thinks these beliefs are true is not to ask him to produce evidence for them, but rather to ask him whether he can live by them, whether he can digest them, whether they constitute food for him' (p. 71). I take it that this serves as an elucidation of a view which Phillips has expressed elsewhere – that in religion truth is to some extent a personal matter ((3) p. 9; (1) p. 150).

I think that Phillips is correct to insist that 'true religion' is not a matter of a corpus of true theological propositions. St John, after all, says that the man who *does* the truth comes out into the light (3.21), while others have insisted that the truth of Christianity is saving truth, i.e. it is truth which has the power to change our lives. But I think that his views involve certain philosophical difficulties, as well as being religiously un-orthodox. We cannot entirely dispense with the element of propositional truth in religion. The early Fathers of the Church clearly intended the Creeds and other doctrinal formulations to express true propositions, i.e. ones giving correct descriptions of actual states of affairs, difficult though it be for us to understand the metaphysical and eschatological strands in them.

The most serious logical difficulty for Phillips' views arises from a situation which I have already noted, namely that different religions often have mutually incompatible beliefs. Now if two people are nourished by beliefs which contradict each other, then one of them is being nourished by a false belief. We cannot, therefore, simply acquiesce in the easy and comforting view that 'The various authentic religious traditions are different reflections of the same truth, and perhaps equally precious' ((3) p. 246, quoting from Simone Weil). Phillips himself is quite willing to accept the fact that some religious beliefs are false: he rejects, for instance, the belief in reincarnation, on philosophical grounds ((4) pp. 11–12).

I imagine that Phillips would meet my point about different religions contradicting each other by a further appeal to Wittgenstein's *Lectures on Religious Belief*, where the latter says that a person who accepts belief in the Last Judgement or regards illness as a punishment is not actually contradicting someone who rejects these beliefs: it is more the case that they are living with different pictures (Phillips does actually appeal to this passage in (4) p. 76). But even if this move is plausible in the case of belief in the Last Judgement (which I personally doubt, for reasons which I have given in Chapter 1) I do not see how it can work in the case of conflicts between different religions or sects about, say, the divinity of Jesus Christ or the infallibility of the Pope. If we take Phillips' way out here, then why not also take it in other cases of conflicts of belief? Thus if you think that London Bridge is still in London and I think it is now in Arizona, we can avoid the bothersome task of finding out where it actually is, and instead peacably agree that we are both simply living with different pictures. The answer, of course, is that Phillips' account is applicable only to religious belief. But is this limitation more than an *ad hoc* response to the fact that religious disagreements seem irresoluble?

Phillips has a further reason for rejecting any definition of religious truth in terms of conformity with the facts ('an external check'): he refuses to allow that there is any single account of 'the facts'. He says that 'Religious language is not an interpretation of how things are, but determines how things are for the believer. The saint and the atheist . . . see different worlds' ((3) p. 132). Some elucidation of this puzzling statement is provided by his account of conversion, according to which coming to see that there is a God involves discovering a new set of concepts or 'universe of discourse', rather than establishing a new fact within a familiar one ((3) p. 19). For the believer the love of God, for example, 'is itself the measure which brings order to whatever is the case' ((3) p. 74) and is not, therefore, a matter of how things go: nothing can render our loving and thanking God pointless, because the meaningfulness of our lives is not dependent on particular events ((1) p. 105). Plainly Phillips is concerned to deny that religious belief is a deduction or conclusion from non-religious facts; rather, our belief constitutes the facts: 'worship of God makes the believer's relationship to other people and the events which befall him substantially different' ((3) p. 55). But I must confess that I fail to understand much of this: Phillips often seems to be reducing God to a mere concept. He is clearly right in insisting that our stock of concepts and beliefs may affect the way we experience the world and, in some cases, the way things happen (particularly in the realm of human relationships). Clearly, too, there can be different responses to the same events and situations. But it is arguable that there are limits to he ways in which we can experience the world. For, on the one side the outcome of past history, the most general facts about nature and the basic requirements of human life seem to serve as natural, immutable boundaries which limit human responses and experience. And on the other side, our concepts and beliefs always have a history. Hence we need to ask how and why the religious 'universe of discourse', which supposedly structures the believer's experience, ever arose in the first place.

CONCLUSION: SOME QUESTIONS FOR WITTGENSTEIN-IANS

In this chapter I have been critical of some Wittgensteinian philosophers of religion, but I would not like it to be thought that I regard their work as lacking in merit. Phillips, for instance, is often both profound and touching in his religious insights, e.g. in his discussions of the nature of forgiveness and the relationship between the love of God and love of our neighbour ((3) pp. 21—9, 194—5). Moreover, he is an acute philosophical critic: many of his shafts aimed at both Christians like Hick and Ramsey and at sceptics like Flew and Hepburn strike home. But their merits are offset by some serious philosophical errors and some unresolved problems which may have led people to underestimate the real importance of much of what they say. I shall bring out the outstanding difficulties by posing some questions which are raised by talk of 'religious language-games'.

(1) Christianity is a response to the life, death and teaching of a historical person. But what is the relationship between the person of Jesus and the forms of life, language-games and other components of the complex system of developed Christianity? In particular, what is the relationship between Jesus and

metaphysical doctrines about a transcendent being?

(2) For that matter, what is the relationship between such doctrines and our own lives? How does faith in a partially incomprehensible being fit into a 'form of life'? Wittgenstein said that 'Only in the stream of thought and life do words have meaning' (*Z.* 173). But people today often find it difficult to connect traditional religious doctrines with their experience and to recover the understanding which led the early Church Fathers to proclaim these doctrines.

(3) Can a Christian ignore metaphysical speculation about the being and attributes of God? Many followers of Wittgenstein ignore or reject ontological speculations and natural theology. But critics have accused them of reducing God to a mere concept or else of making Him inexplicable and unintelligible (e.g. Meynell (3) p. 127, Grant p. 154).

Wittgenstein himself is usually regarded as an enemy of metaphysics, both in his earlier and later periods, and one can certainly cull remarks from his works which seem to express such hostility (e.g. *T.* 6.52–53; *P.I.* 116). But he said to Dr M. O'C. Drury 'Don't think that I despise metaphysics or ridicule it. On the contrary, I regard the great metaphysical writings of the past as among the noblest productions of the human mind' (Fann (1) p. 68). His own *Lecture on Ethics* shows a profoundly metaphysical side of Wittgenstein. Could it not be argued that metaphysics arises through reflection on, and critical questioning of, our ordinary experience? For instance, natural theology attempts to articulate the feeling which people often have that 'all this cannot have happened by accident'. Wittgenstein himself speaks in this lecture of wondering at the existence of the world and seeing it as a miracle (pp. 8, 11).

(4) What is the role of theology? This seems to be a language-game which interprets other previously existing forms of life and language-games, namely those constituting a religion. Wittgenstein's remarks about the role of theology (e.g. *Z.* 144, 717; *P.I.* 373) are rather cryptic. He does not really seem to cater for the kind of language-game which consists of comment about other language-games (see Apel (2), especially pp. 79 f.).

(5) Why are some forms of life and language-games universal human behaviour, while others, e.g. religion today, are only minority interests?

(6) Why does belief in religion ebb and flow? Why have these

particular language-games and forms of life lost much of their popularity today? This is not just a matter of individuals being converted or losing their faith (something which we have already touched on slightly) since we need a sense of history to answer the first question. We need to understand how and why people's responses change and how their religious views are related to their thinking about morality, science and other aspects of life. Why, for instance, do people living in industrialised urban communities tend to lose the concept of 'sacred'? Or why did the religion of the ancient Greeks and Romans pass away? There seem to be various factors one could mention in the latter case: (a) it was superseded by more attractive and powerful creeds, namely Christianity, Eastern cults and philosophies like Stoicism; (b) the gods were depicted as imperfect, and so men came to regard them as not truly worshipful; (c) monotheism usually supersedes polytheism, at least when the latter has nature (as opposed to tribal) gods, since it is simpler to have a single explanation of the world.

(7) Why do religions change, e.g. when their doctrines are refomulated? Again, it is not enough to say simply that language-games appear, change and disappear, since there are reasons for this and we need a sense of history to appreciate them. I mean this in two senses: the formulation of doctrines is one form of men's response to certain events, e.g. the history of Israel and the work of Christ; and, secondly, they gradually developed over several centuries as a result of continuing discussions. We need to reckon with the fact that concepts like 'grace' have a history, and that this is related to the history of men and their culture. K.-O. Apel has suggested that we should supplement Wittgenstein's work with a hermeneutic relating concepts and doctrines to people's experience and explaining their development (Apel (2) pp. 81—7).

(8) The last two questions have raised the issue of the connection between religion and other spheres of life. To put the matter in Wittgenstein's terminology, what is the relationship between the language-games of religion and other language-games?

(9) A particular case of this difficulty is the problem which has beset us throughout this chapter: if indeed religious language-games do have their own kinds of truth and rationality, how are they to be related to those of other fields?

I shall recur to these problems throughout the rest of this book. But I think it is already clear that I regard the last of them as the most serious and that I consider it a grave weakness of the work considered in this chapter that it has failed to back up its contention that religion has its own special kinds of truth and rationality. This weakness stems partly, I think, from the tendency to use the over-simple models of 'form of life' and 'language-game' for complex phenomena like religions. It would indeed solve a lot of problems if we could view different religions as incommensurate 'forms of life'. But the similarity between, say, Christianity and Judaism precludes such a position; and even such disparate religions as Buddhism and Islam have areas of contact and conflict. There are points of comparison, and this is largely a result of something emphasised throughout this chapter, that religions are *families* of 'language-games', 'activities', 'customs' and so forth, which have coalesced and developed over many centuries.

3　A Programme of Work

LOCATING, RELATING AND VALIDATING

In the first two chapters of this book I have discussed the work of Wittgenstein and his followers, and come up with several serious unresolved difficulties. The rest of this book will attempt to go beyond what they have achieved and to meet some of these difficulties. My purpose so far has not been to deny that religion embodies language-games and forms of life, but to point out that such a claim still leaves us with the tasks of elucidating their special nature and of coping with many philosophical problems. I have also, of course, sought to attack certain positions about justification which have accompanied this claim.

In general, I believe that there are three tasks which need to be tackled if we are. to produce a viable Wittgensteinian philosophy of religion. These are to characterise the language-games and forms of life of religion by explaining their place in our lives and experience, to relate them to other language-games, and to deal candidly with the problems of truth and justification. I shall call these three tasks 'locating', 'relating' and 'validating' respectively, and will devote the rest of this book to discussing them. But it will help matters along if I first briefly mention some of the issues involved.

Locating
We may explain the meaning of religious concepts by relating them to other concepts, but sooner or later there must be some reference to our experience, to facts about human nature, life

and history, or to characteristics of the universe (the word 'reference' is deliberately vague because, as we noted in Chapter 1, there may be different relations between language and the world). If we could show how religion 'latches on' to certain facts, we would have gone *some* way to answering the question of why people continue to play religious language-games. Such facts might be very general ones about the nature of the universe or about human life, with the religious element consisting in a peculiar response to them (e.g. wonder at the existence of the universe, or thanks for one's own existence). Thus it is possible that a religion might be characterised by its being a special response to ordinary aspects of human life, somewhat as Wittgenstein considered that mathematics has no proper subject-matter, but is rather a method for exhibiting essential features of the civil use of language, a technique rather than a body of information (see Shwayder, § 8). On the other hand, some religions appeal to unique historical facts or to special religious factors and experiences. Christianity, for instance, arose as a response to the life, death and Resurrection of Jesus Christ (hence some Christians boast that their religion is 'based on facts').

The followers of Wittgenstein whom I discussed in the last chapter do not give a lot of help on this question. D. Z. Phillips, for example, does allow that religion is a response or a reaction to the world, but he describes the objects of these responses in very general terms – as the whole of life ((3) p. 190), as the common human experiences of joy and sorrow, hope and despair ((1) p. 40), or as significant but ordinary events like birth or death ((3) pp. 97, 100). Although writing from a Christian standpoint he rarely alludes to the life, death and resurrection of Christ, and says little about the light they throw on human experience. Similarly, Peter Winch says that religion, like the Zande magical rites, related to a sense of the significance of human life, particularly birth, marriage and death (Winch (3) pp. 36 ff.). True enough, but one needs to distinguish between 'religion' and particular religions. Most of what Winch and Phillips say about religion would be just as applicable to a primitive nature or family cult as to a developed religion (this is partly due to the poverty of the religious and theological examples chosen, a poverty which they share with many contemporary philosophers of religion).

Phillips' failure to explain the relationship between the present life of the Christian believer and the historical events on which his faith is based is an example of the neglect of *particular* historical facts which is found among many other contemporary theologians, and which stems perhaps from Lessing. People wonder how one can base metaphysical and theological claims on contingent historical events. I shall say something about this question in the next chapter, but for the moment I want simply to stress that those who appeal to particular facts, e.g. about Christ's life, do not necessarily regard religious doctrines as *deductions* from them; rather, the facts are a *necessary condition* of Christian theology. Clearly the doctrines of Christianity are not simply deduced from descriptions of the life, teachings and death of Christ — the situation is much more complex than that. We must distinguish between the historical facts and our theological speculations about their implications. But the actual historical crucifixion, for example, is a necessary condition of theorising about the Redemption or the Atonement, and of many other Christian concepts, beliefs and practices. In general, I think that there is some causal and logical connection between the present responses, activities and beliefs of Christians, and certain historical events; any complete description and understanding of Christian 'forms of life' must take into account such connections.

I regard the point which I have just made as an exemplification of what Wittgenstein meant when he said that 'If we imagine the facts otherwise than as they are, certain language-games lose some of their importance, while others become more important' (*O.C.* 63), and when he maintained that the formation of concepts different from the usual ones will become intelligible if we imagine certain very general facts of nature to be different from what we are used to (*P.I.* p. 230; cf. *B.B.* pp. 61–2). Of course, he did not make this point in a religious context; but he did give several examples: if lumps of cheese tended to shrink sometimes when put on the scale, then fixing the price by the turning of the scale would lose its point (*P.I.* 142); similarly, the technique of measuring is made possible and useful by certain physical and psychological facts: if confusion intervened, e.g. if rulers tended to alter in length, measuring and calculating would lose their character and their point (*R.F.M.* II. 74–5; V. 1–2); if houses started turning into steam or cattle speaking, if water started behaving differently, our language-games would change (*O.C.* 513, 558; see Sherry (2) pp. 164—65 for further examples). Now the significance of his point for Christianity is this: if it were to turn out that Jesus Christ never existed or that he was much different from his portrayal in the Gospels, then the Christian religion would lose much of its point (there is, of course, some latitude here: I do not think that we have to insist upon the veracity of every miracle story, while others may question whether belief in the Virgin Birth or the empty tomb is obligatory for Christians).

The truth of the Christian religion also, I think, depends on certain facts about the present and the future, though it is difficult to specify their nature. But we can at least rule out certain possibilities: both the doctrine of the Holy Spirit and Christ's promise that the gates of hell shall not prevail against his church rule out the demise or the utter corruption of Christianity. This question, however, raises the issue of verification and takes us away from our present concern, which is more with the background of religious practices, etc. The issue of verification will be discussed later; in any case, it does not arise in the case of forms of life and non-descriptive uses of language, e.g. commands, prayers and promises, although these do have to be 'located' by showing their context and their purpose.

Phillips, by contrast, thinks that the strength of religion lies in its independence of the way things go. He says that religious belief involves responding to the whole of life and giving thanks, whatever is the case ((2) p. 1; (3) pp. 190, 209). He construes belief in Providence as 'seeing that what is of value cannot be destroyed by the way things go' ((1) p. 124), rather than as expecting some particular happy outcome. The advantage of his position is that it enables the religious person to go on believing, whatever happens. And clearly there is a lot that is very noble in it: it may be seen as an extension of Kierkegaard's insight that love of one's neighbour is eternal, for nothing can take him away, whereas the objects of erotic love or friendship may die or change (Kierkegaard (4) pp. 76 f.). But I wonder whether Phillips' account does full justice to Christ's promise that the very hairs on our heads are numbered and that God cares even for the sparrows. Certainly his understanding of belief in Providence is very different from the traditional view found, for example, in de Caussade's *Self-Abandonment to Divine Providence.*[1] My doubts are increased by his rather unusual view of the virtue of hope: he says that '. . . the believer's hope is not hope *for* anything, moral improvement, for example. . . . It is simply hope, hope in the sense of the ability to live with himself' ((1) p. 67). The suspicion that Phillips has simply abandoned the eschatological strand of Christianity is, of course, confirmed by his rejection of belief in survival after death in his most recent book, *Death and Immortality.*

Besides the categories of fact already mentioned, the Christian religion also, I think, involves a response to certain metaphysical facts. I am thinking here particularly of the presence and activity of God. Of course, such facts are vastly different from historical facts about the life of Christ, but they are nevertheless the objects of religious responses – the worshipper thinks of himself as praying *to* someone, difficult though it be to describe the nature of this being. It is worth noting at this point that the reluctance of Wittgensteinian philosophers to discuss the person and nature of Jesus Christ is parallelled by their reluctance to engage in any ontological analysis of the existence of God. Paul Holmer, for example, asserts that the Christian's confidence in God comes from guilt, prayer and worship rather than from metaphysics, and he attacks theologians like Tillich for seeking to underpin Christianity with an ontology (Holmer (1) p. 143; (6) pp. 368–70). Similarly, D. Z. Phillips describes knowing God in terms of having the idea of God and being able to use religious language (Phillips (1) pp. 18, 50) and he says that coming to see that there is a God consists in seeing a new meaning in one's life and coming to understand a new language ((3) pp. 18–19). But these remarks raise questions about the mode of God's existence: can we, for instance, appropriately describe Him as an 'agent' or a 'power', or as 'personal'? In what do His acting on the world, His giving and loving, consist? Is He transcendent – would He still exist if people stopped using religious pictures, if religious language-games passed away? Did He exist before the human race emerged? The answers to these questions are unclear: it often seems as if Phillips is *reducing* God to a concept or to some aspect of the world: he says that prayer *means* talking to God ((1) pp. 38, 79), that renunciation, forgiveness, etc. *are* God's reality ((4) p. 55) and that the ability

to give thanks in all things *is* God's goodness ((3) p. 209). But a
traditional theologian would have preferred to speak rather of
God's 'presence' or 'activity', in order to do justice to the
notion of a transcendent God acting in and upon the world (see
R. T. Allen, p. 4). He would have seen men's courage or
forgiveness as caused by, or as expressive of, God's goodness,
rather than as *identical* with it.

This unclarity about God's ontological status is seen particularly in Phillips' treatment of prayer. He condemns as super-
stitious prayers which seek to influence God's will ((1) p. 121):

> When deep religious believers pray *for* something they are not
> so much asking God to bring this about, but in a way telling
> Him of the strength of their desires. They realise that things
> may not go as they wish, but they are asking to be able to go
> on living whatever happens.

Hence, for Phillips, petitionary prayer is best understood as 'an
expression of, and a request for, devotion to God through the
way things go' (p. 121). He seems to envisage that the spiritual
benefits received by believers in prayer will enable them to do
good in the world, so that God's power is essentially the power
of men's love for each other. He condemns the tendency to
identify the will of God with anything natural as the 'Naturalistic Fallacy' in religion, and stresses that our dependence on
God is not logical or causal but religious ((1) pp. 101, 109). It is
not entirely clear what he means by such a religious dependence, but one of the things it includes is a spiritual relationship
with God in which we realise our need for grace and in which
we request, receive and give thanks in prayer for His spiritual
benefits: 'The goodness of God is located in the help which
comes through prayer, in what prayer teaches one to recognise'
((1) pp. 122–3; cf. p. 71).

Many people feel that Phillips' account of prayer, though
admirable in many ways, fails to do justice to Christian teaching
about petitionary prayer and Providence. I think that the root
cause of this feeling is, again, Phillips' evasiveness on ontological
issues. Is God *affected* by our prayers? Does He act only
through people (through grace), or also through natural events
and, if so, how? Phillips allows that our prayers may refer to
specific events, but he is so anxious to rebut the view that God

is like the parent of a spoilt child who can be deflected from his purposes by entreaties that he fails to define to what extent God is the 'Lord of Creation'. Similarly, his rejection of natural theology (e.g. in (1) ch. 5 and (3) ch. 3) leaves the causal status of God unclear. Now, although Christians may deny that we can make a causal inference to God's existence and may therefore reject natural theology, they must maintain that, in some sense, God is an agent in the world and that He keeps it in being – in other words, that He has some causal status vis-à-vis the world. The doctrines of Creation, grace and Providence cover this question.[2] They describe God's status in terms like 'create', 'sustain', 'depend on', 'care for', 'intervene', 'bring about', 'design' and so on, all of which denote causal relationships.[3] Even if we carry the process of demythologisation to the extent of restricting God's activity to our inner spiritual life and to personal encounters, we still have to explain the mode of His interaction with us. That is why I think that Phillips is trying to have his cake and eat it in insisting that our dependence on God is religious but not causal.

Of course, Phillips' position does have its advantages: it enables him to dismiss the problem of evil ((1) pp. 93, 106). But I suspect that the difficulties which I have just raised will prove to be the most crucial ones for him in the long run. For I can imagine that Phillips might reply to some of the objections concerning religious truth which I raised in the last chapter by developing Wittgenstein's notions of 'grammar' and 'criteria' and applying them to religion. But the ordinary believer is left feeling that the sense of God's independent existence and of His power is lacking.[4]

Relating
Many writers have claimed that theologians who speak of 'religious language-games' must show how these are related to other language-games (e.g. J. A. Martin, p. 110). Phillips realises this problem and admits that there *is* a relationship: 'I am anxious to avoid a position in which religious language seems to be a special language cut off from other forms of human discourse. Religious would not have the kind of importance it has were it not connected with the rest of life' (Phillips (2) p. 196; cf. (1) p. 40; (3) p. 230). But he does not really explain in what the relationship is, for he is generally much more anxious

to stress the autonomy of religion: 'Wittgenstein stressed that each mode of discourse is not part of some all-embracing reality: it is what it is' ((3) p. 133).

Now it is quite true that Wittgenstein denied that language-games have a common essence which makes them a part of language (*P.I.* 65). But he also noted that we use the same expressions in different language-games (*P.I.* p. 188), e.g. we compose poetry using the 'language of information' (*Z*. 160). He even insisted that 'it is essential to mathematics that its signs are also employed in *mufti*' (*R.F.M.* IV. 2; cf. 41); this is an expression of his view that mathematics is an activity or part of our natural history, a practical technique with many applications in ordinary life.

The problem which I have raised is not peculiar to Wittgenstein and his followers. Many other writers have discussed both the general question of the relationship between religion and other departments of life, and the particular issue of the way in which religion takes ordinary words and gives them new uses. Theology may be trying to say something unique, yet it 'must show how religious language can gear into other language, and it must lay bare the points of intersection' (Bernard Williams in Flew & MacIntyre, p. 207). I think that the solution to this problem will involve two tasks:

(1) Showing the relationship between the language-games of religion and other language-games.
(2) Showing how the meanings of terms like 'exist', 'real' and 'truth' in religious contexts are related to their uses elsewhere.

The second of these tasks is, of course, merely a special case of the first.

In connecting religious uses of language with secular ones we are not seeking to reduce the former to the latter: there is nothing incompatible in showing both that something is unique and that it has similarities with other things. Actually, there are two dangers to be reckoned with here: one is that of 'Reductionism', which Phillips counters when he attacks those who have produced anthropomorphic ideas of God; the other might be called 'isolationism' or 'compartmentalisation' (Nielsen (4) pp. 201, 204). In stressing the autonomy of religion one risks isolating it from the rest of our life. Now I think it would not be unfair to say that, despite his occasional disclaimers, Phillips' account nerertheless leaves religious language rather like a balloon floating in the air without any attachment to earth. It seems that here we must steer between two hazards; but I do not think that this is impossible. It may be true that concepts like 'God', 'grace', 'prayer' and so forth only make sense within the language-games of religion, in the same way that we can only explain the function of chess pieces by explaining the rules of the game in which they are used (to use a favourite example of Wittgenstein's). All the same, this does not mean that the games must be viewed in isolation. To pursue the analogy of chess, we can explain why people want to play it, what its history is, what similarities it has with other games like draughts, whether other games are more interesting or taxing, how well designed the pieces are and so on — while at the same time bringing out its unique features.

In order to relate religious language-games to other language-games I think that we first need to differentiate between special religious or theological terms and words which have uses in other contexts. I would suggest the following rough and ready division of types of 'religious language':

(1) Specifically religious terms like 'God', 'Holy Trinity' and 'Hell' in Christianity (other religions have their own particular terminology).
(2) Metaphysical terms, e.g. 'omniscient', 'infinite' or 'spirit'.
(3) Analogical terms, i.e. terms from ordinary language used outside their normal contexts, e.g. 'father', 'cause', 'make', 'redeem', 'real' and 'truth'.
(4) Ordinary terms, e.g. 'death', 'peace', 'crucify' and very common words like 'and', 'but', 'all' and 'not'.

Most discussions of 'religious language' concentrate on (1) and (2) because the most difficult problems centre round them. But for the moment I wish to concentrate on the last two categories, since these are highly relevant to Winch's and Phillips' claims that religion, like other fields of discourse, has its own criteria of logic or rationality, and that the meaning of words like 'exist' or 'real' depends on the context.

I have already criticised the first claim, and I think that my criticism may be reinforced by noting that the use of logical operators like 'not', 'and', 'some' and 'all' is the same in religious language as in other language, so that it cannot be literally true that religion has its own logic.[5] This statement perhaps needs qualifying slightly, since many Christian doctrines involve paradoxes or logical problems: the doctrine of the Trinity, for example, raises difficulties about criteria of identity, while the term 'God' seems to share the properties of both a proper name and a description. Still, traditional theologians have usually discussed these issues individually and have been careful to explain and justify any odd or stretched use of language; on the whole they would not sympathise with the blanket claim that religion has its own standards of logic and rationality.

The second claim is a reasonable one; but here I find it surprising that Winch and Phillips have omitted to mention the question of analogy. Mediaeval treatments of analogical predication discussed the relationship between God's 'existence', 'love', 'wisdom' and 'goodness', and those of His creatures. They may be viewed, therefore, as attempts to explain how religious language is to be related to non-religious language. I shall discuss their contemporary relevance further in Chapter 7.

Phillips' position is made even more difficult by his rejection of any natural theology or metaphysics of the traditional sort. Of course, I quite sympathise with his rejection of crude apologetical uses of natural theology, such as attempts to boost religion by making capital out of gaps in current scientific explanations. A 'God of the gaps' has little religious significance, and there is always the risk that an alternative scientific or philosophical explanation may be found for the particular problem in question, as the Darwinian theory of natural selection made some of Paley's arguments obsolete. But many proponents of natural theology regard it as an adjunct of religious faith rather than a foundation: it can be seen as an attempt to clarify some of the central concepts of religion by relating them to our ordinary experience. Many people find difficulty in understanding a purely 'Biblical' theology and feel the need for a philosophical account of the concepts involved in their religious beliefs — '*fides quaerens intellectum*'. I do not see that such an approach need be crude or reductionist, or that it necessarily violates the autonomy of religious faith. Again, most traditional philosophical theologians avoided these pitfalls by emphasising the analogical character of many statements of Christian doctrine: terms like 'love' or 'maker' are not attributed to God in quite the same way that they are attributed to men (in any case, such terms have a wide range of uses even in non-religious contexts: think of all the different kinds of relationships which may be described as 'love').

If we reject all traditional metaphysics and natural theology, do we not run the risk of having a concept of God which is completely inexplicable and unintelligible? This question was asked by the respondent to Phillips' paper 'From World to God?' (see Grant p. 154) who went on to compare some of Phillips' views with those of Karl Barth.[6] There are indeed many parallels, e.g. in their views on natural theology and the justification of religious beliefs, and it is perhaps surprising that Malcolm, Phillips and Winch have not said more about this question. But it is also worth noting that many of my criticisms parallel those made of Barth. For instance, Hugo Meynell, commenting on Barth's view that the *analogia entis* is the invention of antichrist because it is impertinent to subsume God and man under the one concept 'being', has remarked that if we deny that *'es gibt'* can apply to God, then presumably we must apply *'es gibt nicht'* to Him (Meynell (2) pp. 40 f.). This comment is very relevant to my criticism of the suggestion that religion has its own criteria of logic. Likewise, his observation that if the doctrine of Creation has no implications of a scientific or existential nature, then it is hard to see what meaning it has (ibid. p. 155), is highly relevant to my remarks about the need to connect religious language-games with other language-games and with facts about the world.

Validating
This is the most difficult of the three tasks which I have mentioned, since it raises a host of problems concerning truth and justification at different levels. It is also the most contentious task, since many philosophers, whilst agreeing with the need to 'locate' and to 'relate' religious language-games, would strenuously assert that the enterprise of justifying them is a misguided one, for we can only justify particular moves within them. Here I must say that I am simply using 'validate' as a shorthand term for dealing with the fundamental issues of

truth and justification raised in the last chapter. I argued there that we cannot evade such problems by simply labelling religion as a 'form of life' since the question is not about 'religion' but about *particular* religions; and in any case it is probably, I think, more faithful to Wittgenstein's usage to say that religion *includes* forms of life than to say that it *is* one.

Now whilst it is simply a fact of nature that people tell jokes, make promises, hope, give or obey orders and report on past events, and it would indeed be silly to ask for a justification of such practices, it is nevertheless true that individual cases can be appraised in different ways: jokes can be funny or crude, hopes groundless, orders pointless or immoral, and reports of events untrue or graphic. We consider that certain conduct merits praise, reward and punishment. Furthermore, there are *some* practices that can be evaluated as a whole: ones like pity, love, thanking and forgiving are recommended, not just in particular cases (we consider them appropriate, praiseworthy or obligatory, depending on the circumstances), but also *in general*. We do criticise those who fail to show pity and affection and consider that people should give thanks or show forgiveness. It is difficult to say how far we can *justify* ourselves here, but it is certainly true that we regard people who fail to make these responses as harsh and insensitive and that we try to teach children to be loving and forgiving and so on. If these responses are indeed 'forms of life', then it seems that they can sometimes be appraised as wholes (*contra* Wittgenstein). Of course, some civilisations (e.g. ancient Sparta) have depreciated responses like pity. But if we found some men who were constitutionally incapable of these responses or who behaved oddly by rejoicing at pain or insulting their friends, we would be inclined either to deny that they were human beings or at least to classify them as deviant beings.

It seems, then, that the procedure of justifying a human response has two stages:

(1) Showing what the relevant facts are ('locating').
(2) Arguing that the response is appropriate, praiseworthy etc. We must not simply say that 'This is what we do!', or rather we must not say this too early in the chain of explanation.

Not surprisingly, especially interesting and difficult cases arise in the case of religion. Is it appropriate to pray for the dead or to the saints? The sixteenth century reformers differed from their predecessors on this matter. When is worship an appropriate response? Presumably this 'form of life' has no point unless what is worshipped actually exists and is indeed worthy of worship.[7] Hence we are faced with the problems of the existence of God and the nature of Jesus Christ — we can only decide what response is appropriate to the latter when we know who and what he is. A religious sceptic might argue that the response of worship is *never* appropriate and that the practice as a whole is pointless. He would not be disposed to accept the claim that practices like praying, worshipping, blessing and cursing are fundamental parts of 'natural history' or 'forms of life', like chatting, commanding or greeting people. Just as practices like pity or forgiveness can be recommended, so other practices can be condemned as irrational or pointless, not just in particular cases but in general.

Another interesting and difficult case is Phillips' parallel between seeking for a foundation of religion and trying to justify science. We have seen that this parallel breaks down, as Phillips himself recognises, because of the diversity of religions. But is it even true that science cannot be justified? In the last chapter I distinguished between the absurd question 'Is science true?' and the sensible question 'Why pursue science?' Now a developing country might well ask itself whether it was worthwhile to set up universities and to encourage scientific research, or a young person choosing a career might debate the merits of a career devoted to science. A number of considerations are relevant: science is interesting, it enlarges our knowledge and understanding, its applications help to eradicate poverty and disease, and so on. Of course, such considerations involve reference to existing moral principles and values which may themselves require justification; and it is doubtful whether one could provide anything resembling a tight, knock-down demonstration. But still, the matter is at least open to discussion.

When we move on to talk of 'language-games' further problems arise. If people refuse to think or talk about religion, what sort of gap is left in their 'conceptual map' and in their lives? Could religion pass away, as witchcraft has almost done, at least in the Western world? What kind of truth is to be claimed for religious beliefs, and how does one reach it? A science might contain a lot of truths and yet not be essential for most people's happiness — botany, for example. The doctrines of religion, however, are clearly of such importance that, if they are true, they are essential for everyone to know. Conversely, a thing may be essential without containing any truths: the Highway Code is essential but it contains few truths, since most of it consists of recommendations and prohibitions, as opposed to statements of fact.

The mainstream of Christianity has insisted both that its beliefs are extremely important for human life and that they are true; moreover, the truth claimed is at least similar to other kinds of truth. Now if we insist that religion has its own special kind of truth, we are in danger of isolating religion from other spheres of life and thereby perhaps trivialising it — again, this is really another case of 'relating': in the previous section I was dealing more with the relationship between religious and non-religious concepts, whereas now I am more concerned with the truth of judgements. This question becomes particularly murky when we try to relate religious explanations to other explanations. I have already mentioned two examples in Chapter 1: Wittgenstein's example of a man falling ill and regarding this as a punishment sent by God, and Bernard Williams' example of a people so regarding a famine. We found that it *can* be irrational to view something as a divine punishment: another example occurred in my own home town in 1967, when a clergyman said that Britain's economic troubles, particularly the devaluation of the pound, were sent by God as a punishment for the immorality of the 'permissive society'. But Britain's economic position subsequently improved without any corresponding improvement in general morality, so the required connection between immorality and economic troubles apparently does not exist. It seems, therefore, that there must be some point in introducing religious concepts and explanations, that they relate to other kinds of explanation, and that their truth is not 'autonomous' because it may depend on the outcome of events.

Perhaps, however, I am going a little too fast here by glossing over terms like 'autonomy' and 'special kinds of truth' and failing to distinguish two different theses:

(1) The view that each religion uses its own sacred books and traditions as the touchstone of truth, and that it is not philosophy's task to decide between different religious 'truths', for there is no single objective norm to which we can appeal. This, as we have seen, is Phillips' view: he maintains that religious truth is a personal matter, by which he seems to mean that a religion is true for me if it embodies beliefs which provide spiritual nourishment and by which I can live. This position has many difficulties and finally founders, I think, on the fact that different religions sometimes have incompatible beliefs. Phillips, therefore, is in effect divorcing his concept of truth from the principle of non-contradiction — something which Wittgenstein also seems willing to do in the case of belief in the Last Judgement.

(2) The view that there are different kinds of truth, e.g. scientific, mathematical, moral, literary and religious. I regard this view as much more worthy of consideration than (1) and will discuss it fully in Chapter 8. We shall have to consider what Kierkegaard meant by 'subjective truth' and how it relates to his 'objective' and 'eternal' truth in God. We shall also have to consider the notion of 'saving truth', as well as some modern views, e.g. Cantwell Smith's contention that a religion *becomes* true if a person appropriates it to himself, interiorises it and thereby transforms his life.

When people claim that there are different kinds of truth, it is not always clear whether they mean that the words 'true' and 'truth' have several different *senses*, or whether they just mean that there are different kinds of evidence and fact in different fields so that varying types of verification or investigation are called for. If the first claim is insisted upon, then it will be necessary to show how the different senses of the words are related to each other — unless we are to suppose that they are completely equivocal. The second claim is a more moderate one: in the case of religion we would have to show what kind of facts we are dealing with, what concepts and 'method of projection' are being used, and what kind of verification is appropriate.

The obvious comment should perhaps be made at this point that in discussing the question of religious truths we are not attempting to prove that any particular religious belief or religion is true — we are not doing apologetics — but rather to show in general terms what kind of truth we should expect to be claimed for religious beliefs.

A PARALLEL WITH ETHICS

The three tasks which I have just outlined will necessitate our discussing the questions of ontology, concept-formation, analogy and truth. Now I think that it is interesting and important to note that three similar tasks arise elsewhere: many recent writers on ethics have attempted to locate, relate and validate moral discourse. Thus the programme which I have laid down for philosophers of religion, particularly those writing from a Wittgensteinian standpoint, can be paralleled in the field of ethics. About forty years ago Logical Positivists espoused some version of the Emotive Theory of ethics, which identified moral judgements with expressions of feeling. If taken seriously, this theory removes ethics from the realm of further philosophical enquiry, since expressions of feeling are a species of 'brute fact'. But during the last twenty years or so ethics has been reinstated as a serious branch of philosophy by writers like Stephen Toulmin, R. M. Hare, Kurt Baier, Marcus Singer and Mrs P. Foot.[8] They have started by pointing out the inadequacies of the Emotive Theory of ethics. For example, Ayer lumped together moral and aesthetic judgements; but several subsequent writers, e.g. Stuart Hampshire (in Elton pp. 162–3) have pointed out that there are important conceptual differences between ethics and aesthetics: the latter is 'gratuitous', in that a person may go through life without making any judgements of aesthetic appreciation. Such a life might be very impoverished but by no means unheard of. But it is very difficult to dispense with moral language, since we all make decisions and perform actions which affect other people, and moral principles are rules for guiding such decisions and actions.

More positively, the writers whom I have mentioned have given a fuller and truer account of the role of morality in our lives. But this brings me to the first point in my parallel between ethics and philosophy of religion.

(1) Locating. What is the *Sitz im Leben* of moral discourse? I have remarked that recent writers have largely agreed that moral judgements are not expressions of emotion but rules or

decisions for regulating our conduct. But this by itself, though perfectly acceptable, is not particularly remarkable; it needs developing, and indeed it has been developed, in at least three ways. First of all much attention has been paid to the 'logic' of rules, commands and other forms of 'prescriptive language'. Secondly (and more relevantly to our present enquiry) much work has been done in 'moral psychology', particularly on problems relating to the nature of human action, intention, will and so forth. If we are to speak of evaluating human conduct and character, we need to have a clear idea of what distinguishes an action from a physiological process, how intentions and motives are related to actions, what makes something voluntary and purposive, and how we distinguish an action from its consequences (see E. D'Arcy for this last question, which is important for the problem of assessing responsibility). Lastly, we need to define the scope of morality by distinguishing moral principles from other rules, e.g. those of etiquette and prudence. Winch is making a good point when he says 'it does not seem to me a merely conventional matter that T. S. Eliot's trinity of "birth, copulation and death" happen to be such deep objects of human concern' (Winch (3) p. 39). But if we define ethics in terms of a certain subject-matter (as compared with Hare, who prefers a more formal definition in terms of being prescriptive and universalisable), to what extent are we committed to some form of natural law?

(2) Relating. If ethics deals with human needs, desires, intentions, actions, character and so on, its vocabulary will be fairly wide. One of the weaknesses of writers like Moore and Ross was that they tended to make ethics into an isolated language-game by concentrating on a handful of terms like 'good', 'ought' and 'right'. This tendency impoverished the subject, as well as raising in its crudest form Hume's old problem of how we move on from an 'is' to an 'ought'. It also impoverished political philosophy, by concentrating on one or two concepts like 'justice' or 'natural rights' in isolation.

Recent writers have cast their net more widely, analysing the terms from philosophical psychology which I have mentioned and also ones like 'unscrupulous', 'saintly', 'heroic', 'weak-willed', and 'need'. Such an examination shows both that the 'language-games' of ethics are highly complex and that they touch and overlap with other language-games in many different ways (the problem of moving from 'descriptive' to 'evaluative' terms remains, but is is questionable whether this distinction can be preserved in its old simple form). For instance, J. Rawls has argued that classical utilitarianism is unable to account for the idea of fairness, which is a fundamental component of the concept of justice (see Rawls, ch. 1). Other writers have pointed to the links between the latter concept and ones like 'natural rights', 'equality', 'freedom' and even 'public interest' (see Gewirth (1)). We can only understand such concepts by considering the whole network of which they are a part.

Mrs Foot and one or two other so-called 'neo-naturalists' would go a step further by claiming that we can make a direct logical inference from statements about human needs, wants, 'flourishing' and harm to ones about the rightness, goodness, or wrongness of actions. This has given rise to much controversy, particularly with Professor R. M. Hare, about the question of moving from descriptive statements to prescriptive or evaluative uses of language.[9] It also raises the question of the possibility of some form of theory of natural law, like that espoused by Professor H. L. A. Hart.[10]

(3) *Validating.* As in the case of religious belief, so in the case of ethics, this is the most difficult and contentious of the three issues which I have raised.[11] Some moral philosophers have tried to provide philosophical justifications of particular moral principles. But usually discussions have been more general and have simply sought to show that rationality does operate in the sphere of ethics. Such discussions on the role of reason in ethics embrace the questions of how we deal with conflicts between different moral principles and how we ultimately justify them. But it is difficult to point to any generally agreed conclusions of the debate, except for the point that not just *any* principle can be regarded as a moral principle. For example, R. M. Hare and M. Singer have sought to show that the Principle of Generalis-ation and the concept of Universalisability provide a method of discriminating between suggested moral principles. They have, I think, succeeded in showing that principles prescribing lying, injury or racial discrimination would involve their proponents in inconsistency or self-frustration, but they have not provided a method for dealing with those principles which depend on fundamental decisions about one's style of life or ideals, or about the kind of society which is to be produced. The other

writers whom I have mentioned seem to be moving towards some form of naturalism or theory of natural law.

Many of the recent writers whom I have mentioned are seeking to attack relativism in ethics (a position which I find to be more common today among non-philosophers than philosophers). One of the things to be decided here is to what extent we must look for universally applicable and rationally justifiable moral principles and to what extent morality is a question of personal ideals or styles of life. My remarks here are relevant to a question which is often raised: could there be two different and mutually exclusive sets of principles, both of which could be called 'moral principles'? Does it make sense to speak, as social scientists often do, of 'different moralities'? Rush Rhees says that Wittgenstein considered that although we resolve moral dilemmas by appealing to moral rules, it makes no sense to ask whether ethical systems, e.g. Christian or Nietzschean ethics, are right — how would we decide?[12] Such a question is like asking which of two standards of accuracy is the right one (Rhees (2) p. 100). I think that Wittgenstein's view is plausible in the case of personal ideals, but much less so in the case of fundamental principles concerning human life and health which seem necessary for any society. It is here that a theory of natural law becomes tempting.

Wittgenstein's views on justifying moral principles are similar to his views on religious belief: in both cases he seems to opt for some form of relativism through his insistence that no ultimate justification is possible. Certainly he is correct to stress the personal element in these areas. But I am left feeling unhappy about such a limitation of the role of rational argument in ethics and religion. I shall return to this issue in Chapter 8.

First I want to tackle the other two problems which I have mentioned, those of 'locating' and 'relating' religion. I shall devote the next three chapters to the former, since it is the more complex (though not necessarily the more difficult): besides considering the facts which form the background of religion, we shall have to consider how religious concepts are formed and their place in a religious way of life.

4 Locating: I The Background of Facts

The question 'How does religion relate to the world?' needs to be broken down into a number of separate questions. Most obviously, there is the question of what religious propositions are about: what is their subject-matter? Religious language has several strands, so presumably many kinds of facts and contexts must be taken into account. But is there a special religious or metaphysical subject-matter, e.g. God, His attributes and actions, or is religion just a special response to ordinary life or to history? Since, however, religious belief is not just a question of accepting certain propositions, but involves behaviour and non-propositional uses of language like prayers and commands, we need to re-phrase these questions. Using Wittgenstein's terminology we might ask: what is the area of life in which religious language-games and forms of life occur and make sense? What are the contexts and surroundings of the concepts which religious people use? What features of the universe, what aspects of human life and history must we consider? In the case of Christianity, how do we relate the forms of life and language-games of present-day Christians to the person and life of Christ?

These are the questions which we shall have to consider in this chapter. I have already touched on their relevance to the philosophy of Wittgenstein and his followers, and I think that it is by now clear that I regard Wittgenstein's insistence that the possibility of a language-game is conditioned by certain facts as an extremely important insight. I have tried to relate it to religion by stressing the importance of certain facts for the emergence and continuance of the latter: in particular, there is often a causal and logical connection between certain historical figures and later religious practices or beliefs. I have criticised those who fail to show how religious activities and language-games are connected with facts about history, the world and human experience. But now, to see what these connections are, let us look more closely at the ways in which behaviour and uses of language occur in certain contexts or situations, both generally and in the case of religion.

TYPES OF CONTEXT

Many human responses occur only in certain surroundings: we give thanks for gifts and for happy events; we hope for pleasant things in the future and fear unpleasant things; we expect both pleasant and unpleasant things, but our expecting implies that we think that the outcome is reasonably certain (whereas one can fear or hope for the remote and the unlikely). We rejoice at good things and are resigned to suffering. Sometimes there can be different responses to the same situation (though perhaps only one of these may be appropriate or praiseworthy): I can, for instance, repent of my sins, or I can be indifferent to them or even proud of them. Conversely, one can make the same response in different situations — though it is important to see that there is often a conceptual link between the response and the context, so that we need to distinguish cases where the background merely suggests or facilitates a particular activity from ones where there is a logical connection between the two: clearly, for instance, it makes no sense to speak of my repenting for your sins, for things I regard as right, or for future events (cf. Z. 519, 'Only someone who can reflect on the past can repent'). There are perhaps one or two responses which are appropriate whatever the circumstances — a Christian would instance love and acceptance — but these are few, because the variety of our experiences evokes a variety of responses.[1]

This point is relevant to Wittgenstein's teaching about the intimate connection between language and the activities of our lives, and also to what he says about 'surroundings' or contexts. He maintains that intending, expecting, loving, and hoping occur only in certain situations: 'Could someone have a feeling of ardent love or hope for the space of one second — *no matter what* preceded or followed this second?' (*P.I.* 583; cf. 581, 337). Similarly, he argues that we can only be said to pretend, to give presents and to play chess in certain situations, and that our saying something in a play is very different from saying it in real life (*P.I.* 33, 250, 268; *Z.* 397). Legal concepts, too, presuppose a 'scaffolding of facts', i.e. a normal human background (*Z.* 350).

More generally, Wittgenstein argues that certain contingent facts place limits on the possibility and nature of our language-games. Although, as we saw in Chapter 2, language-games cannot be justified or criticised as wholes, it is nevertheless true that both natural events and human needs are necessary conditions and that if these conditions were otherwise than they are, our language-games would be different: 'Indeed, doesn't it seem obvious that the possibility of a language-game is conditioned by certain facts?' (*O.C.* 617; in the next section he says that induction is made logically possible only by a certain regularity in occurrences). Even when things are a matter of convention, the concention may be determined by our situation and requirements — this is what I take to be the meaning of his remark that although essences are a matter of convention, there may be a *deep* need for a convention (*R.F.M.* I.74).

In the last chapter I quoted several other examples of the way in which language-games depend on facts about the world. As regards facts about human nature, Wittgenstein says that the limits of Empiricism are 'ways in which we make comparisons and in which we act' (*R.F.M.* V. 18): presumably he has in mind ungrounded behaviour and parts of our 'natural history' like eating, playing and bringing up children (*P.I.* 25, 467; *O.C.* 110). He brings both kinds of fact together in a way which is very interesting and important for the present context in his comments on Frazer's *Golden Bough*: he says that although we cannot explain practices like kissing pictures of loved ones, burning effigies or striking the ground with a stick in anger except by connecting them with familiar instincts, we can point out the importance for man of changes in the seasons, birth, sex and death. Given these facts and his natural tendency to be a 'ceremonial animal', it is hardly surprising that he weaves rituals round birth or marriage (*On Frazer*, pp. 236, 239).

Wittgenstein is not saying that our surroundings force us to have certain practices or language-games (though in *P.I.* p. 204 he does speak of a concept forcing itself upon us), but that they are necessary conditions: both our everyday life and the practice of science depend on an unnoticed background of natural regularities. The language-games we play with colours, for instance, depend on the constancy of colour properties and on the regularity of human reactions (*L.P.E.* p. 306). Moreover, the task of describing our language-games will involve a reference to the context: we cannot explain the phenomenon of hope, since it is a basic fact of human life which must simply be noted (cf. *P.I.* 655); but we can connect it with other facts, e.g. that people want certain things, that they cannot predict the future and so on. Similarly with repentance or forgiveness: these two are 'proto-phenomena' which cannot be explained, but they can be connected with other phenomena like our feelings of guilt or desire to make amends. In other words, they are responses to experience; although they are not *compelled* by the facts, they do presuppose a certain background in our lives.

Now there are many different kinds of religious response and activity: men celebrate weddings and funerals; they have sacraments and sacrifices; they commemorate certain formative historical events and hierophanies; they worship God and devote themselves to His service, particularly by pursuing love and justice in the world. But all of these responses occur against a background of facts about the world and are to some degree dependent on it. Moreover, God is regarded as active in various ways in this background. Let us, therefore, proceed by classifying the objects, persons, events and states of affairs which constitute the latter. There are many possible classifications, but the one which seems most useful to me at this point is that of the unique or non-recurrent, the recurrent, and the world as a whole. These three categories include everything there is, though a fourth possible category is that of the transcendent. Let me explain this classification a little further:

The Unique

Here one thinks especially of unrepeatable historical events, of particular human lives and actions, and also perhaps of miracles, religious experiences and prophetic revelations. Judaism and Christianity are both often described as 'historical religions' because they owe their foundation to certain past events, in the one case the ancient history of Israel and the institution of the Mosaic law, in the other the life, death and teaching of Christ. Both these religions too attach considerable importance to miracles; but then this is true of most other religions. Likewise, many other religions honour particular prophets or teachers, and regard certain 'revelations' given to their prophets or mystics as normative (such revelations may be about any of the three features of our classification, e.g. about particular individuals – Christ's appearance to Saul on the road to Damascus, about recurrent features of the universe like the value of suffering or the nature of life after death, or about the significance of the whole universe and its history). Finally, at the most individual level, each believer can probably point to certain events in his or her life which may be regarded as having religious significance; such events are often described as 'religious experiences' or 'providences' and may include unusual encounters with people, coincidences, mystical experiences and certain crises or turning-points in life.

Many contemporary Christian writers tend to play down the significance of unique historical events because, like Lessing and Wittgenstein, they have qualms about basing so much on so little, or becase they find it difficult to see what connection is to be established between past events and our present lives. If God only reveals Himself at certain times and places, how can He be a God of the here and now? What sort of causal connection do the doctrines of the Resurrection and the Atonement posit between Christ's life and death on he one hand, and the moral choices, spiritual growth and happiness of present-day believers on the other? Such difficulties lead them to put more weight on my second category:

The Recurrent

Nearly all religions respond to recurrent features of the world and events: they praise the beauty and harmony of nature, they recommend love and holiness, they seek to inculcate spiritual renewal, and they ceremonialise significant stages in life, especially birth, marriage and death. Theists regard natural regularities as laws decreed by God and even, perhaps, as signs of His convenant with Noah. Of course, the irreligious person responds to these features and events too, so the difference between the religious and the irreligious person must lie in the nature of their responses: one can have a special response to very ordinary things. But even within the class of religious believers we need to reckon with many different kinds of response, according to the circumstances and temperament of the individual believer and the nature of the religion which he professes. For instance, primitive men worship trees as sacred, but theists see them as the beautiful creation of a loving God who deserves thanks and worship, while natural theologians might see them as evidence for the fact that there is such a God (cf. St Augustine, *Confessions*, V.4).

The most difficult question for the theist in this connection is to understand how God is present in the world and to see why one should point to one class of facts rather than another as signs of His presence or activity. Austin Farrer remarked of those who would restrict God's activity to he spiritual life that 'No one any longer believes in a god of lightning; people are still inclined to believe in a god of enlightenment. God does not blast us, he inspires us; if we are going to talk paganism, he is Apollo, not Jupiter. Very well: but if Jupiter is dead, Apollo is dying. Jupiter was exploded by meteorology; Apollo is eroded by psychology' (Farrer (2) pp. 16 f.). Farrer thinks, therefore, that God's action must be taken to be universal, though this is not to say that His presence comes home to us with equal clarity at every point in the universe: 'There is more theology to be dug out of a saint than out of a sandpit . . . Believers will read God's action into everything; they will not pretend that it everywhere equally strikes them. Great tracts of experience may seem flat and godless; the light breaks on us in occasional bursts of godhead' (ibid. pp. 17 f.). Now I agree with Farrer that God's presence must be taken to be universal; but I think that he has failed to explain why it strikes us on some occasions rather than others: surely it is because He is more active in some cases? We see more of Him in a saint than in a sandpit because His grace and love have more scope for action in the former. I do not think there is anything absurd in this, and I take it that some such view is necessitated by the claim that God *is* love or goodness, since these are more evident on some occasions than on others.

Mention of God's universal presence brings us to our third category:

The World as a Whole

In the *Tractatus* Wittgenstein says 'Not *how* the world is, is the mystical, but *that* it is' (6.44, Ogden trans.) and again, in his *Lecture on Ethics* (pp. 8, 11), he speaks of wondering at the existence of the world or seeing the world as a miracle. He concludes that this is nonsensical, since it only makes sense to wonder at the existence of particular things, and yet that this tendency to 'run against the boundaries of language' and to 'go beyond the world' is an inevitable tendency of the human mind, and one deserving respect.

These remarks of Wittgenstein do not amount to a belief in the doctrine of Creation but they do, I think, express the state of mind in which such a doctrine naturally arises. Perhaps Malcolm was thinking of such passages when he remarked that although Wittgenstein did not accept any religious faith, 'I think that there was in him, in some sense, the *possibility* of religion' (Malcolm (1) p. 72). One might also mention again Wittgenstein's remarks in his *Notebooks* that 'The meaning of life, i.e. the meaning of the world, we can call God . . . To believe in a God means to see that the facts of the world are not the end of the matter. To believe in God means to see that life has a meaning' (pp. 73 f.), though I think that these would involve a consideration of the doctrine of Providence as well as that of Creation.

When we assent to a doctrine of Creation, we are thinking not of any feature of the world, whether unique or recurrent, but of the universe as a whole, and we are seeing this as being dependent on God both for its beginning and for its continued existence. In Chapter 3 I pointed out the close connection of this doctrine with the cosmological arguments for the existence of God, the latter being an inverse form of the former (as the teleological argument is an inverse form of the doctrine of Providence). In both cases we have examples of the way in which religious belief can involve consideration of the world taken as a whole.

The Transcendent

Since God is regarded as standing apart from or outside the world, we cannot properly include Him in any of the three categories mentioned so far. He is, however, related to the objects, events, features of the world, etc. which fall into these categories: the doctrine of Creation asserts that He is related to the world as a whole, that of General Providence states that He upholds the laws of nature, while that of Particular Providence points to His love of individuals and His working through historical events. All these doctrines assert that God is somehow present and active in the world, i.e. that He is immanent as well as transcendent. The doctrine of Transcendence claims that God is not dependent on the world, that He preceded its existence, and that He could annihilate it and yet continue to exist Himself.

The fourfold classification which I have given of religious contexts or situations has not dealt adequately with two important topics, namely religious experience and eschatology I think that the former notion needs 'unpacking', since it includes several different things, e.g. mysticism, paranormal or psychical phenomena, growth in spirituality and awareness of grace or holiness in other people. Each of these can be treated, I think, in terms of my classification. The question of eschatology is more difficult: much Jewish eschatology was 'this worldly', i.e. it concerned the future of the nation of Israel and the realisation of a universal peace and justice, and J. Moltmann has recently argued that much Christian eschatology is of this type; he criticises existentialist theology for assigning faith its home in the 'subjectivity and spontaneity of man' (p. 313) and forgetting about the political expression of Christian love. All of this is well said, but Moltmann and most other contemporary writers are less satisfactory on the 'other-worldly' aspects of Christian eschatology. Traditionally, Christians have interpreted the notions of the Kingdom and Lordship of God, *parousia*, Heaven and the life of the Resurrection in terms of a non-earthly realm. (Reductionist theologians will, of course, quite cheerfully interpret them as expressions of the hope for a future political millennium, couched in the language of an obsolete cosmology.)

I think that the most interesting and the most troublesome of my four categories are the first and last: much Christian theology is concerned with pointing to the significance of particular events, while philosophical theology finds its most serious problems when wrestling with the question of Transcendence. Moreover, it will be interesting to see whether Wittgenstein's philosophy is relevant to either of these two topics. Let us therefore consider them a little more closely.

THE SCANDAL OF PARTICULARITY

It has become something of a commonplace in recent years to contrast Greek modes of thought with Hebrew. R. A. Markus, for example, claims that the Greek philosophers saw God's power in the order and regularity of nature, while the Jews saw it in the unique and extraordinary events (Armstrong & Markus, p. 7). Many writers have ascribed the Greeks' preference for cosmology here to their lack of a sense of history, while others have argued that the two peoples had a different concept of time. R. G. Collingwood considered that Herodotus' creation of scientific history was very surprising in view of the Greeks' metaphysical tendency to look down on the world of change — Plato would have said that there could be no knowledge of what is transitory, but only opinion, while Aristotle considered that poetry is more valuable than history because it extracts universal judgements from the facts, but even poetry is deficient in that it does not provide us with scientific reasons for events (Collingwood (2) pp. 20—4). Mircea Eliade contrasts the cyclical conception of time, held by the Greeks and exemplified in Indian and Greek myths of the eternal return, with the Judaeo—Christian conception of historical time which has a beginning and an end; he also claims that Christianity goes even further than Judaism, in that it regards the Incarnation as having sanctified historical time (Eliade (1) pp. 110—12). Hence the early Fathers of the church, e.g. Origen and St Augustine, rejected the cyclical view of history.

These are all theories, with varying degrees of plausibility (I am inclined to think that the Greek/Hebrew contrast has been overdone). But certainly there can be no doubt that both Judaism and Christianity place great emphasis on particular historical events and that early Christian apologists had difficulty in coming to terms with certain Greek philosophical ideas, particularly with reference to the Incarnation. More recently, philosophers have pointed to three problems raised by the historical character of Christianity.

(1) How do we *understand* unique events, since they are not classable and therefore capturable in human concepts? R. G. Collingwood described the view that individuality as such is unintelligible as a 'positivistic prejudice' (Collingwood (2) p. 150), but actually it goes back to Aristotle who considered that there could be no scientific knowledge of particular sensible substances since their existence was contingent: demonstration and definition are of necessary truths (*Met.* Z. 15, 1039 b 27–1040 a2).

Many historians have tried to prove that their craft is 'scientific' by claiming that it can extract general laws from history. Even if this was a valid claim, it would not be to the point here, since we are dealing with events which are supposed to be unique and yet of inestimable significance for all men.

(2) Historical knowledge is at best only highly probable, since it deals with contingent facts; therefore there is an element of risk involved in a historical religion and all its doctrines must be regarded as fallible. I have already remarked that many contemporary theologians are keenly aware of difficulties of this kind and that they prefer to rest the weight of their case on something other than historical facts, e.g. present religious experience. Bultmann, for example, says that 'This interpretation of the cross as a permanent fact rather than a mythological event does far more justice to the redemptive significance of the event of the past than do the traditional interpretations. . . . The real meaning of the cross is that it has created a new and permanent situation in history.' (Bartsch, i, p. 37). Many different lines of thought lie behind such a view, of course, but one of them is surely, as Professor D. M. MacKinnon describes it, 'a desire to escape from bondage to that which could have been otherwise' (Mackinnon (1) p. 87).

(3) How do we go about building a theology on such facts? Lessing raised this difficulty in its classic form when he queried the legitimacy of jumping from historical judgements to 'metaphysical and moral ideas' (Lessing, p. 54). It is relevant to many different questions, e.g. the relationship between our present spiritual life and past events, the way in which there can be several theological theories about a single historical event (e.g. theories of the Atonement), the relation between the earthly and the transcendent, and the connection between 'theory-laden' theological terms and ordinary language. Wittgen-

stein made a similar point to Lessing's when, speaking of Christianity's reliance on historical fact, he said that these are not ordinary facts, subject to doubt and empirical text, for 'they base enormous things on this evidence' (*L. & C.* p. 58).

Not all philosophers and theologians would be equally perturbed by these problems, since many of them regard Christianity's historical foundation as its glory and its strength. To Wittgenstein's claim that the facts are not subject to doubt they would reply that our commitment in faith precludes our doubting the truth of the Gospel records, just as a husband does not normally question his wife's fidelity; but in both cases one can admit that *in principle* doubt is possible, for historical events can be misreported and wives can be unfaithful. To his charge that Christians base enormous things on the evidence they would naturally reply 'well, why shouldn't they, since the events in question are of an extraordinary type?' God's revelation is an unexpected and unmerited grace, so we have no claim to expect anything more than what we have. In any case, man is a historical being: historical events are not simply physical changes, and man is endowed with a memory which enables him to see and retain the significance of such events. After all, a single event often has great significance in changing an individual person's life, e.g. with regard to his marriage or career; and secular history is full of the record of single lives and indeed single events which have decisively affected the future of whole nations. Novelists and playwrights have appreciated this fact as well as historians. There is no need, therefore, for theologians to be embarrassed at resting so much on so little, since there are plenty of parallels for this elsewhere.

Such considerations, which I would expect a follower of Kierkegaard or Barth to stress, are very cogent, but they do not entirely remove our difficulties, particularly those occurring under (3) with regard to the building of a theology. These difficulties could, I think, be removed only by developing a philosophy of revelation. A really satisfactory account of revelation would have to go beyond itself by showing how the activity of God through historical events and prophetic revelations is to be related to His activity in the public and repeatable aspects of the cosmos, e.g. through the laws of nature, and also to His presence in men's hearts and minds. If the Jews looked for God in history and the Greeks in cosmology,[2] then it would seem that people today are neither Hebrew nor Greek, since they tend to look for God in religious experience, e.g. mysticism, spirituality and self-transformation. That is why I have preferred to make a new distinction between the unique, the recurrent and the world as a whole, rather than to use over-worked and misleading distinctions like those between reason and revelation,[3] history and cosmology, dogma and religious experience, or natural and supernatural.

FORMS OF LIFE AND THE TRANSCENDENT

The other question which I set aside for comment was that of transcendence. Writers like van Buren or J. A. T. Robinson allege that metaphysical doctrines involving reference to transcendent beings and their activities are a particular source of difficulty for people today. The former seeks to reinterpret such doctrines, and describes his programme thus: 'I am trying to argue that it [Christianity] *is* fundamentally about man, that its language about God is one way — a dated way, among a number of ways — of saying what it is Christianity wants to say about man and human life and human history' (quoted in Mehta, p. 55). Such a programme might be called an attempt at theological reductionism (though there are other kinds of the latter, cf. Helm, pp. 43f.). Whilst some people are led by their lack of understanding of the metaphysical parts of religious language to join the Logical Positivists in regarding religious doctrines as nonsense, Reductionists, however, prefer to say that they are really disguised statements about something else.

Not all Reductionists would go as far as van Buren: many fairly orthodox Christians apply Reductionism to only one or two particularly difficult doctrines, e.g. that of hell. I can remember hearing a few sermons in the 1950s giving a nearly literal interpretation to Christ's words about hellfire, reminiscent of the sermon in Joyce's *Portrait of the Artist as a Young Man*. But more recently preachers have tended to avoid the subject altogether or else to dwell on the isolation and misery of the unloving personality. Rudolf Bultmann often says things similar to van Buren, e.g. 'I *am* trying to substitute anthropology for theology, for I am interpreting theological affirmations as assertions about human life', but he goes on immediately to say 'What I mean is that the God of the Christian revelation is the answer to the vital questions, the existential questions' (Bartsch, vol. 1. p. 107) and in general he stops his programme of demythologising short of certain central Christian doctrines. I am inclined to think that D. Z. Phillips might be classified as a 'Partial Reductionist' because of his views on Providence, petitionary prayer, hope and immortality, on which I have already commented.

The overwhelming attraction of Reductionism is that it enables us to simplify our ontology and thereby avoid many thorny problems. If religious doctrines are really about ethics and psychology, then questions about transcendence can be shelved, or even dismissed as the product of an outdated 'two worlds' cosmology. But many people feel that this is to let out the baby with the bathwater.

It is, of course, often difficult to tell whether a particular formulation manages to capture the substance of a doctrine, so we must be careful about rejecting suggested analyses as Reductionist and therefore as inadequate (cf. Thornton). Still, many Reductionists are quite frank about their rejection of the traditional understanding of many Christian doctrines, and certainly writers like van Buren fail to do justice to the variety of Christian beliefs. Like many other easy answers to serious problems, Reductionism may turn out to be only a cowardly and short-term solution.

It is one thing to claim that Reductionism is religiously unorthodox, and another thing to show that it is philosophically untenable. The problem is that statements about transcendent beings are incompatible with the view of most philosophers since Kant that man cannot claim knowledge of things which are beyond his experience. Moreover, there are difficulties of ontology as well as the more familiar ones of epistemology: for if God is transcendent, i.e. spatially and temporally unlimited, immaterial, independent and mysterious, then how can He be related to our finite and material world? Does the notion of a transcendent cause make sense? These problems lead Reductionist theologians to dismiss talk about transcendence as the relic of an obsolete 'two worlds' cosmology or else to interpret it in terms of levels of depth in human experience. In doing this they are following Bonhoeffer, who asserted that the transcendence of epistemological theory has nothing to do with that of God, for 'God is the 'beyond' in the midst of our life' (Bonhoeffer, p. 93).

Wittgenstein considered the question in his earlier philosophy, but took a Kantian line: 'what can be said' is restricted to propositions of natural science, so that those who speak metaphysically have failed to give meaning to certain signs in their propositions (*T.* 6.53). Questions about God and ethics belong to the realm of what can be shown but not said, for they lie outside the world (*T.* 6.41, 6.421, 6.432, 6.522). This presumably means that religious believers would be committed to absolute silence with regard to God's attributes and activities, for otherwise they would utter meaningless propositions.

His later philosophy, however, offers a more flexible approach. His remark 'Only in the stream of thought and life do words have meaning' (*Z.* 173) suggests that he would accept language about the transcendent as meaningful, provided that we could show that it has some role in our life. And indeed his own *Lectures on Religious Belief* offer a partial solution to the question of how a form of life might involve reference to the concept of a transcendent being. There he argues that believing in the Last Judgement does not consist in believing in a future event for which there are grounds or evidence, but rather in living with a picture before one's mind, a picture which regulates our life (pp. 53—9). He suggests, too, that belief in one's immortality is like living with the idea that a task has been given to us, a task so grave that nothing, not even death, can take away the responsibility for its performance (p. 70). Norman Malcolm gives another variation on the same theme: he suggests that we might get the idea of an infinite and perfect being from our feeling of great guilt. A guilt which is too great to be removed by the forgiveness of another human being might be removed by 'a forgiving mercy that is limitless, beyond all measure', and this idea is one important feature of the Jewish and Christian conception of God (Malcolm (2) pp. 60f.).

Now we could generalise these suggestions and argue that believing in a transcendent being consists in living with a picture before us which regulates our lives. Certainly much of the language of the Bible, e.g. 'Whither shall I go from thy Spirit? Or whither shall I flee from thy presence? If I ascend to heaven, thou art there! If I make my bed in Sheol, thou art there' (Psalm 139, 7—8) and 'For as the heavens are higher than the earth, so are my ways higher than your ways and my thoughts than your thoughts' (Isaiah, 55.9) suggests some aspects of the concept of transcendence very graphically. We could go on to construct similar pictures for other features of the concept and its correlative perfections: a love, for example, that is so great that it created and sustains the whole universe, cares even for the sparrows, will comfort a man even in his blackest despair, and endured the agony of the Cross.

We could go on to suggest that the form of life of one who lives with such pictures involves many different responses, but especially that of worship. This will include both fear and love, for these are the appropriate responses to the unseen judge who is also infinite love. Conversely, the response of worship demands an appropriate object; there is a logical and religious requirement that the objects of worship be supremely holy and good, for otherwise worship would become idolatry. If we could show that perfection entails transcendence, we could construct a logical chain as follows:

worship → holiness → perfection → transcendence.

One could go quite a way along this path, but I think that its limitations are already plain. All it has shown is that *if* we are to worship, then we should worship something that is good, holy, etc. (and conversely, *if* there is anything that is holy and perfect, then we must worship it). But *is there* actually anything that is truly worshipful? What is the point of believing in an infinite love and Providence unless there is some reason to think that there is indeed a power which is somehow active in the world? Here we are returning to our earlier criticism of Wittgenstein, and of Holland and Phillips. If we do not believe that there really will be a Last Judgement of some sort, then surely the picture is nothing more than an *als ob*?[4] Despite Wittgenstein's condemnation of apologetics one still keeps wanting to ask why people want to live with such pictures, whether it is reasonable, and what the ontological status of the entities depicted in them is supposed to be.

Wittgenstein himself says that the question of reasonableness does not enter into the matter, and thereby quite clearly disclaims all questions of verification and ontology. But this seems to lead to a complete relativism, in which we say that some people live with these pictures and some do not and that is all there is to it.[5]

If such a position seems unsatisfactory, then there are two directions in which we could go in order to give substance to the concept of transcendence. One is via natural theology, the other by an analysis of some kinds of religious experience. The first way is the way taken by Norman Malcolm, in his reconstruction of the Ontological argument; it is also the way taken by Aquinas. The latter presented a double argument (neatly summed up in *S.T.* 1a. iv. 2) for God's transcendence and perfection: he argued from examples of limited perfections in this world to the perfection of their creator, and he also deduced God's non-spatiality, eternity and other perfections by an *a priori* argument. The latter proceeds by eliminating characteristics which cannot apply to God, e.g. composition, change and materiality; then Aquinas shows that God is 'pure existence subsisting of itself', and argues that He must therefore contain within Himself the whole perfection of being, since all perfections are embraced in the perfection of existence; likewise, His being a pure form necessitates His being infinite (see *S.T.* 1a, articles iii, iv and vii for the stages of this argument, which I shall critically evaluate in Chapter 7).

Alternatively, we might look for features in men's experience of the world which lead them into the form of life called worshipping transcendent being. If we say that there is no point in worshipping unless there is something worshipful in the world, then clearly we must look around and see if we can find anything truly worshipful. This is surely one of those cases when men's responses are dependent on facts about the world, so that if the facts were different, the responses would change and the language-games or forms of life in which they feature would also change or pass away.

Such an approach could have a variety of starting-points, e.g. mysticism, experience of the numinous or sacred, or meditation on the life of Christ, the object of the exercise being to point to some element in our experience which we consider to be a manifestation of a transcendent being. In the next chapter I will consider whether certain religious concepts, particularly those of 'spirituality' could serve our purpose.

CONCLUSION

In this chapter I have discussed Wittgenstein's insight that many concepts can be applied only in certain circumstances and that many customs, forms of life and activities presuppose certain contexts or 'surroundings'. I have sought to apply this point to religion by arguing that religious beliefs and practices presuppose particular contexts in life and often also particular historical facts. All that I have claimed so far is that the situations and facts are *necessary conditions* of religion.

My classification of them has not touched on the problems of how doctrines are formulated and how they might be verified or falsified. But then these questions do not arise at this stage: one might say that we are now concerned with phenomenology, in that we are merely trying to give a logical classification of the different kinds of fact to which men can give a religious response and so we are describing the occasions of religious belief, etc. rather than deciding what constitutes evidence. However, the first three categories are relevant to the question of falsification, since they enable us to give a reply to Flew's query 'What would have to be the case for you to stop believing in . . .?'

If religion is a response to something, then it cannot be true that religious believers are oblivious of the facts. Again, this exemplifies the point that the possibility and utility of certain language-games and forms of life depend on facts about the world. (The boldest answer to Flew's question about what difference the existence of God makes would be to follow one of the participants in the original *University* discussion and point to the world as a whole: if God did not exist, there would be a considerable difference — there would be no world at all!)

Such an approach is compatible with great theological latitude, since we are merely saying that certain facts are the *necessary* conditions of religious practices or beliefs, but not that they are *sufficient* conditions. The bare fact that Jesus was conceived and born is a presupposition of the doctrine of the Incarnation; it does not, however, *entail* the doctrine or any particular interpretation of it (e.g. Kenoticism), so that anyone wishing to put forward these will need to take into account many other facts and arguments. This point is relevant to Hugo Meynell's claim that the Christian religion has certain truth conditions, because it both appeals to past facts recorded in the Bible and makes predictions about the future life after death, and that it is therefore in principle falsifiable. (Meynell (1) pp. 247—9). Now Meynell's argument does, I think, do the job it is designed to do, which is to refute the claim of Flew and others that Christian doctrines are unfalsifiable. But it leaves us with Lessing's and Wittgenstein's problem of how we make a type-jump from facts about Christ's life or the world to conclusions about a transcendent being. To put it in logical terms, Maynell has shown, for instance, that

Jesus Christ is God → Jesus Christ is sinless

Thus, by *modus tollens*, it follows that if Jesus Christ never existed or was an evil man, then Christianity is falsified (Meynell (3) p. 39). But unfortunately, since affirming the consequent is invalid, we cannot use the above entailment to show that since Jesus Christ is sinless, therefore He is God. In other words, Meynell has only shown that facts about God entail ones about the world, and has not proved that we can construct an entailment running the other way (he does, however, realise this deficiency and seeks to remedy it by showing that 'type-jumps' occur in other contexts, e.g. from statements of observation to the laws of physics, or from reports about publicly observable behaviour to judgements about a transcendent human mind (cf. (1) p. 216; (3) pp. 127f.).

Clearly, therefore, religious doctrines are not simply deduced from the facts, although the latter may constitute necessary conditions. But why and how do people go on to build a religion on them? What is the relationship between ordinary descriptive language and the 'theory laden' terms of theologians? Wittgenstein drew attention to an analogous problem in mathematics when he said that although certain physiological and psychological facts make calculation possible and give it its point, this does not mean that the propositions used in calculation are empirical ones (*R.F.M.* v.15). Could two different religions arise from the same situation — we have admitted that there can be different responses to the same facts? Why do people regard certain events as revelations? How comparable are religions which arise from different revelations? How did people form the concept of God?

The existence of these questions is one reason which leads me to say that a description of religious contexts and situations is a matter of phenomenology but no more. Yet the religious believer does feel that if we rightly understand the significance of the facts to which he appeals, we shall realise that they have a certain import which religious doctrines attempt to express. Moreover, he feels that the religious practices of worship, prayer and so forth are appropriate responses to this understanding. I cannot hope to solve the fundamental yet difficult problems which are raised here, but I will at least clear away some of the ground by discussing a topic which follows on naturally from this chapter, namely that of how we attempt to understand the significance of the facts by forming and developing concepts.

5 Locating: II The Formation of Religious Concepts

In the last chapter we considered the different kinds of facts which form the background of men's religious responses. Now I want to link this background to religious language by saying something about how religious concepts are formed. My procedure will be to consider concept formation generally, to criticise certain theories about it which are found among both theologians and philosophers, and then to consider some of the special problems of religious concepts. But it might be as well to say first a little more about why the subject is both so difficult and so important, and to differentiate between the various kinds of religious concept. In Chapter 3 I suggested a rough and ready division of types of religious language, and I think that this will still serve our purposes in the present context:

(1) Specifically religious concepts, e.g. 'God', '*Brahman*', 'heaven', 'holiness', 'sacrament', 'devil' and 'pilgrimage'. Professional theologians also use concepts like 'transubstantiation' or 'hypostatic union' which may well be unknown to the ordinary religious believer. But many of these concepts belong to my second category:
(2) Metaphysical concepts, e.g. 'omniscient', 'infinite', 'transcendent' and 'spirit'.
(3) Analogical concepts, e.g. 'father', 'life', 'cause', 'make' or 'love'. Many terms which we think of as specifically religious, e.g. 'redeemer', 'revelation', 'grace', 'salvation' and 'Providence', might be classified as analogical because they originally had a non-religious sense, even if they have now largely lost this.

(4) Ordinary concepts, e.g. 'death', 'peace', 'just', 'crucify' or 'forgive'.

I will concentrate here mainly on the first category, since the question of analogy will be discussed in Chapter 7 and the other two categories are not specifically religious. The most obvious problem is simply that much traditional religious language fails to communicate anything to a large number of people today, and this is manifested in a variety of ways: outsiders allege that religious language is meaningless or that religion is 'irrelevant', or they fasten on particular issues, arguing, for example, that modern views about punishment and responsibility have rendered the concepts of redemption and atonement obsolete. Religious believers prefer to speak of a difficulty in understanding: ordinary people often find it hard to make sense of the Church's creeds and doctrines, while theologians are troubled by many traditional theological concepts and their associated doctrines, e.g. 'revelation', 'faith' and 'justification' (they are also, of course, troubled by questions of verification, but these are not our main concern at the moment). Now in so far as these difficulties are ones of understanding, the question of concept formation is highly relevant, for understanding is largely a matter of grasping concepts, and religious understanding is no exception. If indeed there is such a thing as a special religious understanding, this must be partly a consequence of the fact that religion employs special concepts.

The difficulties which I have mentioned are widely realised, both at the ordinary pastoral level and by professional theologians, but the response is often superficial. A minority is content to reiterate the traditional view that religion requires a special understanding which is a gift of the Holy Spirit and consists of a special illumination of the intellect whereby the believer is granted the grace to comprehend the truths of the faith; such an understanding is not available to those outside the church, for it is taught by the Spirit, not through philosophical learning (cf. I Corinthians 2.11—14). At the other end of the theological spectrum there is much talk of 'demythologising', of 'outdated thought-forms' and of reinterpreting the essence of Christianity in terms meaningful to modern man. But the proposal to re-express an old truth in new concepts raises many problems: the acquisition of a new set of concepts is not like that of a new set of clothes. Usually a concept becomes obsolete when people realise that nothing answers to it or find its explanatory value exhausted, e.g. 'fairy', 'magical power', 'ether' or 'phlogiston'. But it is difficult to see how one could show that concepts like 'sin', 'holiness', 'grace' or 'redemption' have become obsolete in quite this way.[1] Of course, I have admitted that many religious concepts seem outdated to a great number of people today, but this is the fact to be explained rather than the explanation. Unmusical people do not understand musical concepts and non-Freudian psychiatrists refuse to employ Freudian concepts, but in neither case do they argue that the relevant concepts are obsolete.

The question of concept-formation is relevant to several more traditional religious and theological issues. Most immediately, it arises for missionaries who have to make Christian hymns, creeds, doctrines and so forth intelligible to primitive peoples: difficulties may arise not only with reference to religious concepts like 'Holy Spirit' (e.g. when a people has no suitable term other than that which denotes the spirits of the dead), but also in the case of simple concepts like 'city' or 'shepherd'.[2] Such difficulties of translation occur also among more advanced people: there is a lot of interest in hermeneutics today, but actually this science goes back to Dilthey and Schleiermacher, who wished to recover the true sense of great historical documents by reconstructing their historical and psychological background, and indeed to scriptural exegetes of an earlier period.

The question is also relevant to the problem of doctrinal development. The theological formulations of the Church often use concepts which are not found in the scriptures, e.g. 'original sin', 'transubstantiation' and 'Holy Trinity'. Their proponents regarded them as expressing something which was at least implicit in the original revelation. But the modernists raised the question (which is still with us today) of whether the traditional formulations might be replaced by others. If the concepts and definitions of the faith merely symbolise or evoke the believer's inner and direct experience of God, and if such expressions are determined by social and historical conditions, then it might seem that the experiential core is the important thing and that the traditional formulations might be dispensed with.[3]

But the question of concept formation is also relevant to

many very interesting philosophical problems: why do we have the concepts we do? Could we have a different set of concepts? Are there some concepts or categories which are essential to any rational thought whatsoever? Why can some people do without a particular batch of concepts, e.g. aesthetic or religious ones? Do our interests influence our use of concepts? Can the same truths be expressed in different concepts? How and why do concepts change and develop? And, most basic of all, what is it to have a concept — if we define it in terms of 'recognitional capacity' or 'being able to follow a rule', then will we not have to say that dogs have concepts? To what extent is having a concept a matter of thinking in images, making verbal judgements or behaving in certain ways?

Not all of these problems are relevant to our present concerns, but it is worth making some connections with what has gone before. Most obviously, the question of concept formation is related to my discussion of language-games in Chapter 2: those who make the 'this language-game is played' move apparently fail to realise that many religious concepts have a relatively short history and have acquired many accretions of meaning in the course of their evolution.[4] For instance, even such an apparently common and untechnical concept as that of 'supernatural' arose relatively late in the Church's history.[5] The question of 'forms of life' is also relevant: practices like pitying, forgiving, hoping, repenting and expecting presuppose that one has concepts like 'pain', 'guilt', 'amendment', 'past', 'future' and so on — indeed it might be argued, for example, that doing penance or apologising *is* to have the concept of sorrow. In the case of religion there is a logical link between practices like fasting, prayer or worship and concepts like 'sin', 'holy', 'Providence' and 'God'. This is simply because our behaviour and institutions express our beliefs and purposes. I should also mention Wittgenstein's later views on 'picturing' which we briefly discussed in Chapter 1: of course there can be special kinds of description, e.g. mythical or symbolic, which do not embody a special vocabulary. But very often there are special concepts associated with certain modes of description, and these concepts have their own 'grammar' and 'criteria' which must be grasped if the concepts are to be applied properly. Lastly, the question of concept formation is relevant to that of verification, since one can verify a statement only if one understands the concepts being used and knows the conditions of their correct application.

Since the topic of concept formation is relevant to so many other important philosophical and theological issues, it is unfortunate that in recent years it has not had the attention it deserves. In particular, it is regrettable that philosophers of religion have largely ignored it: since one of their tasks is to straddle the gap between philosophy and religion, a question like this is clearly very important for their endeavour.

CONCEPT FORMATION: DESCRIPTION, UNDERSTANDING AND EXPLANATION

Having a concept clearly involves much more than using language: if we say, for instance, that a married couple have no concept of fidelity, we mean that their relationship with each other lacks certain features, and that this lack is shown forth in their behaviour; similarly, having the concept of time is not simply knowing how to use tenses and temporal expressions. In this chapter, however, I am concerned more with the formation of concepts than with their exercise, and I think that the easiest way to tackle this subject will be to concentrate on linguistic issues. We seem to be faced here with three kinds of question:

(1) How were our concepts originally formed? (a historical question).
(2) How did we learn to use the concepts? (a question of educational psychology).
(3) What is the logical analysis of our concepts? (a philosophical question).

The first question is sometimes regarded as being of little philosophical interest, since no one knows or particularly cares when mankind first began to use concepts like 'red' or 'next to'. But I shall argue that in many cases it is a very important question philosophically: not only in the case of religious and theological concepts, but also in that of ethical, political, legal, scientific and aesthetic ones, since many of these have been introduced into our language because people have discovered new facts or techniques, developed laws and institutions, had fresh insights or devised explanations. Likewise, the second question is sometimes brushed aside as a 'genetic' (as opposed to an 'analytic') question, and so not really philosophically important. But Wittgenstein used to say that asking how words are learnt and how we would teach a child their use is one way of finding out their meaning (see Fann (1) p. 54; also *L. & C.* p. 1), so it would seem that this consideration might often throw light on question (3).

One should not, I think, attempt any *general* answer to the question of why we have the concepts we do, since there are so many different kinds of concepts, depending on human purposes, beliefs and activities, as well as facts about the world and its history. But three considerations are particularly relevant to our present concerns: we use many concepts to describe, to understand and to explain. These three terms, however, cover a variety of situations, so I shall try to bring out the complexity of the question by giving a wide range of examples from different fields under each heading.

(1) Description. The simplest kind of description might seem to be that of a single object like a hat or a house. But a full description of even a simple object will involve reference to its situation, size, colour, history and so forth, i.e. all the Aristotelian categories. And if the object happens to be of artistic interest, a whole barrage of complex concepts may be called into play, e.g., 'chiaroscuro', 'Baroque', 'perspective' and 'tonal gradation'. If we are describing a person, the situation becomes even more complicated since we are unlikely to restrict ourselves to his or her appearance: we shall probably employ moral and psychological concepts like 'brave', 'deceitful', 'neurotic', 'sense of humour' and 'inferiority complex'.

When we come to describe relationships, processes, events or situations in which several objects or people are concerned, we shall introduce further levels of concepts from history, sociology, politics and economics: ones like 'military defeat', 'inflation', 'democracy', 'culture', 'industrial relations' and 'class structure'.

We use all these concepts to define and to classify what we have seen, but 'seeing' is no simple matter: painters are trained to notice more in nature than ordinary people do, while writers try to capture the feeling of unique and transient experiences. Critics and connoisseurs try to develop their awareness of the qualities of a work of art and to discern similarities and differences between a number of works or periods. In all these cases there is a special sensitivity which consists in seeing things which the ordinary layman does not notice: the great critic and art historian Heinrich Wölfflin used to remark that 'a man sees only what he is looking for'. A similar sensitivity is required by historians who seek to describe all the aspects of an important event or to capture the flavour of a particular period; by novelists and others who set themselves to describe human conduct and motives; and indeed by anyone who wishes to acquire self-understanding and to expand his consciousness (to use a phrase of R. D. Laing's). Iris Murdoch wisely remarks, 'We need more concepts in terms of which to picture the substance of our being: it is through an enriching and deepening of concepts that moral progress takes place' (Murdoch (3) p. 20). Now it might be the case that her remarks, rather than Alasdair MacIntyre's cultural/sociological approach, provide us with the key to the question of why people have or do not have certain concepts.

(2) Understanding. We try to make sense of our experience by classifying and connecting things: we point to similarities, differences and relationships, we subsume particulars under universals, we use models, analogies and metaphors, and we interpret the significance of events by assessing their implications. People often speak of 'insight' in this connection, perhaps imagining that this is some special mental faculty: but I think that having an insight usually amounts to noticing a significant fact of the types just mentioned or to hitting upon a new explanation. There are a variety of examples which spring to mind here: realising the difference between pride and self-respect, noticing features in a wide range of works of art which exemplify 'mannerism' or 'romanticism', putting a general construction on someone's life and character, seeing that different diseases have similar symptoms or causes, or observing the implications of a country's class structure. In mathematics, too, new concepts can be invented: Wittgenstein alleged that mathematical proofs involve conceptual change: 'a proof introduces a new concept . . . puts a new paradigm among the paradigms of the language, like when someone mixes a special reddish blue, somehow settles the special mixture of the colours and gives it a name . . . the proof changes the grammar of our

language, changes our concepts. It makes new connexions, and it creates the concept of these connexions' (*R.F.M.* II, 31; cf. IV. 45).

I am not suggesting that we use a special set of terms to understand things, a set which is different from those used to describe or explain them. My point is that the perception of similarities, connections and relationships often brings with it the use of a new vocabulary. Moreover, differences in understanding result in disputes about the application of terms: there may be controversy, for example, as to whether a particular action constitutes an example of hypocrisy, unfairness or cruelty, or whether a work of art embodies a specific style or quality; this situation arises both because the individual case is unclear and because there are often several different criteria for applying a concept. Similarly with explanations: the formulation of laws and hypotheses often involves the introduction of a fresh descriptive vocabulary. Still, this does not mean that all concepts can be simply labelled as 'descriptive': as we shall see, a scientific theory is often judged by its predictive and explanatory value, rather than because all its terms can be correlated with specific aspects of reality (strictly speaking, it is *statements*, e.g. scientific theories, rather than concepts, which explain things). Theoretical terms and statements have only an indirect content or reference, and we judge them by their applicability (Toulmin (2) pp. 169–73). Moreover, a consideration of my remarks in Chapter 1 about names and essences, surroundings and criteria, and the variety of descriptions should warn us against the error of seeking a one-to-one relationship between language or thought on the one hand, and the world on the other (not to mention the special difficulties occasioned by recalcitrant cases like ethical and mathematical concepts, or ones like 'time').

The special connection between using concepts and understanding or insight seems to be this: a person's mastery of concepts is an index of the level of his understanding, for learning is a matter of seeing connections as well as acquiring facts: 'Concepts help us to comprehend things. They correspond to a particular way of dealing with situations' (*R.F.M.* V. 46).

(3) Explanations. Part of the task of understanding a body of facts consists in finding explanations: we look for causal

connections between events and form theories or frame hypotheses which we hope to verify by experiment or observation. The most interesting and philosophically contentious question here is the status of theoretical terms, i.e. terms like 'electron' or 'neutron' in physics, or 'mass point' and 'rigid body' in classical mechanics, or 'absolute temperature' and 'Carnot point' in classical thermodynamics. Empiricists have always found such terms an embarrassment and have usually tried to reduce them to ordinary empirical concepts by rules of translation or else to regard them as 'useful fictions'. But most contemporary philosophers of science are satisfied if there is a partial link with empirical data and if the theories in which they are used are fruitful in explanations and predictions (see for example, Hempel (1) pp. 42–9).

An interesting case in point is that of Freud, who introduced terms like 'id', 'super-ego', 'Oedipus complex' and 'libido'. Such terms do not correspond to any observable processes or entities, hence some critics, e.g. Karl Popper ((2) pp. 161–2) have argued that they have no scientific status and are really no better off than terms like 'Zeus' or 'Apollo'. Quite clearly Freud himself would not have liked such a parallel since he claimed to be giving an empirical account of our mental life: 'The teachings of psychoanalysis are based on an incalculable number of observations and experiences' (Freud, p. 1). He admitted that terms like 'super-ego' were theoretical, in that they do not denote observable entities, but he considered that man's behaviour reveals the state of his psyche in the same way that certain behavioural symptoms reveal that state of intestinal disorder called 'indigestion'. He hoped eventually that psychoanalysis would unite with physics and physiology, so that psychological states might be correlated with the physical organisation of the brain and the nervous system; eventually people would be able to predict all mental events, both conscious and unconscious, by studying neurological mechanisms. These expectations have not been realised yet and are unlikely to be realised in the way that Freud hoped, because he was employing an unusually crude physical model for the mind. On the other hand, some philosophers of science, e.g. A. Ellis, have argued that Freud's theories may be described as 'empirical' because they are in principle falsifiable and because their theoretical terms can be connected with observable behaviour by means of operational definitions.

This issue is relevant to theology, since a number of philosophers of religion have argued that language about unseen religious beings is perfectly justifiable because it is analogous to talk about theoretical entities in science. Hugo Meynell, for instance, compares the doctrine of the Trinity to the theory of relativity, claiming that they are both 'rather regulative principles for the manipulation of the conceptual schemes within which they occur than references to particular facts dealt with by the schemes' (Meynell (1) p. 175; cf. Smart (1) p. 8). It is perhaps rather ironical that they should take this line, in view of Popper's attempt to pour scorn on Freud's theoretical constructs by comparing them to Homer's mythical gods! Certainly they are right to argue that talk about unseen entities is not necessarily meaningless. Moreover, the parallel between 'God' and theoretical terms is drawing our attention to something which is religiously very important, namely that God is both unknowable in Himself and yet to be regarded as the source of holiness and other perfections in the world. But it should be pointed out that unobservable entities in scientific explanation are spatio—temporal and can therefore parallel only God's immanence but not His transcendence. Later on in this chapter we shall have to consider those philosophers who not only plead that theological terms are meaningful even though they fail to refer to directly observable entities, but go on to claim that such terms and the doctrines containing them have a positive explanatory value.

ABSTRACTION AND SEEING AS

Now that we have seen that concepts are formed and used for so many different purposes, we can dispose of two views which have found favour with philosophers and theologians at different times, which I shall call 'Abstractionism' and the 'Grid theory'. The first of these says that our concepts are abstracted from our experience, the second that our concepts are 'given' and that they structure our experience. I think that each theory has many different faults of its own, but that both of them fail to do justice to the fact that many of our concepts, particularly religious and theological ones, have evolved very slowly and have gradually changed during their history.

The view that concepts are abstracted from our experience has often gone hand in hand with the view that they are images and that thinking is a process of manipulating them. Locke, for example, defines thinking in terms of 'ideas' (*Essay,* II.xix), a term which is used interchangeably to denote the objects of perception and those of thought, thereby creating much confusion (cf. *Essay,* II.viii.8 and Bennett, p. 55). Newman applied Locke's thinking to religion when he spoke of the 'ideas' of divine objects granted to us in the Gospels being genuine images of their originals, in the same way that sense impressions are caused by material objects, and when he defined theological dogmas as '. . . propositions expressive of the judgments which the mind forms, or the impressions which it receives, of Revealed Truth' (*U.S.* XV, § § 10, 22). Similarly, his definition of doctrinal development as a process in which '. . . what was at first an impression on the imagination has become a system or creed in the reason' (ibid. § 20) probably owes something to Locke's view that the mind 'compounds' complex ideas out of simple ones (*Essay,* II.xii.1).

As described so far, Newman's model naturally invites the comment that if things were as simple as that, it is difficult to see how any religious disputes or doubts could ever arise! Fortunately, he qualified it a little later in the same sermon and to a greater extent elsewhere. Subsequent philosophers have come to stress the importance of activity, with respect both to the original acquisition of concepts and to their exercise. They emphasise that acquiring knowledge is an active process, involving attention, selection, grouping, organising and experimenting; hence one's acquisition of concepts depends partly on one's interests — there may be many different ways of classifying a body of data. Likewise, exercising a concept is not a matter of contemplating ideas or images, but of being able to describe, recognise or understand things (see Price (1) pp. 342–5). The blanket term 'abstraction' fails to do justice to the complexity of the processes involved. Moreover, there are many cases where it simply will not fit: most obviously, theoretical terms in scientific explanations, mathematical and ethical terms; but also 'family resemblance' terms (one does not form the idea of a 'game', for example, by abstraction, since there is no common property possessed by all games) and analogical terms like 'Cold War' (cf. Schon, pp. 15, 54f.), not to mention ones like 'not' or 'all', about which Jonathan Bennett rightly remarks (p. 98) that:

> Abstractionist accounts of such concepts as negation and totality always have a surrealist air about them, not because plausible examples of allness and notness are hard to find, but rather because someone who lacks these two concepts cannot do what the abstractionist account requires him to do — namely to notice that *all* those things share a feature which is *not* possessed by this other thing.

Recent philosophers have also criticised another view which is usually favoured by Abstractionists and which I shall call 'Reductionism': this is the view that complex concepts like 'democracy', 'jealousy', 'tragedy', 'revolution', 'neurosis' or 'murder' are compounded out of simpler concepts. This view has been applied by Carnap to theological concepts, as we shall see in a moment. It derives from Locke's claim that 'complex ideas', however abstruse, are derived by combining and comparing simple ideas of sense or reflection (*Essay*, II. xii) and from Leibniz's ideal of an *ars combinatoria* (though Leibniz was more concerned with the logical analysis of concepts than with their genesis). Subsequent philosophers, especially Russell in his logical atomism period, have refined and elaborated the theory. Generally speaking, they have tried to work out in epistemological terms the logical view that all complex terms can be defined in terms of simple ones. Thus Carnap, for instance, wished to establish a 'constructional system' of objects and concepts, in which all concepts are derived from certain fundamental ones. His 'genealogy' runs as follows:

(1) Our own sensations and mental states.
(2) Physical objects: our recognition of these depends on perception, hence (1) is more basic than (2).
(3) Other people's mental states: we only recognise these by observing people's behaviour, which is a case of (2).
(4) 'Cultural objects': in this category Carnap includes religion, since this is based upon physical documents, psychological processes, etc. (see Carnap (2) § § 1—2; (3) § 6).

Unfortunately Carnap did not give any examples of how he would derive religious concepts from reports like 'this red now', and it is difficult to see how he would carry out his programme in the case of concepts like 'grace' or 'redemption'. Of course, it is certainly possible to define these concepts in terms of other concepts. But Carnap wants something more than this obvious point, for he wishes to provide an epistemological analysis in terms of 'simples'. Now Wittgenstein pointed out that the words 'simple' and 'composite' are used in an enormous number of different ways: the simple constituent parts of a chair may be the bits of wood of which it is made, the molecules or the atoms, depending on the context; 'white' may be regarded as simple or as consisting of the colours of the rainbow; the length of 2 cm may be simple or it may be seen as consisting of two parts, each 1 cm long (*P.I.* 47).

Wittgenstein's frequent emphasis on the importance of 'surroundings', which I have discussed in Chapters 1 and 4, may also be regarded as an attack on the idea of reductive analysis, in so far as he is drawing attention to the fact that the use of many concepts presupposes a particular context. To learn the meanings of 'giving a present', 'pretending' and 'acting in a play' we have to understand a complex human situation and not just passively watch what is happening. Wittgenstein applied this line of thought to many psychological concepts, arguing for example, that we do not learn the meaning of the word 'think' by watching ourselves while we think, for, if we did, 'It would be as if without knowing how to play chess, I were to try and make out what the word "mate" meant by close observation of the last move of some game of chess' (*P.I.* 316; cf. 337, 583). We have already seen the relevance of this for theology, but it is worth reiterating the point in the present context: many religious concepts presuppose a particular background in our life and should not, therefore, be studied in isolation from the relevant practices, beliefs and contexts.

The second theory which I have marked out for attack, and which I have christened the 'grid theory', is usually associated with Idealism, just as the first is usually associated with Empiricism (incidentally, in attacking Abstractionism I am not attacking Empiricism as such, but certain aspects of eighteenth century British Empiricism and its heirs). Cassirer, for example, said that 'Idealism has always arrived at juxtaposing to the *mundus sensibilis* another cosmos, the *mundus intelligibilis*, and at defining the boundary between these two worlds' (Cassirer, p. 86). Hence he saw science, art and religion as functions by means of which a particular form is given to reality, and concept formation as playing a vital role in this: concepts are formed by selection rather than abstraction and many of them are already present in our inherited language which does not merely 'follow the lead of impressions and perceptions, but it confronts them with an independent action: it distinguishes, chooses and directs, and through this action creates certain centres of objective intuition' (p. 301). From this it follows that there are many different ways of structuring experience.

There are many versions of this kind of theory, some of them held by people who would not regard themselves as Idealists. Brian Wicker, for example, says that the world is not just 'given in perception' but is 'structured . . . by our own capacity for, and use of, language', and mentions Wittgenstein as a proponent of this view (Wicker, p. 15; we shall discuss this view of Wittgenstein shortly). Likewise, Peter Winch thinks that our concepts, which we inherit through our membership of the linguistic community, 'settle for us the form of our experience' (Winch (1) p. 15). K.-O. Apel has remarked that such writers seem to be producing a new transcendental philosophy, in which language-games define the limits of the possibility and validity of meaning and understanding (Apel (2) p. 85). Of course, they all derive their views ultimately from Kant, though they go beyond him in treating *all* concepts as *a priori* and in emphasising the role of our inherited culture.

One should also mention at this point, I think, the view that religious faith is an interpretation or a construction put upon experience, since this view brings up an important aspect of Wittgenstein's thought which we have not yet considered, namely his remarks on 'seeing as'. In Part II, § xi, of the *Philosophical Investigations* Wittgenstein mentions Jastrow's 'duck-rabbit', a drawing which can be seen as either a duck or a rabbit. John Hick has applied this example to religious belief, suggesting that belief in many religious doctrines may be construed as seeing the world or interpreting our experience in a certain way. Accepting the doctrine of Providence, for example, involves experiencing the events of our lives and of history as mediating the presence and activity of God (see Hick (3) pp.

142 ff; (4) p. 53). Now since the same event can be described in different concepts (cp. 'Luckily he was wearing a seat-belt, so he wasn't injured' and 'Because of God's Providence he was wearing a seat-belt . . .') we are naturally faced with the question of why we should choose one interpretation rather than another. Since the world can also be seen as the playground of a malicious demon, there is no point in seeing it as the veil of the divine unless we have some good reason to believe that God does actually exist. Hick answers this objection by introducing the idea of Eschatological Verification: events after death will show that our interpretation has been the correct one.

It is important to see that Hick has both modified and gone beyond Wittgenstein's ideas (I suspect that he owes more to other thinkers who have stressed the role of 'interpretation' in faith than he does to Wittgenstein). The latter employed the examples of the duck-rabbit and the puzzle-picture (where we see faces in the foliage of trees) in order to draw a parallel between 'seeing an aspect' and 'experiencing the meaning of a word'. He certainly did not think that every case of seeing is one of seeing as, for he remarked that I cannot try to see a conventional picture of a lion *as* a lion, any more than a F as that letter, though I may well try to see it as a gallows, for example (*P.I.* p. 206). Likewise, it would, he claims, be ridiculous to say at the sight of a knife and fork 'Now I am seeing this as a knife and fork' (*P.I.* p. 195). Hick, on the other hand, contends that all experiencing is experiencing *as* (see Vesey, pp. 24–5); one of his reasons for claiming this is that, if it is true, it disposes of the objection that since you can only see the duck and rabbit aspects of the duck-rabbit if you are already conversant with the shapes of those two animals (see *P.I.* p. 207), so you can only see an event as an act of God if you first know by direct acquaintance what an act of God is like. Hick maintains that we learn to use the concept 'act of God' as we learn to use other concepts, i.e. by acquiring the capacity to recognise exemplifying instances, though he realises that there are immense differences between this concept and ones like 'rabbit' or 'fork' (Vesey, p. 27).

Clearly Hick has gone beyond Wittgenstein in making his notion of 'experiencing as' cover such diverse cases as identifying a fork, realising that there is a rabbit over there and seeing something as an act of God. And in so doing, he has raised many serious problems. Normally we confine the concept of 'interpreting as' to a restricted range of contexts, and hope that subsequent experience will check our interpretations. But how does Hick's widened concept of 'experiencing as' differ from imagination? How do we *identify* acts of God on different occasions (indeed, *what is it* for something to be an act of God?)? Why is it that even religious people find difficulty in doing so, whereas no adult in the Western world has any difficulty in recognising forks as forks?

These problems also serve, I think, to show up some of the weaknesses of the grid theory. Theories of this type do more justice than Abstractionism does to the fact that our concepts are learnt through our education and that they lead us to discriminate and to select different aspects of experience, according to our interests. But this advantage is offset by many defects: in particular, the theories fail to explain how anybody ever came in the first place to form the concepts which we have.[6] In the case of terms like 'exist', 'possible' and 'thing' it might be claimed that these are essential for any rational discourse and that their source is in the mind itself (to use a question-begging phrase). But clearly religious concepts are not in the same boat since most of them have had a relatively short history and many of them have changed their meaning: for example, the concept of 'redemption' has travelled a long way from its origin in he Hebrew '*goel*', acquiring new accretions of meaning in the Psalms, Isaiah and the New Testament. The writers of these works did not simply passively inherit the concept and use it to interpret the facts, but they developed it in the light of their experience and understanding. The experiences of the Exile and the Prophetic Movement contributed to this development. Similarly, St Paul developed the concept of 'grace' in order to do justice to the event of his conversion and to his experience of life in Christ, and the Church has developed Christological concepts to understand and explain the significance of Christ's life, work and death. Clearly we need a much more complex model of concept formation if we are to do justice to such a process of development.

Neither of the theories which I have discussed does justice to contemporary philosophy of science. Clearly, terms like 'electron' or 'super-ego' were not simply abstracted from observations; nor are they merely ways of interpreting raw data.

Their inventors formulated them to do a particular job, namely to explain things, and they usually sought to show that their interpretations entailed certain checkable observational consequences. Likewise with art: critics who invented concepts like 'tactile values' or 'Mannerism' may have enabled us to see pictures in a new way, but this new vision depends partly at least on the noticing of distinctions and similarities which have hitherto been overlooked. This suggests, perhaps, that we should look for some kind of middle position between the two theories: concepts are 'given' in our language, but they develop as time goes on in response to our experience; sometimes new ones are introduced, while others become obsolete.

Wilhelm Dilthey seems to have had such a middle position in mind when he referred to the 'circulation' between experience, understanding and representation of the world of the mind in general concepts (Dilthey, p. 145). He thought that understanding involves a double relationship between individual facts and general truths: for instance, we understand figures like Bismarck by appealing to our general knowledge of men and history, but such knowledge in turn depends on our vivid grasp of individuals (p. 142). Likewise, our own self-understanding depends on our knowledge of others, and vice-versa (p. 145).

Whichever theory of concept formation we choose, it will have to do justice to the fact that many concepts, including aesthetic and religious ones, are dispensable in that many people manage to do without them.[7] Now while this may show that there is no one set of concepts which forces itself on everyone or which is somehow 'read off' from reality, it does not sanction the opposite extreme of a complete relativism – you have your concepts and I have mine. For our different ways of arranging and classifying depend, partly at least, on the structure of the world: we see the duck-rabbit as a duck or as a rabbit only because it is indeed like both these animals (see Ward, p. 466). The theist will claim that he sees the world as the veil of the divine only because God is present in the world and this presence can be discerned to some degree. It seems, then, that we must reconcile these two views:

(1) Many different language-games can be played in the same world, so that men have a variety of conceptual systems;

(2) Nevertheless, concepts may have a point, and so their use

can be justified to some degree. Conversely, their loss has
a reason and is rarely caused simply by a 'gestalt-switch':
the concept 'ether', for instance, was abandoned for
experimental reasons.

In some cases, indeed, a person may well feel that the facts
ask to be construed in a certain way, even though not everyone
does construe them so. Certainly, scientists, connoisseurs of art
and religious people will wish to claim that their special
concepts enable them to notice and describe features of the
world and human life which other people miss.[8]

RELIGIOUS CONCEPT FORMATION

My conclusion, then, is that religious concepts are neither
simply abstracted nor inherited through our language, culture or
mental structure; rather, they have developed through time as
men have sought to describe, understand and explain their
experience. In this respect, at least, they are similar to moral,
aesthetic and scientific concepts. But they also have some
pecularities, which I will now try to bring out. I shall take as my
examples Christian concepts, since I am best acquainted with
them; but much of what I say will apply to the concepts of
other religions.

One point to which I have alluded intermittently is that
religious concepts, like aesthetic ones, are optional in the sense
that not everyone uses them; yet both kinds of concept claim a
relation to reality. Now aesthetic concepts describe the features
of works of art; but what do religious concepts describe? The
answer to this question was partly provided in the last chapter,
when we divided all that exists into four categories: the unique,
the recurrent, the world as a whole, and the transcendent. I
think that most religious concepts can be classified in terms of
these categories (though ones like 'heaven' or 'hell' are hard to
classify). But the most characteristic and difficult feature of
religious concepts is that many of them involve reference to
more than one category. For example, Christian concepts are
often seeking to interconnect the life of Christ, the presence of
God in the world and man's experience. Of course there are
parallels elsewhere for concepts which link together different

kinds of fact, particularly in the philosophy of mind. In Chapter 1 we saw that terms like 'expect' or 'hope' involve reference to inner mental processes, bodily behaviour and a certain situation or surroundings in life.

The first category, that of the unique, includes historical events such as the history of the Jews in the Old Testament, the life, miracles and death of Christ. Here we have to deal with concepts like 'Messiah', 'Incarnation', 'Resurrection', 'Redemption' and 'Atonement'. Now if the birth of Christ was an event like any other birth, or his death was like the assassination of Abraham Lincoln, there would be no problem other than that of how to describe and classify a historical event, and certainly no problem of concept formation. But it is not clear in what sense the Incarnation and the Resurrection were 'events', since in both cases we are supposedly dealing with divine interventions in history having extraordinary implications for mankind. Similarly, the term 'Redemption' does not simply denote a past event but an ongoing process: using a legal analogy, it attempts to link several kinds of fact as shown by this diagram:

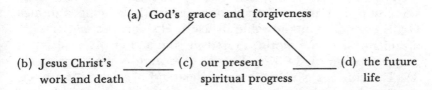

(a) God's grace and forgiveness

(b) Jesus Christ's work and death   (c) our present spiritual progress   (d) the future life

The problem with this concept is that we know only (b) and (c), but not (a) and (d), and that we do not know the nature of the links which I have symbolised with straight lines. I had such examples in mind when I said that the formation of concepts attempting to link facts of different kinds is one of the most characteristic features of Christianity, particularly its Christological concepts, which attempt to grasp the significance of Christ's work and to explain his relationship to God and the world. Such concepts were introduced gradually over a long period of time, and Christians would justify this by claiming that theological understanding, like any other form of understanding, is a slow process: subsequent generations may read more significance into past events than their contemporaries were aware of or could put into words (see Moran, pp. 87–8,

138—9). But such claims need to be supported by some account of the nature of revelation and the development of doctrine.

The second category, the recurrent, includes concepts involving reference to our experience today: the concept of 'Providence', for example, points to purpose in our lives or to patterns discerned in nature; 'sin', 'reconciliation' and 'atonement' arise from our feelings of guilt and our desire for God's forgiveness: 'grace', 'holiness' and other concepts concerned with 'spirituality' describe the self-transformation and the new life which the Christian faith aims to produce. But none of these concepts, any more than those of the first category, is merely descriptive of features of our experience. Most of them are explanatory, in that they are trying to interconnect different types of fact in the way already described (one of the weaknesses of most 'empirical theologies' is that they oversimplify the relationship between concepts and reality). For instance, the concept of 'grace' tries to link the spiritual strength and sanctification of men with the love of God and the redemptive work of Christ. In Orthodox theology it is related to the concept of 'deification' ($\theta \acute{\epsilon} \omega \sigma \iota \varsigma$): grace is regarded as the 'deifying energies' which the Holy Spirit communicates to man, thereby penetrating and transforming his whole being; although God's essence is unknowable in itself, His energies and activity are manifest in the world; moreover, the action of grace serves as a revelation of the Kingdom of God in advance (Lossky, ch. 4). The concept is difficult to understand because it is seeking to provide an explanation of a rather peculiar sort. The main philosophical problem in such cases is to show that they really do provide an explanation and that one is needed: the charge is frequently made that religious explanations are vacuous, or else that there is an alternative non-religious explanation available.

The problem of explanation, however, is most acute in the case of our other two categories, namely the world as a whole and the transcendent. Many theologians have claimed that the existence of God has explanatory value. G. F. Woods, for example, argued that the doctrine of Creation explains why the world exists, why there is something rather than nothing (Woods, ch. XV). Others claim, more generally, that their religious beliefs make most sense of things.[9] Sometimes, too, people argue that God's existence explains particular facts about the world or history, e.g. the emergence of intelligent life through evolution.

Such an approach attracts fire from both philosophers and theologians. The former naturally protest that the existence and love of God are compatible with *any* state of affairs in the world and cannot, therefore, serve as a genuine explanation because they fail to provide for prediction and discovery.[10] Moreover, physicists and other scientists who appeal to unobservable entities in their explanatory theories usually try to link at least some of their terms with observational terms, e.g. by correspondence rules or operational definitions. Hence those who claim a parallel between theoretical laws in science and religious doctrines must provide such rules or definitions for terms like 'God', 'Holy Trinity' and 'grace', point out what particular states of affairs they wish to explain by them and how theological explanations differ from other ones.

The religious objectors claim that an explanatory God is merely a 'God of the gaps', who is religiously inadequate and anyway liable to be supplanted when an alternative scientific explanation is found (Bonhoeffer, pp. 103—4, 121). This objection may perhaps be regarded as a modern version of Pascal's preference for the God of Abraham, Isaac and Jacob to that of the savants and philosophers. It is, I think, more a criticism of apologetical arguments which use God as a working hypothesis than of more metaphysical approaches like that of Woods. A different kind of criticism comes from some Wittgensteinian philosophers of religion: they object to the practice of discussing the existence of God as if it was simply a philosophical problem or hypothesis instead of trying to understand the situations and 'forms of life' in which people speak of finding God, dwelling in His presence or feeling His absence. In general they emphasise the importance of paying attention to the circumstances in which religious people use their concepts, to their 'grammar' (in Wittgenstein's sense) and to the criteria of their application.

I think that the religious objectors are right in suggesting that the term 'God' is part of a complex conceptual scheme. One might develop this point, and also relate it to the question of theological explanation, by showing that the conceptual system has taken many centuries to develop and has been used in many very elaborate arguments: think, for example, of the complexity of the Epistle to the Romans, with its teaching about grace and justification, and its argument that the Law has been fulfilled in Christ. Now St Paul's arguments may be bad and his conclusions false, as indeed any religious or theological judgements can be; but, if there are mistakes involved here, they cannot be obvious ones and their refutation would not be a *simple* matter. This complexity has been disguised in contemporary philosophical theology, particularly by the poverty of the examples it chooses: too often philosophers discuss the question of God's existency or His love for us without seeking to connect the concept of love with those of grace, reconciliation, redemption and salvation, and without appreciating the kind of situations in which God is spoken of as acting or being present.

This line of thought still leaves us, however, with difficult ontological problems, which I mentioned in Chapter 3 (e.g. with regard to God's transcendence). Now the comparison between theology and theoretical concepts or explanations in science is trying to meet these problems, by suggesting that a system of religious belief is like a scientific theory in that it only needs to 'touch down' at some points in our experience (though unlike it in that we do not seek to test religious beliefs through experiments). That is why I regard the philosophical objections as more serious — though I think they point more to the incompleteness of the comparison than to its impropriety. It is unfortunate that many contemporary philosophers of religion have suggested the parallel without working it out in detail or explaining how it could be developed and how far it is to be pushed. I shall say more about the role of ontological models describing unseen entities and their role in religious belief in the next chapter.

As regards the issue of explanation, I think that two points are worth mentioning at this stage. In the first place, religious concepts and explanations differ from most scientific ones in being personal (cf. Woods, pp. 170–2). Hence they do not necessarily compete with each other, and indeed religious explanations may be regarded as supplementing scientific ones. Those who put God to the test (e.g. Charles Bradlaugh, who pulled out his watch and challenged God to strike him dead within five minutes) fail to reckon with the fact that He is personal and so does not necessarily have to reveal Himself or act according to fixed laws. Secondly, we do not always adhere to a scientific theory because predictions derived from it have been confirmed by further observations and experiments: in some cases we adopt a theory because it is simple, wide in its scope, illuminating, fruitful in solving puzzles, internally coherent and externally consistent, and because it provides a familiar and manageable picture or model (this is not to say, of course, that we may not also hope at the same time that future events will make the theory more probable or even certain – a point which is very relevant to the question of eschatological verification). Wittgenstein claimed that Freud's and Darwin's theories were of this type, offering a 'synopsis' or a connected 'representation' of the facts, rather than a scientific hypothesis (*Moore/Lectures*, p. 316). Of course, this still leaves us with the philosophical problem of establishing in a more precise and systematic way the standards which would enable us to decide between different representations and explanations.

THE CONCEPTS OF SPIRITUALITY

So far I have tried to show the different types and uses of religious concepts, and also the way in which the conceptual scheme of any religion must be viewed as a whole. But why should we adopt such schemes, since it is possible to do without them? Have I not merely shown how religious concepts *might* arise, but not how they *should* arise?

This obvious objection raises a host of difficulties which take us away from the subject matter of this chapter into the realm of apologetics and comparative religion. My purpose in this chapter has not been to prove that any particular set of concepts is the 'right' one, but simply to point out the importance of the question of concept formation for philosophers of religion: it is, in my view, one of the growing edges of the subject, despite the fact that relatively little attention has been paid to it. It would require another book, and indeed a whole life's work, to continue from this point and to explain how religious concepts have been formed, how they are used, to what facts they are related and the nature of the connection. In any case, it is unlikely that any *general* account of the matter is feasible, beyond the kind of schematic outline which I have provided. Despite these reservations, however, I will endeavour to say a little more about the way in which religious concepts 'latch onto' the world, and will choose a particular group, namely those relating to 'spirituality'. I choose this topic because it is important in itself, because it has not been widely discussed recently, and because it is arguable that an understanding of these concepts is the road to the understanding of more complex religious concepts.

By 'spirituality' I understand a way of life in which people attempt to acquire holiness and an awareness of the presence of God through prayer, meditation and other spiritual practices. The subject has been neglected in contemporary philosophical theology (in Britain, at least; much of what writers like Tillich and Bultmann say is highly relevant to the question), but it has made a welcome return in Professor H. H. Price's recent work, especially his final Gifford Lecture. There he argues that we may partially verify theism by making what might be called a 'devotional experiment'. The procedure is to take the hypothesis that God created the world and loves each one of us, and to suppose that it is true. By meditating on this hypothesis and praying, we develop our spiritual capacities. One who does this for a long time 'will himself become a different kind of person, and will begin to have experiences of a sort which he has never had before' (Price (2) p. 485). These experiences provide evidence of God's existence and attributes, especially His love (pp. 474 f., 480 f., 483–5).

Price rests the weight of his case on these personal religious experiences, and I do not propose to investigate this aspect of his argument. But he also appeals to the phenomenon of sanctification or personal transformation: spiritual people have a certain serenity and inward peace which others admire: '. . . the existence of such persons is in practice the most persuasive argument in favour of a religious world-outlook' (p. 475). Now what is the nature of this 'argument'? In the main, Price seems to be arguing that the radiating love and serenity of saintly or 'spiritual' people are important because they attract others and so make them disposed to investigate the claims of theism, and because they are the visible fruits of genuine religious experience (Price (2) p. 475; (3) pp. 58, 68 f.)

There is, however, another line of thought which seems to be at the back of Price's mind: the quotation given from p. 485 suggests that personal transformation is part of Price's 'devotional experiment' and that he regards both it and inner religious experience as evidence for God's existence and attributes. Certainly it is tempting to appeal to spiritual transformation as evidence for the existence of a transforming power, i.e. God. Yet clearly such a line of argument would be fraught with great difficulties. It is not perhaps to the point to object that different religions with mutually incompatible dogmas produce a similar sanctity in their adherents, for we are simply concerned with *theism*. But it is unclear whether a man who acknowledges the sanctity of some religious believers and yet refuses to admit God's existence is making a *mistake* and, if so, of what kind. Surely it could be argued that the existence of saintly people merely shows that all men have certain latent capacities which can be developed, but not necessarily that there is some external power which fosters this development? Moreover, even if we do personify the source of this sanctity (assuming that there is a source) it remains to be shown why we should call it 'God' or 'the Holy Spirit' rather than, say, 'Apollo'; or why we should identify the God who heals and nourishes our souls with the God who created the world (as Price does in (2) p. 482, although nothing that he has said proves that there *is* a creator), or with the God who raises men from the dead. And why should our self-transformation provide evidence of God's omniscience or eternity? Clearly the answer to these questions would have to be that the God who can transform men must have these other attributes and powers. But an independent argument for monotheism would be needed at this point.

I shall return to some of these questions in the next chapter. For the moment I shall say that it is probably a mistake to try to link the question of spirituality with that of verification (in general, I think that much contemporary philosophical theology suffers through its premature concentration on the question of verification).[11] I also wish to claim that the topic of religious experience is only part of the question of spirituality: it is unfortunate that they are often identified and that they have become tangled up with apologetics, like so much philosophy of religion (I am thinking of textbooks which have a section on 'the argument from religious experience' — usually following one on revelation). I would prefer to proceed at a slower pace and to deal with the question of *understanding*, rather than with those of verification and religious experience. The connection which I would like to establish is simply that many religious concepts involve reference to spiritual transformation, and that many religious doctrines attempt to describe and explain the possibilities of acquiring such a transformation. Hence a consideration of this topic is valuable in giving us an understanding of one important strand in many religions. Sometimes this transformation is described in special religious terms, but often metaphorical or analogical terms are introduced, e.g. 'light', 'life', 'love' and 'father'. One may go on to conclude that some experience of spiritual transformation is required in order to fully grasp the relevant concepts and doctrines, and that there are levels of depth in our understanding of religion, depending on our level of spirituality, but I think that such conclusions would require an independent argument.

By 'spiritual transformation' I understand a transformation of the whole personality, and I make this comment in order to clear away a misunderstanding which may well have contributed to the unpopularity of the topic of spirituality today. This misunderstanding consists of the assumption that spirituality is something 'inward' and that it is, therefore, purely a matter of one's interior life and not one's outward life and behaviour. Fortunately this misapprehension is less common today than it was a few years ago, largely due to the popularisation of some of Bonhoeffer's ideas — though it still tends to be perpetuated in many discussions of 'religious experience'. After attacking people who used God as a stop-gap in scientific explanations, he went on to deal with those who would give him a domain in our private interior life. He remarked (Bonhoeffer, p. 118):

... it must be said that the Bible does not recognise our distinction of outer and inner. And why should it? It is always concerned with the *anthropos teleios*, the *whole* man, even where, as in the Sermon on the Mount, the Decalogue is pressed home to refer to inward disposition. It is quite unbiblical to suppose that a 'good intention' is enough. What matters is the whole good. The discovery of inwardness, so-called, derives from the Renaissance, from Petrarch perhaps. The 'heart' in the Biblical sense is not the inward life, but the whole man in relation to God. ...

This is why I am so anxious that God should not be relegated to some last secret place . . .

Kierkegaard, I think, anticipated much of this in his attack on Bishop Mynster's idea of 'hidden inwardness' which I mentioned in Chapter 1 and related to Wittgenstein's attack on the Cartesian account of the mind, summed up in the slogan 'An "inner process" stands in need of outward criteria' (*P.I.* 580). The point is not that there is no such thing as the interior life or 'inward remaking', but that these things are only genuine if they are manifested through outward behaviour. The New Testament is quite clear on this point, and uses very forthright language to describe the total self-transformation to which Christianity aspires. The Gospels speak of 'change of heart' (μετάνοια) and 'rebirth', while St Paul speaks of 'newness of life' (Romans 6.4), 'a new creation' (Galatians 6.15) and a '. . . new nature, created after the likeness of God in true righteousness and holiness' (Ephesians 4.24; cf. Colossians 4.10); he also describes this transformation in terms of the fruits of the Holy Spirit – love, joy, peace, etc. – and of Christ being formed in us (Galatians 4.19; 5.22–3). St Peter even speaks of our sharing in the divine nature (II Peter 1.4; cf. II Corinthians 3.18).

It often seems that such strong and clear language is not taken entirely seriously. There are perhaps theological reasons for this: the stress on justification rather than sanctification in some churches, the fact that the Bible sometimes speaks of our sanctification as merely consisting in being believers (e.g. I Corinthians 6.11; 7.14) and the already mentioned tendency to stress the inward working of grace. But the main reason is the sheer human fact that it is so difficult to achieve real holiness (as opposed to timid attempts at self-improvement): as Nietzsche said, 'They don't *look* redeemed'. Perhaps, however, we have been fortunate enough to meet once or twice with saintly people who do some justice to St Paul's words. Such meetings are a very touching experience, which Newman describes (*G.A.* pp. 402–3)[12] graphically:

And all of us, the more keenly we feel our own distance from holy persons, the more we are drawn near to them, as if forgetting that distance, and proud of them because they are so unlike ourselves, as being specimens of what our nature may be, and with some vague hope that we, their relations by blood, may profit in our own persons by their holiness.

But sanctity has a theological significance as well as a religious importance, and this is well brought out in Karl Rahner's essay, 'The Church of the Saints'. Rahner argues that although the Church is the church of sinners, of those *in via*, she is also the church of 'eschatological salvation' and 'of victorious grace'. Hence she must say (Rahner, p. 94) that:

> God really *has* redeemed, he really *has* poured out his Spirit, he really *has* done mighty things for sinners, he *has* let his light shine in the darkness. . . . She must not declare this merely as a *possibility* provided by God . . . as if one could merely 'presume' that God has poured out his Spirit without giving any evidence at all of his mighty wind and his tongues of fire.

For Rahner, the saints show forth God's work, and they also serve as 'the initiators and creative models of the holiness which happens to be right for, and is the task of, their particular age' (p. 100).

To avoid the difficulties about verification which I mentioned earlier, I would prefer to express Rahner's point in a different way: we need to be able to teach people the meaning of terms like 'sin', 'holiness', 'grace', 'redemption' and so on. Of course, people may learn these in different ways, but the advantage of the saints is that they provide us with public and recognisable examples. I think that an experience such as the one described by Newman is valuable for giving us some understanding of religious concepts — I say *some* understanding, because even fairly simple concepts like those just mentioned are, to use N. R. Hanson's phrase, 'theory-laden' and, as I shall shortly point out, they often have difficult metaphysical implications. For example, sin is not merely immorality but an offence against God; and the Old Testament ascribes holiness primarily to God and predicates it of people, places and objects only in so far as these are related to God's work (Exodus 30.28—9, Leviticus 9.44). Still, the terms do involve some reference to men's moral state, and in virtue of this they have passed into ordinary language.[13]

By starting with simpler concepts like 'holiness' we enable our theology to 'touch down' (to use a phrase of Ian Ramsey's). We can then go on to more complex concepts like 'redemption', 'salvation', 'grace', and 'Holy Spirit'. These concepts are much more difficult to grasp because they are parts of a complex theological system and they relate to facts of many different types — historical, eschatological and metaphysical. But all of them involve some reference to the possibility of our self-transformation (I take it that the main thrust of Bultmann's work has been to remind us of this). 'Grace', for example, although a technical theological term describing many aspects of God's relationship with mankind, does denote a power which may transform the lives of saintly people, a source of strength, love and faith (I Timothy 1.14; II Timothy 2.1).

We could, I think, even use my approach to gain *some* understanding of God's transcendence, though this is a more difficult and contentious matter. The connection might be established in the following way: saintly people have a quality of spirituality consisting of an inner joy and peace, depth of character and radiating love which deeply impress those around them. Sometimes this quality is part of a natural and spontaneous innocence, but usually it has resulted from years of prayer, reflection and self-discipline, often accompanied by great suffering. If we congratulate them on their goodness and spirituality, they may well plead that it is the grace of God working through them. Now the concept of grace is used to indicate that our lives can only be transformed through the operations of a power which is not part of our own resources or under our own control. Moreover, this power operates at different times and places, with no apparent causal connection between these occasions. Socrates spoke of himself as God's gift to Athens, and others have thought of the saints and prophets as men inspired by the Holy Spirit and given the task of bringing their contemporaries to an awareness of God. The coming of such men seems to be unpredictable and inexplicable in terms of natural causes, and so people speak of them as having been 'sent' by God. This gives us the idea of God as a transcendent power. The connection which I have outlined may be expressed in a scheme such as this:

Saintliness — external source (perhaps called the 'grace of

God') — transcendent power (transcendent because operating unpredictably and at widely separated times and places)

I am not putting forward this scheme as a proof that there *is* such a transcendent power, but as a suggestion of one way to acquire the concept of such a power.[14] It is perhaps tempting to use the paradigm case argument at this point and say '*this* is what we call the grace of God', but such a move may result in Reductionism, or else it raises the question of whether one can base ontological claims on mere linguistic usage.[15] For even if it were legitimate to hypostatise the power of grace by saying 'There is a power which works through saintly people, and *this* is what we call God', we would still have to go on to prove that this power is identical with the traditional conception of God as Creator. In other words, we would have to provide a link between the cosmological and the spiritual strands in religious concepts and doctrines.[16]

I shall return to this difficult subject in the next chapter, when I discuss the place of ontological doctrines about a transcendent being in the religious way of life. The main purpose of this present chapter has been to continue the task of 'locating' by relating religious language to facts about the world, human life and history. Roughly speaking, this chapter has concentrated on one side of the relation, namely language, while Chapter 4 dealt with the other side. My discussion has tried to add substance to the claim that religious language-games, activities, etc. are responses to certain facts and that they involve the formation and use of concepts in an attempt to understand these facts and their implications.

We are still left with many problems, especially with regard to the 'theory-laden' character of much religious and theological language, the nature of verification and the question of the relationship between different religions (this last difficulty concerns both sides of my discussion: not only do different religions use different concepts, but they claim different facts about the world or history as revelations of God). Moreover, we have to show the *point* of many concepts: we have to bring together this chapter and the last one by relating the concepts to their background and explaining how people come to understand them. This will be the next topic to which I will address myself.

6 Locating: III The Religious Way of Life

One of the cryptic references to theology in Wittgenstein's work goes 'How words are understood is not told by words alone (Theology)' (Z. 144). He does not explain the reference to theology, but the surrounding passages enable us to grasp his general point. In the previous section he had asked what gives meaning to a configuration of chess pieces (a favourite example of his) and what distinguishes paper money from mere printed slips. He goes on to investigate what is involved in understanding music, poetry and language generally. In all these cases significance depends on the surroundings and use in our lives: 'Only in the stream of thought and life do words have meaning' (Z. 173). We have already seen how Wittgenstein maintained that language is part of an activity or form of life, and that meaning and sense are not something internal and mysterious.

It seems natural to pursue Wittgenstein's point by arguing that we come to understand religious language through some direct acquaintance with its associated forms of life, activities, customs, institutions and surroundings. And indeed we find such an argument among some of his followers. Peter Winch, for example, contends that an understanding of prayer and monasticism can be gained only by those who have some religious sympathy and knowledge of religious beliefs; this is part and parcel of his general argument that we understand social practices and institutions by grasping the rules which govern them rather than by the experimental and observational method of the natural sciences (Winch (1) pp. 23, 83 ff.). Similarly D.

Z. Phillips criticises many philosophers for failing to examine the contexts of religious beliefs, e.g. when they assume that they can settle the question of whether there is a God or not without trying to understand the form of life of which belief in God is a fundamental part (Phillips (2) pp. 4, 63). Such an understanding is gained by participating in the form of life, though one may, of course, eventually find it unattractive. But such a rejection by someone who knows the story from the inside is very different from the urbane scepticism of a detached philosopher, for Phillips claims that 'There is no theoretical understanding of the reality of God': we may love Him, fear Him, or rebel against Him, but we cannot remain neutral – hence the remarkable claim that 'understanding religion is incompatible with scepticism' ((2) pp. 75, 79).

A fuller and less extreme version of this view is found in the recent work of Paul Holmer, who has outlined a distinctive approach to the question of religious understanding, relying heavily on Kierkegaard and Wittgenstein. Much of this work consists of a polemic against those who claim that traditional religious language is meaningless. Holmer argues that a 'learning how' is needed in the religious life, and that a lack of understanding of religious concepts is caused by a loss of religious interest and practice. He too appeals to Wittgenstein's insight that some language belongs intimately to a form of life and cannot be understood independently of this (Holmer (12) p. 118); from which he argues that we untie the knots in our understanding of religion and theology by achieving a 'greater congruence between our thoughts and our form of life', for 'to think right requires that we live right' ((14) pp. 30, 35).

Holmer also appeals to Wittgenstein in support of his contention that we need no special science of meanings or interpretation in order to understand religious language ((1) p. 170). Words acquire their meanings as part of a natural process of human interaction. Now the basic language of Christianity is that of fishermen, tax-collectors and tent-makers, and is learnt by practising the religion. The meaning of its concepts may fail to be discerned by outsiders, including philosophers and even theologians, because they confuse learning *about* faith and religion with learning *to be* faithful and religious ((1) pp. 12, 18; (5) pp. 253–9). Erudition is of limited value here, for 'Tolstoy learned Hebrew and Greek to translate the Scriptures for himself and then was chagrined to discover that there were people ignorant of the ancient languages who understood specific texts better than he and in virtue of something else' ((12) p. 118).

This something else was a moral, religious and aesthetic sensitivity, depending largely on qualities of character rather than education. Hence Holmer argues that learning how to use religious concepts is a matter of learning how to be truly religious — to be contrite, forgiving, long suffering and so on. A man who reads the Old Testament without understanding it needs 'pangs of conscience, a sense of contrition, even a sense of wonder', rather than mere background knowledge of the text ((12) pp. 117—18). Likewise, we learn concepts like 'God', 'sin', 'grace' and 'salvation' through a complex of reactions, stimuli and responses in 'a religious context of worship, faith and concern' ((5) p. 257). Again, if they seem meaningless, this may be because we have lost sight of the relevant practices and the context with which they are associated.

This view of religion entails that the theologian's role is mainly descriptive rather than speculative. Holmer cites Wittgenstein's remark that 'The work of the philosopher consists in assembling reminders for a particular purpose' (*P.I.* 127), and argues that theology's role is to help us to learn how to be religious and to *understand* religious concepts, beliefs and practices, 'precisely to root believers firmly in the Christian life' ((6) p. 369). Naturally, such a delineation of the theologian's role brings him into conflict with many contemporary schools of thought: most obviously, with the 'God is dead' and other radical theologians, but also with more traditional views. A lot of recent work is speedily dismissed: 'It is unfortunate that the so-called theological revival in our time . . . has been primarily one more way to attract the talkative bright college set' ((6) p. 367). Holmer's main target, however, is those theologians who consider that we need to underpin religious language with a comprehensive metaphysics and ontology; and his greatest wrath is reserved for Tillich. He criticises them for over-intellectualising religion — as if one had to have beliefs of a transcendent sort and to engage in idle speculation in order to acquire the scriptural virtues of patience, courage, hope and faith, and to have one's life made anew by Jesus Christ ((6) pp. 368 f.). If people lack religious understanding, will they be any better off if we give them a transcendent metaphysics or some other meaning scheme, substituting, for example, 'being' or 'ground of being' for 'Father in Heaven'? Of course, Tillich was right to see that the traditional teaching on sin and God's redemption is hard to understand, but: 'The lack of understanding has never demanded an ontological explanation. According to Christian theology and the Bible, understanding comes with putting oneself more securely in the moral context that the Bible describes, not in a still more abstract and general kind of enquiry' (Holmer (1) p. 143).

I have much sympathy with the line of thought which I have just summarised, and particularly with its development by Paul Holmer, but I think it raises many problems. I will devote the rest of the chapter to the three most serious ones, concerning, respectively, religious understanding, concepts and the place of metaphysics.

(1) The writers whom I have discussed stress that participation in the religious way of life is requisite for a full understanding of religion. Now the claim that 'only insiders can understand' is a move which tends to be the last gambit of a defeated apologist and it naturally arouses suspicion. Exactly what is the insider's advantage here? Just *what* does he understand? Concepts? Doctrines? Activities? And exactly how does the development of one's moral and spiritual life influence one's religious understanding? Certainly there is something unedifying about a professional theologian whose personal life shows little real religious spirit. But what is the nature of the 'greater congruence between our thoughts and our form of life' which Holmer thinks will help us to untie the knots in our theological understanding? Exactly how does our becoming more saintly help us to make sense of highly technical theological controversies, e.g. those of the Reformation or of the early Councils of the Church? If people lose their faith do they lose their religious understanding (as Phillips (3) p. 46 asserts)?

It could be argued that the importance of religious understanding has been exaggerated in recent philosophy of religion: one thinks of the retort of a philosopher at Oxford: 'It's not that I don't understand Christianity, I don't *believe* it.' Some of the religious difficulties which people have are ones of understanding, but many are not, or at least not in the sense meant by Holmer, Phillips and Winch: I am thinking of difficulties about proofs for the existence of God, immortality, miracles, moral theology, the Problem of Evil and so forth.

(2) Holmer says that concepts like 'God', 'sin', 'grace' and 'salvation' depend upon the interaction of human responses and language. True enough, but these concepts differ widely from each other. We found in the last chapter that there is a wide variety of religious concepts: consider, for instance, the great difference between concepts used to describe spiritual transformation and those concerned with eschatology and cosmology. Now if indeed the later Wittgenstein showed that there is no *general* answer to the question of how language 'latches on' to the world, then we can only proceed by analysing particular religious concepts. We need to treat concepts individually, explaining how they are learnt and how they are related to our experience.

(3) What is the place of metaphysical doctrines in the religious way of life? In Chapter 2 I suggested that any 'Wittgensteinian' philosophy of religion is going to have difficulty in accommodating the metaphysical strand in Christian doctrines, and indeed this is borne out by most of the work which has been produced so far. Yet the existence of ontological statements about the Trinity and the nature of Christ in the Creeds and other teachings of the Church suggests that the Christian theologian, at least, cannot dispense with metaphysics, as Holmer apparently desires. We are faced, therefore, with the need to explain how these traditional formulations are to be understood and what role they play in the practice of the ordinary believer.

UNDERSTANDING FROM WITHIN

In discussing the view that only believers can fully understand religion, I think that we need to distinguish two theses. Firstly, a theological one, that only a minority of people have received the gifts of faith or spiritual transformation which constitute the inner conditions necessary for the understanding of religious doctrines, and that this fact may be accounted for in terms of doctrines of predestination, grace, etc. Secondly, a philosophical thesis that concepts need to be learnt and that this learning involves having certain experiences, understanding certain forms of life, taking part in certain activities and so on.[1]

The second thesis may be applied to both religious concepts, beliefs, etc. and to secular ones. In the case of the former it can either be applied by itself, or else be supplemented by the theological thesis, since the two are not incompatible; one might, for example, explain the fact that only certain people have the experiences necessary for an inner understanding of religious concepts by appealing to a doctrine of Election. Of course, other theological explanations are possible besides this one: the philosophical thesis is consistent with several theological theses — or with none. Let me say a little more about both of them:

(1) In the Gospels we are confronted with the problem that only a small number of Christ's contemporaries acknowledged him, the others 'seeing they do not see' (Matthew 13.13). This blindness is explained mainly in terms of their hardness of heart (John 12.39—40); in general, the Gospels make religious understanding a function of moral character: 'Blessed are the pure in heart, for they shall see God' (Matthew 5.8); 'He who does what is true comes to the light' (John 3.21). St Paul developed this idea into the doctrine that religious understanding and discernment is a grace or gift of the Holy Spirit: he speaks of a mystery, in which all the treasures of wisdom and knowledge are hidden (Colossians 2.2—3), which has now been revealed to himself and to the holy prophets and apostles, through the Spirit (Ephesians 2.3—5). The full knowledge of God's revelation is to be acquired through the gift of a spirit of wisdom (Ephesians 1.17), and also through love (Colossians 2.2; Ephesians 3.17—19). Spiritual things can only be learnt spiritually and not through philosophical learning: the Christian message seems foolishness to the Greek philosophers (I Corinthians 1.17—25; 2.7—14).

St Paul's remarks raise a host of theological problems concerning the nature of faith, grace and religious knowledge which have occupied theologians since his time[2] and have produced numerous schools of thought.[3] Aquinas distinguished firmly between truths which are accessible to rational investigation, which include the fact that God exists, and those which have been divinely revealed; the latter require the grace of God for their understanding in faith. The Holy Spirit manifests to our understanding the depth of meaning in revelation and unfolds its implications for us (*S.T.* $2^a 2^{ae}$ viii, 4—5). Aquinas followed

St Augustine and St Anselm in claiming that we acquire this understanding through faith — *credo ut intelligam* — and that it presupposes a pure and holy life (*S.T.* 2ᵃ2ᵃᵉ. viii. 7, 8 ad 2).

Calvin addressed himself more directly to the question of why religious understanding is available to only a minority of people. He grasped the nettle firmly and argued that the Fall had corrupted the human intellect, so that only the Elect, whose minds have been illumined by divine grace, can understand the truths of the faith (*Inst.* II ii. 12, 18—21). This amounts to extending the doctrine of grace to the cognitive sphere as well as the moral, though it could be argued that the other writers whom I have mentioned did this implicitly to some extent. Barth took a less rigid line, but he too maintained that the Word of God can be grasped only through the grace of faith: he agreed with Luther that any man may hear the Word, but feeling it inwardly is the work of faith, a secret doing of Christ's (*C.D.* I. i. 198 ff., 211, ii, 233 ff.). While he rejected double predestination, he also rejected Aquinas' view that God's existence can be known by the unaided reason (cf. *C.D.* II. ii. 171 ff. and II. i. 85).

Newman took up directly the New Testament suggestion that there is a link between religious understanding and moral character. He defined faith as 'the reasoning of a religious mind, or what Scripture calls a right or renewed heart' (*U.S.* XI, § 1); commenting on one of the passages which I have mentioned (I Corinthians 2), he claimed that St Paul makes 'a certain moral state and not evidence . . . the means of gaining the Truth' (*U.S.* XII, § 22). This line of thought stayed with him throughout his life, for over thirty years later he wrote (commenting on Montaigne's scepticism) that 'truth there is, and attainable it is, but . . . its rays stream in upon us through the medium of our moral as well as our intellectual being' (*G.A.* p. 304).

Newman's approach is similar to H. H. Price's suggestion, mentioned in the last chapter, that theism is partially verifiable, because a spiritual person has experiences which other people do not have and which he construes as evidence for God's existence and attributes, especially His love. Price counters our suspicions about admitting that there are some facts which can only be verified by spiritual people by pointing out a non-religious parallel: the realisation of certain truths about other people depends upon our moral character. Thus selfishness and unkindness, for example, may lead us to misunderstand and misinterpret people's conduct and feelings, and even not to notice them; so it seems that one's emotional and conative dispositions may affect one's cognitive powers (Price (2) pp. 471 f.).

Price's argument is concerned with verification rather than with understanding (though he thinks that a spiritual person's experiences provide him with a *better* understanding of theism — cf. (2) p. 475). But it resembles the theological arguments which we have considered in that it links intellectual and moral considerations. Moreover, the fact that it does not employ technical theological concepts like 'grace', 'Holy Spirit' and 'Predestination' means that it may serve as a bridge between the theological arguments and the philosophical thesis that one's acquisition of concepts depends on certain factors.

(2) The philosophical thesis asserts that our interests, intelligence, and experience govern our acquisition, understanding and use of concepts; consequently propositions which embody these concepts may be appreciated only by those who are in a position to grasp what is at stake. This does not amount to claiming that these propositions are esoteric, i.e. necessarily available only to a minority of people, since *in principle* anyone with the requisite intelligence, experience and sensitivity can understand them. But in fact only a minority do so. Usually there is not a sharp line drawn between those who do and those who do not understand, since there are levels of depth in the acquisition of understanding. We use terms like 'sensitivity', 'appreciation', 'insight', 'penetration', 'perceptiveness' and 'discernment' to describe the gradations in the level of people's consciousness and comprehension.

The reasons why experiences and truths are not generally available differ from case to case. Consider the following examples:

(*a*) Simple experiences like drunkenness, drug-taking and poverty. Al Ghazali contrasted the drunkard who knows what it is to be drunk, even though he does not know the definition or the scientific explanation of drunkenness, with the sober man who may know about these theoretical matters but who nevertheless cannot be said to know what it is to be drunk (he was making the point that only a mystic can speak knowledgeably about mysticism — see Zaehner (2) pp. 12—13). One could provide many other similar examples, e.g. the knowledge of poverty possessed by a slum-dweller as compared with that of a sociologist (see Carse, p. 151).

These examples merely contrast different kinds of knowledge. There is no real difficulty of concept formation, since people have no problem in applying concepts like drunkenness or poverty, whether or not they have any first-hand personal experience.

(*b*) Mathematical concepts. These are, in principle, available to everyone, but their use presupposes that certain practices, e.g. counting, are established and recognised. The introduction of new mathematical practices sometimes provides us with new concepts (see Wittgenstein, *R.F.M.* V. 49; his example of playing chess is also highly relevant). If someone does not understand the concepts, it is no use trying to explain them by merely providing verbal equivalents, since puzzlement about mathematical concepts (and indeed most other kinds of concept) is not like puzzlement about the use of words in a foreign language. We can only grasp concepts by understanding their function, and this understanding may call for great intelligence.

These remarks apply, *a fortiori*, to many other academic subjects, e.g. physics, though the degree to which mere spectators can understand the concepts employed differs from case to case.

(*c*) Music. This is a very tempting, and often misleading, parallel with religion (see Otto, p. 177, for an example). Here we have a whole area of experience which is available only to those who 'have an ear' for it. Furthermore, there are levels of insight and understanding even among music-lovers, and also a barrage of technical terms employed in writings about music. On the other hand, the tone-deaf man can recognise the *activity* of making and listening to music, even if he does not appreciate musical *works*; moreover, some musical concepts can be explained to him. In many respects, e.g. his inability to follow a melody, he is more appropriately compared with someone who cannot understand a language than with someone who has never had a particular experience at first-hand.

(*d*) People. Our appreciation of works of literature depends on our self-knowledge and on our understanding of other people, their problems and relationships.[4] This in turn may depend, as Price has shown, on certain qualities of character, e.g. sympathy, humility and unselfishness, as well as on a general perceptiveness and intelligence.[5]

(*e*) Religious concepts. Price, as we have seen, applies his point about understanding people to the awareness of God, arguing that moral factors may influence our epistemology in both cases. But I think it should be noted again that Price is mainly concerned with verification (he is providing a version of what has come to be called 'The Argument from Religious Experience'), and not with understanding. He is certainly not arguing that our religious experience teaches us the meaning of 'God' and other religious concepts. Religious believers do not necessarily rest their faith on such experiences. Moreover, any attempt to base religious understanding on them encounters the difficulty that an atheist *can* use terms like 'God' properly, for he can learn the definition and the attributes of God (not to mention all the general difficulties which Wittgenstein raised about the notion of a private language).

When Wittgenstein made the remark which I quoted at the beginning of this chapter (*Z*. 144) he was not concerned with the issues of verification or of private experience, but rather with the way in which our concepts depend on forms of life, practices, 'surroundings', institutions, etc. Similarly, *P.I.* 19 and 23 are not particularly concerned with the issue of inside participation, but more with the context of language in our lives. So we should be asking ourselves about the dependence and the context of religious concepts, and only secondarily whether a non-religious person can grasp them. Wittgenstein seems to have in mind the way in which concepts like 'authority' depend on the form of life of giving and obeying orders, or the way in which 'sorrow' or 'atonement' are expressed in practices like repenting, confessing, apologising and making restitution, or perhaps the dependence of punishment on concepts of responsibility and desert. A person who had never been taught to command, obey, apologise, etc. would simply fail to understand much of our language and social behaviour: understanding a command, for example, presupposes a knowledge of what commanding is and the realisation that a particular utterance is one. This is not to say, of course, that he could not be trained in these practices by us later on and so learn the concepts, just as a non-mathematician can be taught how to use mathematical concepts. A more difficult case would arise if we found people who lacked the most fundamental of all human forms of life like hoping, intending and believing — if this is possible.

In the case of religion we should look for the dependence or religious concepts on religious forms of life, institutions, etc. such as worship, prayer and penance; and indeed we do find such a dependence: there seems, for example, to be a logical connection between the concepts of divinity or holiness and the practice of worship, in that the latter is stigmatised as idolatry when directed at an unworthy object; and the practice of confession presupposes a grasp of concepts like sin, guilt, repentance and forgiveness. Similarly, beliefs embodying such concepts are presupposed in religious practices. The form of life of theistic worship, for instance, depends on the belief that God exists, and that He has certain attributes and relationships with creatures. The question of which comes first, beliefs or practices, presents us with a chicken-and-egg situation. I suppose that logically the beliefs come first, in that the quickest way to explain the point of religious practices is to describe the beliefs they express: if people understand belief in God, then we can explain to them the point of worship and other practices of theistic religions, and also go on to concepts like 'sin', 'holiness', 'grace' and 'Creation' (though in the last chapter I have suggested that one can also start from the opposite direction, from the concepts of spirituality). But historically and psychologically the practices may come first: people can adopt religious practices because these express their deepest needs and feelings, and only later consciously articulate the beliefs which the practices presuppose or express.

We are now in a position to say something about the religious outsider. In the first place, it depends on how much of an outsider he is: I am assuming that he is a human being and therefore a user of language. Now clearly a rank outsider (e.g. a man from Mars, or one raised in a totally irreligious environment) would fail to understand the point of a religious ceremony because he would not know the purpose and the 'surroundings' of the actions, the rules for their performance, the beliefs on which they were based, and the intentions of the participants. He would be like a spectator of a chess-game who did not know the rules — or even one who did not realise it was a game (*P.G.* 11). But all of these things can, like the rules of chess, be explained to him: an atheist can attend a Requiem Mass and understand what is going on, provided that he is informed about the relevant beliefs; he may find it strange or unattractive, but that is another matter. More generally, it should be pointed out that we can come to understand the customs of other cultures and the rules on which they are based, e.g. courtly love and chivalry (cf. Apel (1) p. 50, criticising Winch on this score). Anthropologists manage to come gradually to understand several different cultures and religions. Practices which seem pointless and abhorrent to us can be made to seem more reasonable when their context and the beliefs on which they are based are explained to us: I am thinking, for example, of the way in which Mircea Eliade has illuminated the significance of cannibalism and primitive religious practices (see Eliade (2) pp. 46 f., 203).

One can go even further than this: an outsider may sometimes have a better understanding of things than a participant does, for he sees aspects and relationships in human activities which remain concealed from the participants, and he can expose self-deception and rationalisation. D. R. Bell (pp. 119—20) instances the way in which Marx conceptualised the social and economic relations of early industrial capitalism, and thus questions Winch's apparent assumption that the participants' conceptual scheme is the only one possible. The obvious parallel with religion is that someone may understand a religious way of life, and even admire many aspects of it, but reject its description in terms of religious concepts and instead redefine and explain it in terms of psychological and sociological concepts. One thinks particularly of the way in which Freud claimed to give the 'real' meaning of religious behaviour.

What, then, are we to say of the remark by the American author, William Burroughs, that 'what is called "love" is a fraudulent invention of women and the media'?[6] This remark appears cheap and superficial, yet I imagine that it would be difficult to *argue* Burroughs out of his view. On the other hand, those whose personal experience differs from Burroughs' would strenuously resist his redescription. The particular relevance of this example to our present concerns is that it again raises the question of the role of personal experience in religious understanding. I have followed Wittgenstein in rejecting the view that seeks to link such experience with our learning to use religious language: any person can be trained in the religious way of life, learn the meaning of its terms, become acquainted with the relevant beliefs and indeed become deeply learned in theology. Yet it must be admitted that certain things may well be missing: a real religious inclination or interest at the beginning, a conversion or abiding religious passion later on, a moral change, and religious experiences. These things can never be guaranteed, so the believer ascribes them to the grace of God. Now it is the last of them which particularly concerns us here: what is the importance of religious experience?

One answer to this question has been provided by Price, in terms of verification. But another answer was provided by Mill when he said that 'There are many truths of which the full meaning *cannot* be realised until personal experience has brought it home.' Very often people accept something as true but rarely think about it, until some particular experience brings a fuller realisation and appreciation. Newman describes this contrast in terms of 'notional assent' and 'real assent'. Mill's remark does not apply to all religious truths — it does not apply, for example, to historical statements about the life of Christ. But I think that it is applicable to many kinds of religious proposition, particularly, perhaps, to those concerned with spirituality. Religious experience seems to be one factor which helps to produce 'real assent' (which is not to say that it proves the *truth* of religious doctrines: I am more concerned here with the psychology of religious belief than with its verification); for many people it is a characteristic part of the religious way of life, helping to arouse and sustain a deep passion and commitment. Thus it is possible for someone to accept the definition of God as an infinitely perfect being and to believe that he loves mankind, but to devote little thought to the matter. But later some experience seems to bring home the truth of these beliefs: the believer feels that knowledge by description has been replaced by knowledge by acquaintance, that God is a power and not simply an idea, just as someone who falls in love feels that the concept of 'love' has received some new content, that the mere knowledge of the meaning of a word has been replaced by first-hand experience.

Does the religious believer *understand* more through his experience? It depends what is meant by 'understanding'. It is unlikely that his conceptual grasp will be increased. But very commonly 'understanding' in religious writings is used in a wider sense than this, and is used to indicate the full realisation of a truth: when people say that the illumination of the Holy Spirit is required in order to understand the truth of revelation, they mean that some personal experience is needed in order to bring home the truth of beliefs which are indeed already 'understood' in some sense. Thus St Anselm says: '. . . who has not believed will not understand. For he who has not believed will not experience, and he who has not experienced will not know. For the knowledge of one who has experienced exceeds that of one who has merely heard, just as experience surpasses hearing' (*Ep. de Incarnatione Verbi* I (Schmitt II, p. 9) my trans.). Here he is contrasting understanding based on direct experience with that of someone who merely hears words. Something of this use occurs in ordinary speech: when someone says, for example, 'You don't understand my feeling of despair', he does not mean that we do not have the concept of despair, or that we cannot predict and explain actions motivated by despair: rather he means that we cannot really empathise with him because we lack the first-hand experience of deep despair. To use Max Weber's terminology, one can have explanatory understanding (*erklärendes Verstehen*) without the direct understanding of actions' subjective meaning (*aktuelles Verstehen*); cf. Weber, pp. 94f.

This distinction will enable us to see the relationship between the theological thesis about religious understanding and the philosophical one, which I discussed earlier. Religious concepts are not esoteric, for they can be learnt by anyone; and, in principle, religious doctrines can be understood by anyone. But, as it happens, relatively few people have the requisite interest in religious questions or the experiences which serve to establish a real commitment. Now we may simply leave it at that, saying that it is a brute fact that people's experience and interests differ, and therefore their level of understanding does likewise, and that it is the task of some other science, and not of philosophy, to explain why this is so. For instance, psychology can explain what factors of character and personality are relevant and how they are operative. But this may seem an unsatisfactory position, since it fails to specify how religious interests and concepts differ from others. Hence the religious believer will be inclined to give a theological explanation in terms of grace, predestination, etc. The philosopher of religion is in the difficult position of wanting to preserve a theological neutrality and yet being required to bring out the peculiar character of religious concepts.

THE SPIRITUAL WAY OF LIFE

The appropriate conclusion so far seems to be that there is an interdependence between religious concepts, beliefs, activities, forms of life and institutions. The practices of praying to the saints and for the dead, for instance, presuppose that one understands concepts like 'sanctity', 'merit', 'salvation' and 'heaven' and that one has certain beliefs about the effects of prayer, immortality, Purgatory and so forth. These practices only occur in certain contexts and they require certain intentions and beliefs to give them their point. The 'insider' has the advantage of being familiar with these things, but a non-participant can learn how to use religious concepts and to understand religious doctrines, even though he lacks the experiences which many religious believers enjoy and which help to produce real assent.

One could only proceed from this point, I think, by being more specific. I shall endeavour to be so by recurring to the topic of spirituality, understood in the sense of self-transformation (this may include inner 'religious experiences', but these are not necessarily its most significant feature). In the last chapter I pointed out its general religious importance and its philosophical relevance to the question of concept formation. I think that it has a wider philosophical importance than this, since it raises questions about ethics and, as we shall see in a moment, ontology. But the question which particularly concerns me now is the connection between certain religious concepts and doctrines on the one hand, and a religious way of life on the other. An example of the latter would be one in which people feel their own sinfulness and their need of God; they wish to atone for their sins and to seek God's forgiveness; they also wish to come to know Him more intimately and to experience His love; as a result they embrace a mode of life involving prayer, meditation, penance, self-sacrificing love and detachment from worldly pleasures. They may well live in a community because they need its spiritual support or because the possibility which they are seeking to actualise is essentially a communal one. Some of the consequences of the choice of this way of life may be seen by an outside observer if the religious people become outwardly sanctified; but other consequences will be known only by the participants, for they consist in inner experiences which they construe in terms of the presence and activity of God in the soul. Now this way of life clearly involves the understanding of certain concepts, e.g. 'God', 'grace', 'sin', 'holiness', 'atone for' and 'salvation', for many of its constituent practices, e.g. prayer and fasting, depend on them and as a whole it is designed to achieve a spiritual transformation which is described in religious terms.[7] Moreover, the way of life depends on certain doctrines about the consequences of sin, the nature of God, and the life of the soul in this world and the next.

This sketch of a religious way of life should throw some light on the way in which religious concepts are learnt and understood, for I have sought to show their dependence on a context, somewhat in the way in which Wittgenstein sought to relate mathematical concepts to the practices and procedures of that discipline in his *Remarks on the Foundations of Mathematics* (one might also mention again the way in which he showed that many concepts presuppose certain surroundings and an understanding of rules and practices). The important point here is that there is such a dependence, rather than that only the participants can fully understand the relevant concepts and doctrines. Indeed, it should be clear from what has gone before that I think that the latter claim is probably false. Those who lack a religious interest may indeed not know how to use religious concepts and therefore fail to fully understand the relevant activities, doctrines, etc. Moreover, it is probably true that the most direct path to learning about the real point of religion is to participate in prayer, meditation and other spiritual practices, in an attempt to achieve some degree of spiritual transformation and holy living; this participation acquaints one with the background in life which makes religious concepts meaningful. But there is nothing to prevent the outsider coming to understand the religious way of life, particularly by studying the beliefs on which it is based, even though he will lack the experiences and relationships which characterise direct participation.

Still, it should be pointed out that the outsider (who may be an adherent of another religion or someone without any religious commitment at all) differs from the believer in several ways, quite apart from the question of religious experience. He will probably reject the beliefs which support the religious way of life which he is studying. He may well have reservations, too, about the moral worth of many religious practices and ways of life, e.g. asceticism, and he may therefore question particular patterns of 'holiness' or 'salvation' on moral grounds. The clash between religions is not always a matter of conflicting doctrines: it is often a moral conflict, for different religions may describe and recommend different possibilities of spiritual renewal, so that the outsider may have to decide which pattern seems more worthwhile or noble.[8] Buddhism, for example, is concerned with release from the cycle of reincarnation rather than with the overcoming of sin, and so it lacks anything comparable to the Christian concept of 'salvation'. This is not to say that one cannot compare Christian and Buddhist patterns of spirituality with each other, or that one cannot ask questions about the truth of their doctrines — about whether, for instance, reincarnation really occurs or whether following the eightfold path will release us. But it does mean that one's ethical views may colour one's religious sympathies. Moreover, a shift in moral attitudes may have wide repercussions *within* a religion: compare, for instance, the way in which compassion succeeded detachment as the key ethical category in Buddhism, thereby causing a development in religious belief and practice, or the way in which modern views on the justification of punishment affect our feelings about the doctrine of Hell.[9]

The most fundamental difference, however, between an outsider and a religious believer is that the former may very well reject even the vocabulary which the latter uses to describe spirituality, because he rejects the religious ontology pre-supposed in this vocabulary. We saw in the last chapter how spiritual transformation tends to be described in metaphysical language, especially in terms of God's actions on the soul. Moreover, doctrines dealing with this matter are often closely conjoined with other types of doctrine, e.g. eschatological ones. We cannot, therefore, concentrate simply and solely on the topic of spirituality; nor can we treat religious doctrinal systems merely as attempts to describe and explain possibilities of achieving spiritual renewal in this life (though this is *part* of their function) and therefore as verifiable.

The tendency to combine several levels of religious language is particularly exemplified in Christianity: the Nicene Creed, for example, contains within its relatively short span statements of several different types, notably cosmological, ontological, historical and eschatological ones. Christian writers pass easily from one type to another: St John, for instance, makes 'eternal life' both something possessed here and now and something to be realised after death, and he regards the second as a consequence of the first: we are raised after death because of our faith in Christ (John 6.40,47,54; cf. 3.36, 5.21,24, 17.3). Similarly, St Paul regards the presence of the Holy Spirit now as a pledge and anticipation of our inheritance (Romans 8.11,23; II Corinthians 1.22; 5.5; Ephesians 1.13f.); and the Epistle to the Hebrews says that those who have received the Spirit have already 'tasted the powers of the coming age' (6.5). The reasoning behind these moves seems to be that the power which is strong enough to transform men now is strong enough to raise them from the dead (cf. Dodd, Pt. II, § 2; von Hügel (2) pp. 21, 70–7, 367, 396). Thus the experience of spiritual transformation seems to be one source of man's belief in immortality.

Since the subject of spirituality has traditionally carried with it all this additional baggage, it is not surprising that people have come to wonder whether much of it might be jettisoned. We are again confronted with D. R. Bell's point, that the participants' conceptual scheme is not the only possible one. We are also, I think, confronted with the last of the three difficulties raised at the beginning of this chapter: what is the role of metaphysical doctrines about a transcendent God in the life of the ordinary believer? Could one keep the religious way of life and abandon the structure of traditional ontology?

SPIRITUALITY AND ONTOLOGY

Such a question may be seen as an expression of the widespread feeling that it is hard to see the relevance of religious doctrines to the lives of ordinary believers today. Traditional apologists often argued that holiness is one of the marks of the Church, proving the continuing presence of the Holy Spirit in it. Now one may well agree that there is something to be said for an organisation which does produce saintly people (while regretting that they are all too rare) and yet feel puzzled by many of the Church's doctrines. 'True religion' has a nourishing and healing power, and may produce sanctity, but, apart from that, what does the truth of its doctrines consist in?[10] What is the ordinary believer to make of the Chalcedonian definitions, the dispute about the *filioque* clause, and the Reformation controversies about faith, grace and justification?

The aspect of this difficulty which concerns us now is this: granted that spiritual transformation does occur and that there is a mode of life designed to realise it, why suppose that it needs a religious explanation? Or, better, why *describe* it in terms like 'grace', 'holiness', 'nearness to God', 'Holy Spirit' and so on, i.e. in terms of a specific religion, or indeed in terms of any religion at all? Are we not simply providing what Paul Edwards has called 'a bombastic redescription of familiar facts'? Why not just accept that there is a way of spirituality and leave it at that? After all, there may be a purely naturalistic explanation, e.g. in terms of love (which Christianity improperly and unnecessarily hypostatises). We could eliminate the religious terminology by speaking of 'evil' and 'heroic virtue' instead of 'sin' and 'holiness', and replace 'grace' by 'sudden and unexpected moral improvement'.

It will not do to reply that there is no one 'right' way of describing the world, and that traditional religious language cannot be shown to be *mistaken*. For the whole point is that this language is 'theory-laden' with metaphysical concepts and that it makes ontological claims, especially about God's existence and attributes. Unless, therefore, we are willing to acquiesce in Reductionism, we must admit that its claims transcend our experience; and this, of course, is the source of Kant's criticism of traditional religion. It is interesting to note that in one passage Kant presents his objection in a way which is highly relevant to my discussion of spirituality, when he queries the use of the term 'grace': he admits that certain inexplicable movements leading to a great moral improvement do occur in people, but he insists that we cannot distinguish between the effects of grace and nature, because we cannot recognise a supra-sensible object within our experience (Kant (3) Bk. IV, especially Pt. 2, § 2).

I think that Kant is over-stating his objection, since a man may feel the 'givenness' of grace without necessarily wishing to claim any acquaintance with the giver: believers have always admitted that God is beyond our direct experience and full comprehension. Nevertheless, his objection is important in pointing to the fact that the Christian religion does tend to move easily from the spiritual to the ontological. In so doing it raises not only Kant's difficulty, but also the question of how God works through nature and history. It remains to be shown that the God who helps men to achieve holiness (and we are, of course, already moving from spirituality into ontology in hypostatising such a being) is also the Lord of Creation, that He has cosmological as well as spiritual power. A person may feel God's power in his own striving for spiritual perfection or in the spirit of a religious community, but be at a loss to see his hand in a poverty-stricken and disease-ridden world. And yet the considerations about the nature of spirituality which I advanced in the last chapter prevent us from taking refuge in any simple contrast between the 'spiritual' and the 'material', since I have been trying to break down this false dichotomy. We seem to be left, rather, with a contrast between God's presence in mankind and His working through the rest of nature. If we say that God operates in the world through the spiritual resources which men have realised in prayer then we shall have difficulties with the doctrines of Creation and Providence, as well as with many aspects of petitionary prayer, since we will have restricted God's power to the inner life.[11] Even if one is willing to countenance such a restriction, I think that one cannot thus evade the problem of divine causality, i.e. the nature and mode of God's agency.

I think it will be helpful to notice that the difficulty which I have just raised is really two-fold:

(1) Can we reasonably base ontological statements about the existence and attributes of God on facts about human spirituality? What is the link between the spiritual and the ontological strands in religious doctrines or concepts (or, as others would put it, between anthropology and metaphysics)?

(2) What is the relationship between the different types of statement found in theology: eschatological, cosmological, spiritual, historical and so on? When can we justifiably make a 'type-jump' from one to another?

I shall restrict myself to the first question, since the second one takes us too far away from our present concern with spirituality (though it is worth noting that any answer to the first question will contribute towards the second, since it will have said something about God's nature and powers). I cannot, of course, hope to solve such a grave problem, one which takes us right to the frontiers of philosophy of religion. Here, more than anywhere else in this book, we are walking in a mine-field. In any case, my purpose now is not to defend any particular metaphysical doctrines, but rather to show the role of the latter in religious practice. Hence I think it will be sufficient to point out that the tendency which we are considering is understandable from the religious point of view, and that there are parallels elsewhere for the linking of statements of different types and the use of an ontological model to co-ordinate them.

The most obvious parallel is in the philosophy of science: Freud, for instance, constructed a model of the mind in order to explain the complexities of human behaviour. Now it may perhaps be the case that religious thinkers who engage in metaphysical speculation are trying to provide a 'projection' or a 'model' (in the sense of a structure of unseen entities posited to explain what is seen) for describing and explaining the possibilities of spiritual transformation which they believe to be available to mankind. This is not to say, of course, that either Freud or these metaphysicians are correct in their speculations; but I do not think that their *methodology* is necessarily misguided.

This methodology, when applied to religion, is not simply a matter of looking for a coherent explanation of things – I am certainly not suggesting that religious belief consists in the choice of an explanatory hypothesis, for this would indeed produce merely a 'God of the gaps'. The important point is that religious people feel that they are confronted by the reality and power of God; many saints have gone further and have spoken of a penetration or fusion, resulting in a profound change in their nature and a new mode of being. Now the purpose of a religious metaphysics is to supplement this apprehension of God's power and activity by providing an account of His nature. Thus the religious inspiration of the methodology is people's feeling that there are religious forces at work in the world which can take possession of communities as well as individuals, and which can operate through rituals, customs, etc. (see Watson, ch. 4). Now one might simply stop here and say, with Gregory of Nyssa, that 'The word "godhead" signifies activity rather than nature'. But the question surely arises of whether there can be activity without an agent: surely, to use the mediaeval slogan, *operari sequitur esse?* Hence, the next stage is to attempt to give some ontological account of these forces, i.e. to describe their nature and origin. Now such accounts are explanatory, in that they tend to link one kind of fact with another. Thus the concept of 'grace' attempts to link the trasformation of man with the action of God. We saw in the last chapter how, in Orthodox theology, it is related to the concept of 'deification': grace is regarded as the 'deifying energies' which the Holy Spirit communicates to man, thereby penetrating and transforming his whole being.

Theistic explanations differ from scientific ones in being personal: that is to say, they interpret the world in terms of the will and activities of a personal being. Moreover, this being is regarded as infinite and transcendent, not limited by time and space. Hence such explanations cannot allow for prediction or experiment in the simple way that some scientific hypotheses can; furthermore, models using 'love' as their dominant concept will have their own special features and difficulties — love cannot by bought, manipulated, etc. God is neither a predictable mechanism nor a capricious dictator (if He were either, the practice of prayer would be non-existent or very different from what it is).

Clearly these differences create many problems. Religious people use such explanatory models because they feel that the facts demand them, in particular because they feel confronted by a power outside of themselves in the way already suggested; hence they are not satisfied with naturalistic explanations. But others may be sceptical, either because they lack any sense of God's power, or because they do not find that traditional doctrines answer to their religious experience,[12] or because of moral considerations — I have already pointed out how our conceptions of God's attributes are influenced by our ethical views. Any theologian, therefore, who wishes to show that traditional theism is still an appropriate model will have his work cut out for him. Just as in science these are disputes between those who use different theories to cover the same facts (e.g. in psychology), so different religions often enjoin similar ethical ideals and spiritual practices but have dissimilar views about God's nature. There may also be disputes among those who claim to use the same ontological structure: I take it that the controversy over the *filioque* clause was a dispute about relationships within the main Christian model, the Trinity. Such disputes entail that theology cannot simply describe religious concepts, as Holmer suggests.

More radically, critics may suggest that the differences between religious and scientific explanations are so great that they destroy the parallel (cf. Nielsen (8) p. 204). I think that some answer to such criticisms can be given by recalling what I said in the last chapter, that personal explanations form a special category rendering experiments inappropriate,[13] and that in any case some scientific theories cannot be established by experimental predictions — we have to use criteria like simplicity, internal coherence and consistency with the rest of our experience. The issue of transcendence is perhaps not quite the stumbling-block which it appears: God is also believed to be present and active in the world, so presumably *qua* agent immanent in the world (in this case, as the efficient and formal cause of sanctity) He *is* spatio-temporal; the attribution of transcendence specifies that His existence is not limited to worldly activity.

My purpose in this chapter, however, is not to deal with such philosophical difficulties so much as to argue against the religious opponents of metaphysics, e.g. Paul Holmer, that much traditional religious belief embodies metaphysics (in the sense of the construction and use of ontological models) and that it is natural that it should have developed in this way. If God is indeed a power capable of changing men's lives, then surely religious people are committed to a special ontology? If they think that they can discern the workings of the Holy Spirit in their 'new life' then it seems natural to go on to give some account of his nature and relationship to the world and to the Trinity, i.e. his ontological status. It is true, as Holmer says, that the Christian's confidence in God comes from guilt, prayer, worship and so on rather than from metaphysics, and that it may take a lifetime to learn how to use the word 'God' (Holmer (6) p. 370). But one can admit all this and yet still feel that it is legitimate to want to go on and give some metaphysical account of God, as both Tillich and the more traditional theologians who discussed ontological issues did. Such accounts are not attempting to provide a *foundation* for religion, for they are comparatively late developments. But they are designed to increase religious understanding. Perhaps after all the metaphysicians whom Holmer attacks were really trying to say the same things as he is about the power of God and the possibilities open to men, but were using ontological models to describe them. If that is so, then we shall have shown the role of metaphysics in people's religious belief.

EXCURSUS: THEOLOGY AS GRAMMAR

An interesting recent example of the 'only insiders can understand' thesis is S. C. Brown's *Do Religious Claims Make Sense?* In this important book he argues that many articles of faith are 'grammatical' claims, i.e. necessary propositions which specify internal connections and thus 'articulate features of a conception of reality' (p. 49), and that they can only be grasped through insight. Once they are understood they are believed — there is no room for doubt or for verification (pp. 60, 119, 142, 173); nor is there room for loss of faith, for Brown rules out this concept as a grammatical impossibility (p. 147; on the other hand, he does allow for our finding something sufficiently unintelligible to reject it as false, for example, belief in fate). Brown specifies five different types of insight (pp. 173—5), but the religious examples which he provides are cases of our coming to accept something as necessarily true which we previously regarded as contingently so or as false. These include 'God cannot be mocked', 'it is impossible to escape divine punishment', 'the lover is remembered by love' (i.e. God's love) and 'God is an eternal being' (pp. 47, 149—50, 151, 171). All of these claims articulate the standards of intelligibility implicit in the language of Christianity and cannot be imposed from outside of this religion. Although they are necessarily true, they are not analytic, for they are neither descriptions of current usage nor stipulations for new linguistic conventions (pp. 57, 63, 104). Of course, most grammatical propositions are learnt through our acquisition of language, but Brown rightly perceives that grammar can change, and that reasons may be given to justify these changes; we do not simply opt without reasons for new verbal conventions (pp. 59–60, 64, 120).

Clearly the application of Wittgenstein's concept of grammar to theology raises many serious problems. In Chapter 1 I showed that in his jargon 'grammar' is closely related to 'criteria' and concerns the logical structure of our language (cf. particularly *Moore/Lectures*, pp. 276, 295; *R.F.M.* I. 128, V. 29: *P.G.* 23; *P.I.* 251, 370–3, 496, 664); grammatical propositions are necessary propositions which specify essences or internal properties, e.g. 'my images are private' (*P.I.* 251), 'believing is not thinking' (*P.I.* 574) or 'You can't hear God speak to someone else, you can hear him only if you are being addressed' (*Z.* 717). Although these propositions are necessary, Wittgenstein allows for fluctuations in grammar, e.g. when he points out that what now counts as an observed concomitant of a phenomenon can tomorrow be used to define it (*P.I.* 79); and he allows for alternative grammar, e.g. different sets of colour concepts (*Z.* 331, 346, 354 ff.) Does this mean then that there could be alternative religious grammars – that some theologies might allow for our eavesdropping on God (*contra Z.* 717), as Actaeon spied on Diana? Wittgenstein seems to allow for such a possibility, for he remarks that 'God' is used in many grammatically different senses: in some religions it makes sense to speak of God having four arms (*Moore/Lectures*, p. 312) or, one might add, becoming man. Presumably he would have thought that there is no point in asking which god is the real one, for there is no neutral court of appeal. In any case, even in non-religious cases systems of concepts are not imposed by the world. Yet the religious believer will feel dissatisfied here: surely only one true God exists? And surely it is a matter of *fact* that He cannot be eavesdropped upon? Moreover, the fact that God is transcendent differentiates him from the other subjects of grammatical propositions.

The issue which particularly concerns us now is that of understanding. Now I am inclined to think that Brown errs in linking the concepts of 'grammar' and 'insight' and in resting so much on the latter.[14] The important questions here are about how grammar and criteria are established and whether there can be good grounds for changing them. But the concept of insight is too vague and general to explain anything. Brown says that as a result of insight we see things in a new light (p. 60) and

instances the new understanding of human behaviour provided
by Freudian concepts (pp. 117–18). But I have already suggested in Chapter 5 that very specific issues of prediction, explanation, etc. are raised by such parallels, and that they need to
be explored. Moreover, we use 'insight' both of seeing general
conceptual connections and of making particular judgements,
but Brown does not always sufficiently distinguish the two:
how, for instance, does one categorise the 'anti-Christian insight' that there is pointless suffering in the world (p. 145)?

Wittgenstein dimissed appeals to intuition as 'an unnecessary
shuffle' (*P.I.* 213) and his comment seems equally appropriate
to Brown's concept of 'insight': it is unnecessary in the case of
very commonplace grammatical propositions like 'Every rod has
a length' and '3 x 18 in. won't go into 3 ft.' (to give two of
Wittgenstein's examples), which are conceptual truths about the
categorisation of various entities and their essential properties;
and it begs the question in the case of more disputable examples
like 'a machine surely cannot think' (*P.I.* 360) or 'a foetus is a
human life'. Surely propositions like the last two *are* stipulations (I assume that they are not established usage)? This is not
to say that they are arbitrary, for we may be able to provide
reasons for our stipulations. For instance, an opponent of
abortion might argue his case by pointing to similarities between a foetus and a baby, and a Central State Materialist might
contend that if Physicalism is true, then propositions like 'my
pain is red and two inches long' are not in fact ungrammatical;
similarly, someone who thought that a hypocrite is not necessarily insincere (to use an example discussed by Brown) might
defend his understanding of the concept of hypocrisy by
appealing to the role of self-deception. The point is that there is
room for discussion in these cases, and that recourse to the
concept of insight fudges the issues. Moreover, such cases surely
tell against Brown's contention that grammatical propositions
cannot be doubted? We often do wonder whether a particular
concept is applicable, usually because the criteria for its use are
not clearly defined or conflict with each other. But Brown is
committed to regarding this as due to lack of insight and
understanding; just as he is committed to regarding a man who
'loses his faith' as never having had it in the first place (since a
loss of understanding is precluded) — surely rather a drastic and
implausible move.[1 5]

Brown would probably regard the view I have suggested as approaching a conventionalist account of necessary truth, which he rejects because he thinks that such a view fails to account for the fact that the concepts which we have reflect the understanding we have of the world: grammatical claims are *presupposed* in the matter-of-fact claims we make about things (pp. 117–18). But surely one could admit this and regard it simply as a consequence of the fact that *most* necessary truths are acquired as we learn language? Of course, the interesting cases are those where the definition or application of a concept are matters of dispute. Now here Brown rejects conventionalism because he assumes that it cannot do justice to the fact that grammar changes, and that there are reasons for this. But again, surely there is nothing to prevent our saying both that grammatical propositions are stipulations and that such stipulations are rationally justifiable? We do legislate here, but our legislation is based on reasons, for instance analogies or significant facts about the world or human needs. As Wittgenstein said, 'to the *depth* that we see in the essence there corresponds the *deep* need for the convention' (*R.F.M.* I. 74; cf. V. 6 for grammar having a point. In *Z.* 331 he explains that his claim that grammar is arbitrary is directed against those who would make it a matter of verification).

A good topical example which supports my view of grammar is provided by Stephen Toulmin ((2) pp. 188–9): recent medical advances in organ transplant surgery call for decisions about when death occurs: if a man's heart is still beating but his brain has ceased to function, is he dead? Such questions are not simply empirical, nor are they semantic, for our current usage is not sufficiently clear and definite. They call for a decision, but the decision should not be an arbitrary convention but a redefinition of our terms in the light of the relevant facts, i.e. physiological knowledge, legal requirements, etc. Appeals to 'insight' simply beg the question. I suspect that Brown could only really provide an alternative to the view which I am suggesting by developing a view about internal relations and properties very different from that found in recent philosophy.

7 Relating

THE CONTEMPORARY RELEVANCE OF ANALOGY

The second task which I proposed for Wittgensteinian philosophers of religion in Chapter 3 is that of relating religious language-games to other language-games. Of course, religion is not the only area in which such a problem arises: many commentators on Wittgenstein have drawn attention to the need to relate different language-games to each other as well as to distinguish them. Wittgenstein himself noted that there are such relationships (*P.I.* 65), but he said little about their nature. The problem is particularly acute when various fields of enquiry raise issues which go beyond their own boundaries: neurophysiology, for example, seems to pose questions about human freedom and responsibility, while the religious belief in immortality, as traditionally understood, encounters issues in the philosophy of mind, especially with regard to the migration of consciousness (see Pears, pp. 119–20).

Much recent work in theology may be seen as attempting to meet this difficulty, not so much for the reasons I have mentioned, but more through a pastoral concern to avoid separating the language used in religion from other kinds of language and thereby isolating it.[1] Bultmann, for example, insists that theology is concerned with our self-understanding, and that therefore its concepts must be related to those in which the 'natural' man understands himself and his world (Bultmann (2) pp. 96–8).

The problem of relating religious language-games to other ones is distinguished by a special feature: although the former do employ some specifically religious terms (especially 'God') much of their terminology consists of terms like 'father', 'exist', 'love', 'cause', 'make', 'act', 'redeem', 'have', 'good', and 'life' which also occur in non-religious contexts. (Sometimes one can define purely religious concepts in terms of them, e.g. by describing God as the 'infinitely wise, loving . . . Creator', and this is one way of showing people the meaning of many religious concepts.) So it seems that we are confronted with an exemplification of Wittgenstein's remark that we use the same expressions in different language-games (*P.I.* p. 188; cf. *Z.* 160). But the difficulty is that many of these terms do not seem to be used in religious contexts in quite the same sense that they are used in other contexts: for instance, God is not regarded as being a father in the sense of a physical procreator.

What I want to do in this chapter is to see to what extent a consideration of the theory of analogy will help us in our task. I think that the contemporary significance of the theory lies in the fact that, despite its very complex ramifications, it attempts to meet a problem which can be stated fairly simply, namely that raised in questions like: 'How can we speak of God, using terms derived from our ordinary language?'; 'Are the terms used to describe God to be taken in the same sense as in their other uses?'; 'Granted that all human language is inadequate to describe God, yet surely some terms must be at least more appropriate than others?' It is unfortunate, therefore, that there is a dearth of contemporary non-thomistic studies of analogy: although several thomists have produced distinguished contributions on this topic during the last twenty years, few philosophers in the 'analytic' tradition have devoted much attention to it. This omission is surprising, since many writers have pointed out that notions like 'systematic ambiguity',[2] 'open texture' and 'language-strata' which play a considerable role in contemporary philosophy, bear at least some resemblance to traditional theories of analogy. Similarly, several writers (e.g. Kenny (4) pp. 220–6, and Bambrough (1) p. 171) explicitly couple together analogy and Wittgenstein's 'family resemblances'. In both cases there is an attack on the 'tendency to look for something in common to all entities which we commonly subsume under a general name' (*B.B.* p. 17).

Perhaps the reason why non-thomists are suspicious of the theory of analogy is that its treatment of the topic of analogical predication is accompanied by some less acceptable views on ontology and epistemology, especially with regard to the nature of being and God's causal efficacy. I shall remark more fully on these metaphysical views later in this chapter. Certain contemporary thomists seek to avoid these difficulties by pleading that St Thomas' theory of analogy is mainly a question of logic and language, rather than of epistemology or ontology. Fr H. McCabe, for instance, says: '. . . too much has been made of St Thomas's alleged teaching on analogy. For him, analogy is not a way of getting to know about God, nor is it a theory of the structure of the universe, it is a comment on our use of words' (McCabe, p. 106).

I do not, as it happens, agree with this as an interpretation of Aquinas, since I think that his views on analogy are closely tied to his metaphysic of being. But I think that we can salvage a lot of what he says without having to accept the latter. In any case, Aquinas is not the only writer to have discussed analogy, even among the mediaevals. I shall feel free, therefore, to diverge from his views.

TYPES OF ANALOGY

’αναλογία (analogy) was originally a mathematical concept, probably deriving from Pythagoras (see Lyttkens, p. 15). Plato used it in the '*Timaeus*' to describe the mathematical relations between cosmic elements which help to harmonise the universe, e.g. fire : air :: air : water (*Tim.* 32 B–C). He used a similar format to define the general relations between different kinds of knowledge and spheres of reality, e.g. being : becoming :: knowledge : opinion (*Rep.* 534 A), and to express similarities of functions like:

Politics		*Care of the body*
sophistry : legislation	::	self-embellishment : gymnastics
rhetoric : justice	::	cookery : medicine (*Gorgias* 464B–465E)

Aristotle likewise extended it to functional similarities, e.g. the way in which different species of animal have a variety of organs fulfilling the same function, More generally, he argued that distinctions like actual/potential and form/privation/matter apply to everything that there is κατ' αναλογίαν (analogically) (*Met.* Λ. 1070 a 33 ff., 1071 a 3—17). Likewise, the four causes apply to all the categories in different ways (*Met.* Λ. 1070 a 31—3, b 27—35). He listed the different kinds of unity which may be found in he world, and describes unity of analogy as 'where things are related to one another as a third thing is related to a fourth' (*Met.* Δ. 1016 b 34—5).

Aristotle was the first to use what was later called 'analogy of attribution', when he pointed out the many senses of the word 'healthy': it can describe something which produces, preserves or signifies good health, as well as a man who has it. He paralleled this with the many senses of 'being' and argued that just as the primary use of 'healthy' is its application to a man, so the primary use of 'being' is that of substance, since the being of other categories is dependent on that of substance (*Met.* Γ. 1003 a 33 ff.). He did not, however, actually use the term αναλογία in such contexts, but described them as relationships προς ἕν (with one central reference) or ἀφ'ἑνος (with one derivation).

Nowadays the two kinds of analogy which I have just mentioned are described as Analogy of Proportionality and Analogy of Attribution. This terminology is found in Cajetan, who presented it as an account of St Thomas's thought; he further subdivided both types of analogy, the first into Analogy of Proper Proportionality and Metaphorical Analogy of Proportionality, the second into analogy of one thing to another and analogy of two things to a third (Cajetan, § § 3, 17—18, 25—6). Cajetan's account has come under heavy fire in recent years from many thomists who allege that it misrepresents Aquinas's views on analogy. Fr B. Montagnes, for example, lists seven ways in which Cajetan diverges from St Thomas, mostly with reference to their respective metaphysics of being (Montagnes, ch. IV) and Fr G. Klubertanz argues that his division of the types of analogy is over-simple (Klubertanz, pp. 118—45). Both these writers agree that Analogy of Proper Proportionality plays a relatively small part in Aquinas' work and that it does not deserve the attention which is usually paid to it in thomistic handbooks.

A non-thomist will not be particularly worried by the fact that Aquinas did not make great use of analogies of Proportionality, since the Bible certainly uses such analogies. Most of the common descriptions and images of God, as father, creator, light, etc. can be expressed in this form, e.g.

God : His creatures :: a father : his children

Likewise, many of the images which Christ used of himself, e.g. the vine, the good shepherd and the head of a body, can be expressed in a similar form. But a thomist could raise two very serious difficulties here which we shall need to discuss on their own account: how do we know that such analogies do hold between God and the world, and are the terms used in them necessarily 'analogical' in the sense that Aristotle's example of 'healthy' is an analogical term?

Let us briefly discuss the first difficulty. A preliminary point is that most Biblical similes and metaphors, when expressed in the form a : b :: c : d, are Metaphorical Analogies of Proportionality (to use Cajetan's terminology), since God is not taken to be literally a light, a vine, a shield, etc. An Analogy of *Proper* Proportionality is one in which the same term is predicated on both sides of the analogy and is to be taken literally, e.g. Aquinas's example (I *Eth*. vii. 1) borrowed from Aristotle:

vision : the good of the body :: intellect : the good of the soul

But the really serious difficulty, in both cases, is to know how we establish the analogies when dealing with God's attributes or relations. In the case of Biblical analogies we are merely rearranging knowledge which has supposedly been given to us in revelation. But what are we to make of an analogy like this (given by Aquinas in IV *Sent*. 49. 2.1. ad 2):

our knowledge : created beings :: God's knowledge : His essence

Aquinas thinks that God has knowledge essentially (*De Ver*. II.1.), as compared with creatures who have to acquire it and may lose it. This is to be related to his view that God *is* goodness and other perfections, and that creatures only have these perfections through participation (*C. G.* I.31–2). He also says that God's knowledge acts as a cause (*De Ver*. II. 14), and this again is to be related to his view that God's perfections are the sources of creatures' perfections: we participate in His goodness, just as our being is caused by and participates in His being (II *Sent.* 9. 1.1. ad 6; I. *Sent.* prol. 1.2 ad 2). The upshot of this is that the relationship denoted by ' : ' is not the same on both sides of the analogy, since God's knowledge is His essence. Moreover, there are additional connections between the terms on both sides of the analogy, because God's being and perfections are related to ours. But, as it stands, the analogy does not inform us of any of these complications, and still less establish them.

We can now begin to see why contemporary thomists tend to depreciate Analogy of Proper Proportionality and to insist that it needs to be supplemented by other kinds of analogy in order to establish the connection between the terms on both sides of the analogy. Even Penido, who stoutly resisted Descoq's view that Analogy of Proper Proportionality is an invention of Cajetan, admitted that we require Analogy of Attribution along with Aquinas' causal arguments in order to establish the existence of a source of all perfections (Penido, pp. 143–7). Likewise, E. L. Mascall admits that we can only use such an analogy as I mentioned if we have first proved that God does exist, and he argues that the perfections which we attribute to Him and to creatures need to be linked through an Analogy of Attribution (Mascall (2) pp. 109–115). The advantage of the latter type of analogy is that it specifies the relationship between the different terms: for example, living in healthy places on a healthy diet *causes* and *preserves* health in men, while a healthy urine or complexion are *signs* of good health. It is interesting to note that in the case of 'good' Aquinas combines both types of analogy, arguing that creatures have their own intrinsic goodness and that God is the first exemplary, effective and final principle of all goodness in creation (*S.T.* la.vi.4; cf. *De Ver.* xxi.4; *I Eth.* vii.1). Now if we reject Aquinas's account (as we may), we shall either have to give up Analogy of Proper Proportionality altogether, or else provide some alternative way of showing that God exists, that He has various perfections and that these are somehow related to creatures' perfections.

The second objection to Analogy of Proportionality which we must consider is that it is not necessarily 'analogical'. Put in these terms, the objection sounds paradoxical, but it confronts us with an important linguistic issue, namely: what is it for a term to be analogical? Klubertanz points out that although Aquinas's general discussions of analogy diverge from each other because he is tailoring them to particular problems, there is one point which occurs in all of them, that analogy is midway between being univocal and being equivocal (Klubertanz, pp. 35—8). Now one might want to reply here that 'univocal' and 'equivocal' are opposites, so that there is no room for a third possibility. If we follow the *Shorter Oxford Dictionary* in defining 'equivocal' as 'The same in name but not in reality', and 'univocal' as 'Having only one meaning or signification; not equivocal', then it seems that we have exhausted all the alternatives. Aquinas, however, is pointing out that there are some terms which will not fit easily into either category. There do seem to be, as Wittgenstein said, '. . . words of which one might say: they are used in a thousand different ways, which gradually merge into one another. No wonder that we can't tabulate strict rules for their use' (*B.B.* p. 28). The word 'healthy', for example, is not univocal, since it has the three different meanings which we have already noted. But neither is it simply equivocal, since these three meanings are related to each other, whereas a word like 'pen' is wholly equivocal because it is purely fortuitous that we use the same word for a writing implement and an enclosure for animals.

Aquinas went on to argue, following Aristotle, that terms like 'being' and 'good' are analogical: they are not univocal, because they may be predicated in all the categories and because there is no common form or concept covering all cases which can be abstracted and in which all things participate equally; and they are not equivocal, because it is not purely accidental there these words have several different uses — there is a relationship between them. Moreover, in the case of our attribution of these and other perfections to God there are additional reasons for insisting that the terms are not univocal: God is outside any genus, and His perfections are unlimited — indeed, He *is* wisdom, goodness and so on, whereas creatures have them only by participation and in a limited fashion. Those who use ordinary terms of God without realising that they are to be taken analogically are in danger of anthropomorphising Him. On the other hand, the terms are not equivocal because men's perfections have a certain likeness to God's in view of the fact that they are caused by Him and participate in His perfection (see, for example, *S.T.* 1a. xiii. 5; *C.G.* I. 32–4).[3]

Now the point to which all this is leading is that the terms used in a proportionality of the form a : b :: c : d need not be analogical (in Aquinas's sense) or 'systematically ambiguous' or whatever you like to call them. Such a format can be used to express a multitude of things, such as parallel relationships (The Queen : Prince Philip :: Elizabeth Anscombe : Peter Geach), similarity of functions (eyes : sight :: ears : hearing), similes, mathematical proportions and simple parallel predications (see further Klubertanz, pp. 77–86). For a thomist, proportion-alities like 'God diffuses His perfections as fire heat' or 'God is the source of spiritual life as the sun is of physical life' are not genuinely 'analogical', since they do not raise any problems about analogical predication as such. When, however, we at-tribute perfections like goodness, wisdom or knowledge to God, such problems are raised.

We have, therefore, discovered two limitations in Analogy of Proportionality, of which the first is the most serious: it needs to be supplemented by natural theology, revelation or some other form of analogy, and its terms are not necessarily 'analogical'. But I think that this form of analogy will always remain very attractive, because of its Biblical roots[4] and its closeness to the original meaning of ἀναλογία, and because it seems to give us the possibility of reaching out beyond our human situation and dimly apprehending something beyond. Many people like to imagine that the church is a kind of microcosm or model of heaven, or that religious dogmas are, as it were, maps or diagrams of heavenly realities (see Antonia White, pp. 93, 164 for these comparisons).

I shall not say anything further about divisions of analogy into different types. The traditional distinction between Analogy of Attribution and Analogy of Proportionality cer-tainly misrepresents the complexity of Aquinas's views, but it is handy in that it serves to distinguish two fundamentally different issues, i.e. 'focal meaning' in language and isomorphy of relationships, as well as referring us back to the two main sources of analogy in Greek thought, namely Aristotle's discus-sions of πρὸς ἕν predication, and his and Plato's application of ἀναλογία outside of mathematics. Recent Thomist writers (e.g. Klubertanz, pp. 125–44) have argued that many different kinds of analogy occur in Aquinas's work and that these have nothing in common beyond the fact that they are usually defined in terms of '*communis*' or '*communitas*', and that the words used in them are neither univocal nor equivocal. The point which will occur to a non-thomist here is that subsequent philosophers have pointed to types of analogy not found in Aquinas. Wittgenstein's remarks on 'family resemblances' are highly relevant here, as I suggested in Chapter 1: the word 'game' is not simply univocal, since there is nothing in common to all games; but neither is it equivocal, since there is 'a complicated network of similarities over-lapping and criss-crossing' (*P.I.* 66). J. L. Austin concluded his paper 'The Meaning of a Word' by listing many ways in which the same names are used to cover things related in many different ways. Some of these will fit into Aquinas' scheme: I think his example of 'Fascist', which originally had a precise connotation but is nowadays applied to any violent right-wing movement (and indeed as an abusive term for any kind of authority) would be classified by St Thomas as 'resemblance'. But Austin also mentioned the cases of 'youth' and 'love', which may refer to a person or a quality (Austin (1) pp. 39–42).

Rather than try to work out a classification of the various types of analogy, I think that it will be more helpful to proceed now by giving a few examples of the use of analogical terms in religious language. This will give us some idea of what I take to be the contemporary relevance of the question for religion, namely its role in relating 'religious language-games' to other language-games.

EXAMPLES OF ANALOGY

Father and Love

St Paul says that all fatherhood in heaven and on earth takes its title from the fatherhood of God (Ephesians 3.15). Now since God is not a physical procreator, he cannot be our father in the sense that our earthly fathers are; so if 'father' was equivalent to 'physical procreator', then it would simply be false that God is our father. But God is our Creator; moreover, the concept of fatherhood also includes the notions of love, headship of a family (which is suggested by St Paul's play on the word πατριά) and the dependence of his children on the father; and the point of calling God a father is to apply such notions to Him. Like most biblical analogies, this may be expressed in terms of a proportionality: as a father loves his children, so God loves us; as a child depends on its father, so we depend on God.

But in what sense does God love us? And how are we dependent on Him? It seems that these terms are analogical too, so that we are involved in a regress. But in a way the position is easier in these two cases, since the terms 'love' and 'depend on' are already analogical (or open textured, or systematically equivocal) even in ordinary nonreligious contexts. There are many different kinds of relationship described as 'love', and I doubt whether there is any satisfactory definition which would cover all of them. It would be very difficult to explain to a child what mature human love is like: we would ask him to think of his feelings towards his parents, friends or pets and then say 'well, it's like it in some respects, but different in others'. But the result would be highly inadequate, both because of the child's lack of understanding and because here we do not have a likeness between two species of one genus 'love', but rather a family resemblance between two things. Similarly, there are many different forms of dependence: physical support, economic, logical, emotional and so on. Now since the concepts of love and dependence are already so loose, it seems reasonable enough to stretch them to include God's relationship with us, provided that we can point to some similarity with an established usage, e.g. in our need and thanks for His grace.

Causing and Making

God is said to be the cause or creator of the universe, but many modern thomists, perhaps inspired by Barth, have insisted that these terms are not to be taken at their face value, since God's relationship to the world in Creation is a unique relation (see Farrer (1) p. 7, 21–5, for example). We point to the nature of this relation by using as many causal analogies as possible to describe it, to prevent ourselves being misled through taking any one of them too literally. Terms like 'cause', 'maker', 'mover', 'governor' and 'designer' are merely pointing to the direction in which we must look.

This procedure of Farrer and other recent thomists has been questioned by Professor R. Hepburn, on the grounds that they are misusing ordinary language: they are taking terms used to describe natural or human relationships and then 'whittling them away to nothing' by applying them to a bizarre and incomprehensible supernatural relation (Hepburn (2) p. 236).[5]

I think that Hepburn has failed to note that 'cause' and 'make', like 'love' and 'depend on', are already highly analogical: making a fortune, a clay statue, a meal, a decision, a mistake and someone angry are very different activities, and I doubt whether any common definition of 'making' is possible; so it seems legitimate to say that God made the world, provided that we can point to some similarity between His creative action and our own, e.g. our artistic activities in particular. Similarly with causation: the verb 'to cause' is, properly speaking, an umbrella term covering several different kinds of connection between events, actions, objects and persons. Usually we prefer to use specific terms for these connections like 'construct', 'change', 'modify', 'prevent', 'influence', 'originate', 'control', 'father', 'accidentally bring about' and so forth. It will be seen that many of these terms denote actions rather than events, i.e. they are applicable only to human beings or to animals. We may, if we like, lump all these terms together as examples of the relation 'to cause', and then seek to analyse this. But it is notorious that most analyses given by philosophers are either too wide because they cover non-causal relations, e.g. 'constant conjunction', or else too narrow, e.g. Mill's 'sum total of the conditions positive and negative taken together'. It may be that such analyses have failed because they are seeking to include a number of relations under one formula, and such an attempt is bound to fail where we are dealing with a case of 'family resemblance'.

Consider the variety of situations in which we speak of 'causes': usually we describe as causes events which precede others nearby, such that the first are always sufficient conditions of the second. But very often there are several contributory causes of one event, so that practical considerations lead us to pick out one of these and call it *the* cause. Sometimes we speak of objects or persons as causes. Sometimes we may have a continuous process with several other conditions as its determinants, giving us the notion of 'functional dependence', e.g. the heat of the kettle depends on that of the fire and the length of time it has been on it. And sometimes a non-event can be a cause: the lack of a vital rivet caused the bridge to collapse, his absence at the party caused it to flop (see Vendler in Butler (1)).

Since these terms already have so many different uses, we are merely stretching them a little further in applying them to God; this stretching would be justified if we could point to some similarity between God's activity and activities or processes in the world.

Doing and Having

In Chapter XV of the *Categories* Aristotle shows that the word 'to have' has many uses, e.g. having some property, having a husband or wife, having hands and feet, having certain habits or dispositions, or having a certain length, height, etc. Wittgenstein (*B.B.* p. 49) makes the same point and discusses the problem of why I cannot have your pain. I think that a similar analysis might be provided in the case of 'doing' or 'acting'. In all these cases it seems difficult to provide any common definition which will cover all applications of the terms. I think myself that it is most helpful to classify these as cases of 'family resemblance'. We could also express the different senses in terms of a proportionality, but I doubt whether this would be at all useful.[6]

Again, the justification for using such terms of God is that they already have a very wide range of uses in non-religious contexts, and that we are merely continuing an on-going process of stretching. Such a process is in any case a natural feature of any living language, particularly with regard to the development of metaphors: many familiar expressions like 'fit in', 'feel better' and 'upright man' were originally metaphors. D. Schon sees both metaphor and analogy as examples of what he calls 'the displacement of concepts', the process whereby language develops through our bringing the familiar to bear on the unfamiliar (Schon, ch. III; cf. Black, p. 33).

Wisdom, Knowledge, Beauty and Other Perfections

Thomists consider that in applying such terms to God we must employ the *via remotionis* and the *via eminentiae*, i.e. we must purge the terms of their limitations and imperfections and then project them to infinity. Thus in the case of 'knowledge' we remove the limitations of human knowledge, e.g. that it is discursive and acquired only gradually through sense experience, and we extend it indefinitely — God knows all things. Scotus considered, as I have mentioned, that the terms in question are still univocal, but I think that the difference between him and Aquinas is largely a matter of their varying definitions of 'univocal'. Both of them agree in allowing for an 'open horizon' in which we use language to point in the direction in which God is to be found rather than to represent Him.[7]

More seriously, Kant objected that concepts like 'understanding' are derived from our own experience, and that it is illegitimate to proceed to apply them in a new context (Kant (2) p. 57). But I think that a reply can be given to him similar to that already given to Hepburn: although we learn the meaning of words from our everyday experience, it does not follow necessarily that their use is to be confined to the contexts in which we learned them, *provided that* we can give good grounds for extending their use. In the case of perfection terms there is already a great variety in our application of them: we use words like 'strong', 'sound', 'rich' and 'flourishing' in all sorts of contexts.

Curiously enough, many Thomists make a similar assumption to Kant's. Fr Copleston, for instance, writes (Copleston, pp. 129, 131):

If we mean that God is wise in precisely the same sense that a human being is or can be wise, we make God a kind of superman ... the positive content of the concept in our minds is determined by our experience of creaturely wisdom, and we can only attempt to purify it or correct its inadequacies by means of negatives.

This is, I think, to anticipate non-existent difficulties. Just what is this 'precise sense' of human wisdom? And if there is such a thing, who has tried to ascribe it to God? Presumably Copleston is thinking of the facts that human wisdom has to be acquired through experience, is limited and can be lost. If indeed this is our concept of wisdom, we must apply the *via remotionis*. But it is not clear to me that these imperfections of human wisdom are actually built into our concept of 'wisdom' and are part of its meaning.

I believe that Copleston gets into this difficulty because he unconsciously shares Aquinas's theory of meaning, which links the meaning of words to intellectual concepts, which in turn are abstracted from '*phantasmata*' derived from sensible things. Elsewhere I have suggested that if we accept Frege's and Wittgenstein's criticisms of such 'ideational' theories of meaning (to use William Alston's description), then we can simplify matters. If perfection terms do not necessarily imply any limit, then we do not need to follow Aquinas in distinguishing between the 'mode of signification' of words, which we learn from creatures, and the 'thing signified', and then claiming that our intellect is able to soar above the former and to ascribe the latter to God (*S.T.* 1a. xiii.3,6; *De Pot.* VII.2 ad 7). We can regard the *via remotionis* and the *via eminentiae* as already implicit in our use of perfection terms, and not as an extraneous procedure introduced in order to cope with the problem of God's attributes (see further Sherry (4)).

The really tricky problem with regard to God's perfections is deciding which ones are appropriate to Him and what are the grounds for ascribing them to Him. If God is aware of truths, then it is legitimate to ascribe the perfection 'knowledge' to Him. But why should we suppose that He has knowledge? How does He exercise it? Similarly with 'love': how do we discern the actions which exemplify God's love (and other perfections)? As we shall see shortly, the biggest limitation of using analogical predication in theology is that it usually presupposes a special ontology and epistemology. And it is just here that Kant's objections are so formidable.

Presence

The presence of a physical object consists in its occupying a certain spatial location; hence, as Plato pointed out (*Tim.* 52 B), we tend to think that everything which exists must exist in some place. But what about the presence of disease, love, authority and God, to pick a few examples? Well, one might argue that most of these things exist only when objects and persons are present too, so that they are ontologically dependent on the latter: diseases are present only when men are ill (cf. Aristotle, *Met.* Λ 1070 a 22 on the existence of health), while authority is a relationship between men. Love is more difficult, since it is both a state and a relationship, but it too is present only when men are present. But the presence of God is the most difficult case of all: what would it be for God to be absent? Perhaps the easiest way to approach this problem will be by considering at greater length its correlative notion, that of existence.

Being

We saw in Chapter 2 that D. Z. Phillips contrasted the existence or reality of God with that of physical objects, and indeed with that of pictures in one's mind, chances of getting a job and so forth. He criticised Flew and Hepburn for forgetting that the meaning of terms like 'fact', 'exist' and 'reality' depends on their contexts. We found that although there is some truth in this position, it is nevertheless necessary to relate things to each other as well as to distinguish them. More specifically, unless we want to claim that 'real' and 'exists' are completely equivocal, we need to explain how the different uses of the term are connected. Again, this is merely a particular case of the general need to relate religious language-games to others.

Aristotle often noted that the word 'be' is used in many ways: a threshold's or a lintel's existence consists in being situated in a certain way; a faggot's in being bound together; a cocktail's in being mixed; to be ice is to be solidified and to be breakfast or dinner is to be eaten at a certain time (*Met.* H. 1042b15–1043a7). For living things, to be is to be alive (*De An.* 415b13).[8] These are not species of one genus, for being is not a genus (*Met.* B. 998b22–7). On the other hand, there is a relation between the different senses, and Aristotle interprets this in terms of his doctrine of categories: to be is to be a substance of a certain kind, a quality, a relation, a place and so on, but all the other categories depend on substance, for the latter is primary in definition, knowledge and time (*Met.* Z. 1028a33). This primacy is supported by several arguments, for example that one cannot have relations, qualities etc. without substances, and that a substance can change its place, colour, weight, etc. without ceasing to be the same substance (*Met.* Z. 1028a34 f., *Cat.* 4a10–b4).[9]

Aristotle furthermore believed that there are three kinds of substance: sensible and eternal ones, e.g. heavenly bodies; sensible and perishable ones, and the Prime Mover. The first two are partially dependent on the Prime Mover, because he moves the outer sphere of the heavens unceasingly in a circular motion, acting as a final cause in that he is an object of love (*Met.* Λ. 6—7). Thus we have two forms of dependence to consider here:

(1) The dependence (both ontological and otherwise) of the other categories on substance:

(2) The dependence of other substances on the Prime Mover.

These doctrines became the foundation of what came to be called the *analogia entis*, though Aristotle himself never used the word αναλογία (analogy) in this connection (Lyttkens, pp. 52—3).[10]

Aquinas followed Aristotle in regarding substances as being the primary realities on which the other categories depend (IV *Met.* i) and in arguing that 'being' is predicated primarily of substance (*Princ. Nat.* 6), but he diverged considerably from Aristotle in discussing the second aspect of the 'analogy of being', the dependence of different substances on each other or on an outside cause. For him God is not merely a Prime Mover but also a creator on whom all things depend for their continued existence at every moment. Moreover, God is *ipsum esse subsistens* or pure being, in which all other beings participate according to their degree of being. All creatures can be ranged in a hierarchy according to the extent of their realisation of being and other perfections. Their dependence on God can be expressed in two main analogies: an analogy of participation linking creatures to the pure being in which they participate, and a causal analogy linking creatures to the source of their being (Montagnes pp. 34—8, 104—14. Their dependence on God does not prevent creatures having their own specific kinds of existence and goodness: cf. *S.T.* 1a.vi.4; xliv.1 ad1).

This is no more than a thumb-nail sketch of the analogy of being, and it is difficult for a non-thomist to know what to make of some aspects of it. Clearly it depends on certain metaphysical views on the nature of being which are not generally accepted by philosophers today, especially those concerning 'degrees of being'. Moreover, these views are unacceptable to many theologians: Barth objects to the metaphysical aspects of the *analogia entis* rather than to its linguistic presuppositions about univocal and equivocal terms, since he too accepts that we must use analogy when speaking of God (see especially *C.D.* II. i. pp. 224 ff.). But at least it is an attempt to link together the different senses of 'to be' through ontological analysis, i.e. by giving an account of the different things which exist and the way in which they are related.[11] Moreover, the first part, i.e. the arguments for the primacy of substance among the categories, is in close harmony with much recent work: I have already mentioned Strawson, but there is also Professor Anscombe's impressive presentation of the Aristotelian doctrine of substance in *Three Philosophers*.

Now if one rejects Aristotle's or Aquinas's views one can either elaborate an alternative metaphysical account, e.g. Quine's view that the choice of an ontology depends on one's interests and purposes (see Quine (1) p. 19), or else one can just remark that 'exist' or 'be' have many senses and leave it at that. Wittgenstein and his followers seem to take the latter alternative: he remarks that the existential quantifier is used in countlessly many different 'games' (*P.G.* II, p. 453). He contrasts a railway train, a railway accident and a railway law (*B.B.* p. 64), but does not go on to make the obvious comment that the last two are ontologically dependent on the first. Similarly, he distinguishes the existence of a gramophone record of a tune from that of a tune (*B.B.* p. 40; cp. p. 31), but without discussing the connection. The other kind of case which he discusses is that of the existence of mathematical entities (see *Moore/Lectures*, pp. 302–4). Malcolm likewise says: 'It is wrong to think that all assertions of existence have the same kind of meaning. There are as many kinds of existential propositions as there are kinds of subjects of discourse' (Malcolm (2) p. 53).

This is all right as far as it goes, but it fails to attempt to explain how the different kinds of existential proposition are related to one another. In particular, it fails to meet the claim of Aristotle and his modern followers that material objects and persons are primary; if we accept this claim, we will have to explain what God's existence consists in and how it is related to that of other beings. We know how thomists do this. But how do Malcolm, Phillips and Winch do it?

Truths, fact
Phillips claims that notions like 'facts' and 'corresponding to

reality' have several different meanings, depending on the context (see Phillips (1) p. 13, (3) p. 63, and my comments in Chapter 2). This is to be related to his views about the nature of religious truth, which I shall discuss in the next chapter, along with some other writers who argue that religion has its own special kind of truth. But it is worth noting that since the concepts of 'fact' and 'reality' are closely related to 'states of affairs' or 'what is the case', this topic will follow on naturally from the last one which I have discussed, i.e. the different senses of 'being'. It is also worth noting, more generally, that the task of 'relating' throws light on that of 'validating': for if we have shown that areas of discourse overlap, then it follows that there must be some connection between their criteria of evidence, rationality and truth. Thus the grounds for ascribing terms like 'love', 'father', 'exist' and 'active' to God must bear *some* relationship to the grounds used for our normal everyday applications of these terms. Similarly, even if 'God created the world' expresses a unique relationship, its truth conditions must bear some resemblance to those of our ordinary uses of terms like 'make' or 'depend on'.

THE LIMITATIONS OF ANALOGY

This point brings us back again to Flew's claim that theological statements using terms like 'love' die a 'death of a thousand qualifications' because the believer is unwilling to allow that anything will count against statements like 'God loves us as a father loves his children' (Flew & MacIntyre, p. 97). More generally, John Stuart Mill argued that there is no point in using the same terms of God unless they are similar in some respects: in an attack on Mansel he remarked that we have no business employing the words 'Just, Merciful, Benevolent' of God unless we intend to predicate them in the same sense as we do of our fellow-creatures, only in a greater degree (Mill, p. 122).

I think that we can only answer such objections by showing that God does have certain qualities and relationships which are appropriately described in traditional analogical language, and that we are in a position to know this. But this is to take us away from purely linguistic matters into ontology and epistemology. Quite clearly most traditional theologians who have used analogy have been willing to justify it in this way. Aquinas, for example, tied in his use of analogy with a comprehensive natural theology, based on an analysis of God's being and His relationship to His creatures.[12] Barth objects to this, but he still thinks that God is related to his creatures (in His reconciliation and redemption through Christ), and that we can know this through revelation.

Earlier in this chapter I argued that any fruitful use of Analogy of Proportionality in theology presupposes that we have some independent knowledge of God's attributes and activities; we want to avoid trivialities like 'God stands to His things as creatures do to theirs' — and even this triviality presupposes that we have proved His existence. Aquinas, therefore, preferred other forms of analogy in his mature works, and most contemporary Thomists agree that analogies of Proportionality do need to be supplemented by them. But now I must point out that even these other forms of analogy will not stand by themselves, but they too need supplementing since they presuppose that we have knowledge of God's existence and perfections. We know by observation that healthy climates and diets produce good health in men — that is why we call them healthy. But how do we know that God is the first exemplary, effective and final principle of all goodness (Aquinas, *S.T.* 1a.vi.4), the source of wisdom and other perfections (*S.T.* 1a.xiii.6)?

Aquinas has a definite answer to this question, but it is one which creates many difficulties for a non-thomist. Having proved that God exists, he then presents a double argument for His having every perfection,[13] which I briefly mentioned in Chapter 4:

(1) God is the cause of perfections in creatures, therefore He must have all the perfections which He causes, because no effect can have a perfection which its cause does not have (*S.T.* 1a.iv.2).

(2) God is the self-subsistent Being, so He must have every conceivable perfection, 'because not one of the perfections of full existence can be wanting in Him who is essential existence Himself' (*S.T.* 1a.iv.2 ad3).

The first prong of this argument depends on the principle that 'everything brought to perfection pre-exists in the producing cause in a more excellent mode' (*S.T.* 1a.iv.2). This in turn depends on the maxim *'omne agens agit sibi simile'* which was taken for granted by Aquinas and therefore also by most of his modern followers. Montagnes, for example, blandly asserts that 'the resemblance of cause and effect is a general law of causality' (p. 47, my trans.). Not suprisingly, the name 'Hume' is not mentioned in the index of his book, and indeed nearly all the modern philosophers mentioned by him are fellow Thomists. Now it is just this kind of blind refusal to face basic problems that infuriates the non-thomist, making him feel that Thomism is an intellectual strait-jacket designed to constrict the mind and prevent its grappling with real issues. One is just tempted to give some simple counter-examples, like stupid parents producing intelligent children or ugly artists painting beautiful pictures, and to leave it at that.

Such a reply, however, would be over-hasty, though it is no more than dogmatism deserves. In the first place, it does seem to be an essential part of the religious attitude to assume that God has more eminently whatever perfections are found in the world: meeting a person of great holiness or seeing a landscape of great beauty are often profoundly moving experiences, making us feel that they are not the result of mere blind chance; moreover, most creation stories (e.g. Plato, *Tim.* 29 E) depict the creator as making the world in his own image. Secondly, St Thomas does not say baldly that every event must resemble its cause: he qualifies the formula *'omne agens agit sibi simile'* in various ways, since he realises that God can, for example, create a stone without being himself a stone (*C.G.* I. 31; cf. Montagnes, pp. 47 ff.). Moreover, there is a strongly Platonic strain in his work which leads him to speak of 'imitation', 'resemblance' and 'participation': it is God's 'exemplar causality', and not merely his efficient causality, which guarantees that there is an intrinsic likeness between Him and His creatures (see Klubertanz, pp. 54 f., Montagnes, pp. 44—53); and, as I have already pointed out, for Aquinas God *is* goodness, wisdom, etc. so that creatures who possess these perfections to any degree do so by participation.

I have not space here to defend St Thomas' views on causality and participation, still less his views on the nature of being which underpin the second part of his argument in *S.T.* 1a.iv.2, namely that which deduces God's perfections from His self-subsistent being. And, in any case, this is not necessary, since the point which I am trying to make is merely that Aquinas's use of analogy rests on his metaphysical views. We may reject the latter, but if we do this we will need to provide some alternative support, as indeed Barth does; for we must have *some* reason for applying the terms which we do to God.

If we reject both Aquinas's and Barth's views and yet do not wish to remain silent about God and His attributes, we still have some latitude. One possibility might be to base our language about God on an account of religious practice and experience such as I touched on briefly in the last chapter: we might maintain that religious 'forms of life' include prayer and meditation. The religious person feels that these practices provide a new understanding of life and a road to holiness, and that their benefits are gifts of God; hence they speak here of 'grace', and of God's 'love', 'wisdom' and other attributes. They may also speak of God's 'activity' in their souls, of His 'working' through men's hearts, and so on. The advantage of this way of speaking is that it attempts to *identify* examples of God's activity, and thereby to give concrete content to lists of divine attributes: there is no point in describing God as merciful, loving, etc. unless we can envisage what it is for Him to *act* with mercy, love or forgiveness (see Alston, p. 429). The difficulties of this approach I discussed in the last chapter: clearly the sceptic is going to demand why we regard the things mentioned as God's loving actions. An account of God's attributes based on religious experience and ways of life still encounters ontological and epistemological problems.

I shall not elaborate on these tentative suggestions any further, since my purpose in this chapter has not been to provide a foundation for our language about God, but to say something about the question of how such language is to be related to non-religious language: I have concerned myself with the theory of analogy because it seems to offer an important contribution to this question (which is not to say that there may not be other ways of relating religious and non-religious language-games[14]), rather than because I accept its traditional metaphysical basis. But it is worth pointing out that the terms which I have imagined the prayerful man attributing to God are exactly the same as those used by Aquinas in his philosophical discussions of analogy. One would like to think that his extraordinary metaphysical contortions were an attempt to express his own deepest religious feelings: when discussing Barth's rejection of the *analogia entis* Henri Bouillard wisely remarks that the Thomistic method of negation and eminence would merely be a fantastic projection, were we not already moved by the presence of God within us (Bouillard, p. 111). Sometimes indeed Aquinas does seem very dry and remote, and in general theological language often seems far removed from living religion. But much of what he says is in harmony with men's religious feelings: they do regard God as the creator of the world, and envisage Him as both intimately involved in their lives and yet transcendent; and, as I have suggested, they do think that earthly beauty and perfections are signs or expressions of His nature. It seems, therefore that the metaphysical strand of religious language is attempting to do some justice to the spiritual aspects of religion.

8 Validating: Does Religion have a Special Kind of Truth?

AUTONOMY AND TRUTH

In this chapter I shall consider the claim that religion has its own special kind of truth.[1] As it stands, this claim is ambiguous: it may mean that in the Bible and in other religious contexts the words 'true' and 'truth' have a special meaning, in which case we would have to show how this is related to their meanings in other contexts — a particular case of the general problem of 'relating' which we considered in the last chapter; or it may mean that a special kind of understanding and verification is required in religion. Both these claims, and some others like them, have actually been made, so that it will be necessary to disentangle a number of different issues. I shall do this by considering several different versions of the view that religious truth is a special kind of truth. I shall conclude that in so far as this view has any validity, it amounts to one or more of the following three theses, all of which I hold:

(1) Sometimes 'truth' is used in an ontological sense, i.e. synonymously with 'actual state of affairs'. Now it is indeed true that religious doctrines often describe unique states of affairs, like the existence and transcendence of God.

(2) Since these states of affairs are unique, their verification (in so far as they can be verified) may be very peculiar. It often seems very difficult to understand religious doctrines and to see how people can claim to know that they are true. We seem to be dealing with peculiar kinds of evidence.

(3) Even when we can see the relevant evidence, it often seems difficult to understand how the doctrines correspond to

the facts in question. For instance, it is hard to see the relationship between traditional Christological language and the facts recorded in the Gospel about Christ's life, teaching and death. The reason for this is that theological language has, to use Wittgenstein's terminology, a special 'grammar' and 'method of representation': it employs unusual concepts and adopts symbolic and mythological modes of description.

Some of the writers applying Wittgenstein's philosophy to religious problems whom we considered in Chapter 2 seem to hold that religion has its own special kind of truth, though it is difficult to see exactly which version of this thesis they hold. D. Z. Phillips, for example, says towards the beginning of his *The Concept of Prayer* that although mistakes and confusions can occur in religious discourse, these can only be recognised by criteria to be found *within* religion (p. 8). This might be taken to mean that only religious people can understand religion and so recognise mistakes, but the context and the use of the word 'criteria' suggest that something more is meant: and indeed a few pages later Phillips makes the (to me) incredible assertion that 'To say that the criteria of truth and falsity in religion are to be found within religious traditions is to say nothing of the truth or falsity of the religion in question' (p. 27). I discussed this in Chapter 2, and also the account of religious truth found in Phillips' more recent work which owes much to Wittgenstein's *Lectures*. We found that Phillips' views on religious truth are part and parcel of what I called the 'autonomist' and 'no justification' positions, i.e. the view that the forms of life and language-games of religion cannot and need not be justified. These positions are to be related to Peter Winch's claim that different fields have their own 'criteria of logic' and standards of intelligibility and rationality. I pointed out the very serious difficulty raised by conflicts between different religions: if two religions put forward contradictory claims on the same matter and if there is no way, in principle, of resolving the conflict, then the sceptic is going to argue that we have forfeited all right to speak of religious 'knowledge' or 'truth'. Furthermore, the remark of Phillips which I quoted, taken at its face value, seems to imply that one and the same statement could be 'true' within one particular language-game or religion, and 'false' within another.[2] But does such an idea make sense?

Many other writers (both theologians and philosophers) have

argued that religion has its own special sense of 'truth', so let us proceed by considering some examples, taking the theologians first.

THE HEBREW SENSE OF TRUTH

Several recent writers have argued that the Bible means 'faithful' or 'reliable' when it speaks of 'true'. E. E. Schneider, for example, begins a recent article with the promising title 'Truth as the Central Concept of Theology' by saying that although truth must be the prime goal of the theologian, this must not be understood in the legal sense, 'for legal thinking is not related to the truth of the Gospel' (p. 258, my trans.), nor in the scientific sense. He goes on to identify 'truth' with God's reliability and fidelity, made known to us through Jesus Christ. He makes the all too familiar contrast between Hebrew thought and Greek philosophy: 'The "Amen" [as used frequently by Christ in the phrase "Amen, I say unto you"] naturally reminds us of *'emet*, i.e. loyalty and faithfulness, but not at all of the theory of knowledge of the Greek philosophers' (p. 260, my trans.).

Not surprisingly, Schneider makes no reference to James Barr's book *The Semantics of Biblical Language*, where views similar to his are subjected to some criticism. Barr mentions Torrance's view that the etymological root of the *'-m-n* group of words in Hebrew is 'steadfastness', so that *'emet* is not 'abstract or metaphysical truth, but what is grounded upon God's faithfulness, i.e. truth not as something static but as active, efficacious reality, the reality of God in covenant — relationship' (quoted in Barr (1) p. 187). Barr counters with the following arguments:

(1) It is 'excessive etymologising' to offer 'firmness' as the basic meaning of *'emet*. Current usage is a better guide to the meaning of words than ultimate etymology is, and it seems that 'truth' became the standard meaning fairly early on. Hence the word is usually translated as ἀλήθεια in the Septuagint. Likewise, it is misleading to offer 'becoming disclosed' as the standard meaning of ἀλήθεια. This is indeed the etymological root meaning, but it will not do as a translation in phrases like ῥήματα ἀληθείας (words of truth) in Acts 26.25 or εἰπεῖν τὴν ἀληθείην (speak the truth) in Herodotus 6.69, since here

ἀλήθεια is obviously meant to be 'truth' in the sense of the opposite of 'lies' or 'falsehood'.

(2) We must not take religious or philosophical uses as typical. *'emet* is ascribed to God in the Old Testament, but this does not mean that this usage determines its meaning in other contexts: quite often it is used in the everyday sense of 'truth', e.g. in I Kings 10.6. Likewise, although Plato and St John use ἀληθής and ἀλήθεια in some highly pregnant and allusive senses, they also use them in their everyday meanings of 'true' and 'truth', e.g. in Plato, *Apology* 17a, John 5.31, 8.13–14, 16.7.

(3) It is just as wrong to take phrases like 'true friend' or 'true men' in the Bible and to use them to read a 'Personalist' view of truth into Jewish thought as it would be to do the same in English. Even today we speak of lovers remaining true to one another, but we do not on that account argue that 'true' always means 'faithful' or 'genuine' in English.

As regards usages like 'I am the way, the truth and the life', Barr claims that it is not our so-called modern 'Intellectualist' view of truth that makes them so difficult, but the fact that 'I' is a person and 'truth' an abstraction. Such a sentence is not found in the Old Testament and would be just as unusual in Greek or Hebrew as in English (Barr (1) pp. 197f; see pp. 187–205 generally).

In a recent book O. Loretz takes a similar line to E. Schneider, though he is addressing himself specifically to the question of Biblical truth. He rejects any identification of this with 'inerrancy' and instead argues that 'for the Old Testament the "truth" of God is primarily bound up with his faithfulness. Yahweh is the covenant God who not only demands faithfulness from his people but promises to be faithful himself as well' (p. 83). He cites Barr's name in footnotes on pp. 82 and 84, in his list of authorities to back up his conclusions, apparently failing to realise that Barr is attacking precisely the points which he is making!

The general conclusion of Loretz's book is that the truth of the Bible is the same as the truth of God, that is, His faithfulness. The Bible records the covenant which God made and the way He kept His promises; hence 'Scripture is true to the extent it speaks of a God of truth. . . . Since the truth of God is manifested in his faithfulness to his covenant people,

Scripture could only be charged with error if God broke His faith with Israel' (pp. 87, 89). Now this is sheer confusion. Even if Loretz were right in supposing that God's truth is the same as His faithfulness, it would not follow that the Bible's truth must be understood in his supposed 'Semitic sense' of truth. For in one case we have God's actions in history, and in the other (at least as regards the historical books of the Bible) we have written accounts of the former. Now surely a written account is true in so far as it describes correctly whatever it is claiming to describe? So if, *per impossibile*, God betrayed His people and the Bible accurately recorded His betrayal, the Biblical account would be true even though God had proved himself untrue, i.e. unfaithful.[3]

I agree with Loretz's earlier claims (pp. 71 ff.) that the Bible is not literally inerrant, since it does contain errors of detail, legends, anachronisms and human interpretations. But I doubt whether we need go through all his elaborate contortions in order to rescue some element of truth. In particular, I think that we might start by considering the different genres which the Bible contains. This might enable us to see what kind of truth we should claim: for instance, the truth of 'Proverbs' is not going to be that of 'corresponding to historical fact'. Loretz merely remarks that appealing to genres will not enable us to explain away historical errors (p. 78). But who says that we want to explain them away?

A third writer, W. Cantwell Smith, takes a somewhat different line from Schneider and Loretz, since he is concerned with other religions besides Christianity. But, like them, he rejects traditional definitions of 'true' such as 'corresponding with the facts'. He claims that the rationalist and intellectualising emphases of the Enlightenment have made us lay too much stress on doctrine and theology, equating religion with abstract systems of belief rather than with ways of life ((2) p. 76). Instead, Cantwell Smith suggests that the concept of 'religion' be replaced by the two concepts of personal faith and the 'cumulative tradition' ((1) pp. 141, 175; by the latter he means the observable religious systems transmitted from one generation to the next). The former cannot be true in a propositional sense, but only in the sense of being 'genuine': living a 'true' religious life means living a truly human life, a life truly responsive to man and to one's total situation ((2) p. 80).

Similarly, with the latter concept: since religious traditions are ways of life or 'contexts' into which we are born, these cannot be true or false ((1) p. 332); rather, '... religious *truth* is a function of a personal life lived in that context, not of the context itself' ((2) p. 81). From all this it follows that a Christian's religion, if lived insincerely, can be more false than a Muslim's, for 'Christianity ... is not true absolutely, impersonally, statically; rather it can *become* true, if and as you or I appropriate it to ourselves and interiorise it' ((2) p. 68). The question is not so much 'Is Christianity true?' but 'Is *my* Christianity true?' Since truth is equated here with 'genuineness', Cantwell Smith's view entails that the religion of a particular Christian may be more false than that of a particular Muslim ((2) p. 72); and indeed (and even more paradoxically) that my religion can be truer on one day than on another ((2) p. 71).

I think that Cantwell Smith is quite correct in insisting that 'true religion' is not just a matter of a corpus of true theological propositions. St John, after all, says that the man who *does* the truth comes out into the light (3.21), while others have insisted that the truth of Christianity is saving truth, i.e. it is truth which has the power to change men's lives. But all the same, nearly all religions have creeds and doctrines which claim to describe truly how things are, and these play an important role in defining both the individual's faith and the collective tradition. Christianity formulated its creeds centuries before the Enlightenment which Cantwell Smith castigates (he acknowledges this fact, but brushes it aside by attributing it to the influence of 'intellectualist' Greek thought, which, he says, tends to reify, i.e. to conceptualise with nouns: cf. (1) pp. 68, 163). Even Buddhism, the most undogmatic of religions, has the four Noble Truths: all life involves suffering, the adoption of the discipline recommended in the Noble Eightfold Path will lead to its cessation, etc.

Very often different religions are claiming to give answers to different questions, so that their creeds do not necessarily conflict with each other. But occasionally their beliefs do contradict one another, e.g. with regard to reincarnation or the status of Christ. Moreover, the grounds for these differences are often complex: it is no simple 'picture preference' which leads a Muslim, for example, to believe that Muhammad is really the

Paraclete promised by Jesus, or that God did not permit Jesus to suffer and to atone for our sins but rescued him from crucifixion. Thus we cannot acquiesce in the easy view that all religions ultimately express the same truth. I do not see how Cantwell Smith or Phillips or anyone else can get round such cases plausibly.

Of course, one may be attracted to a particular religion for reasons other than the seeming truth of its beliefs — for the beauty of its rituals, for example, or the nobility of its ethical code, or its 'psychic hygiene' (to use a phrase of Jung's[4]), or because one has been impressed by the holiness of its adherents, or (if one is cynical) because it is socially useful. But to adopt a religion *solely* for these reasons would be to abdicate from the question under consideration.

I have discussed the writings of the three authors mentioned above because they have appeared recently and because their views are typical of much contemporary work. All of them seek to evade the traditional view that truths are descriptions of actual states of affairs, and instead opt for versions of Personalism, Pragmatism or Existentialism, seeking to identify truth with 'authentic existence', 'faithfulness' and so on. Now I am not denying the importance of inwardly appropriating the truth and embodying it in one's personal life. But we will still have to give some account of the truth of the propositions involved in religious belief. If we divorce religious truth from ordinary propositional truth, it will be hard to explain why we should continue to use the term 'truth' in religious contexts.

One might, however, claim that the word 'true' already has several different meanings, even when predicated of propositions, so that there is nothing outrageous in claiming a special sense of the word in religious contexts. If 'true' is systematically ambiguous and each discipline has its own kind of truth, then theology is on a par with all the others and need feel no special embarrassment. Such a claim has been made by philosophers, so we shall turn next to an examination of this view.

IS 'TRUE' SYSTEMATICALLY AMBIGUOUS?

F. Waismann wrote that 'the idea of truth varies with the kind of statement . . . it has a systematic ambiguity. . . . Statements may be *true* in different senses, *verifiable* in different senses, *meaningful* in different senses'. (Waismann (2) pp. 113, 116). He instanced geometrical theorems, laws of nature, proverbs, statements about one's own motives, exact quotations, summaries of speeches and a few other kinds of statement, and argued that these all have their own kind of truth. For instance, a geometrical theorem is true if it can be deduced from the axioms of our system, so that the Coherence Theory of truth seems plausible in such cases. A law of nature is true if it is well established by experimental evidence, if it increases our understanding by making new connections, if it simplifies our theoretical system, and if it is fruitful in leading us to predictions and new discoveries. The truth of proverbs and poetry is inseparably tied up with the literary quality of the writing which expresses them.

These conclusions have been applied to theology by A. A. Glenn, who regards them as supporting his own Barthian view that theology is an autonomous discipline with its own form of verification. He cites Waismann and draws this conclusion: 'Therefore, when Karl Barth writes that theology has its own proper verification corresponding to its own particular objectivity, he is reflecting epistemological conclusions of contemporary analytical philosophers' (Glenn, pp. 102 f.).

I myself do not think that 'true', when predicated of propositions, is systematically ambiguous; and I do not think that the facts which Waismann mentions support this conclusion, for the simple reason that he has confused 'truth' with 'verification'. It is indeed true that we verify proverbs in a different way from physical laws (surely Waismann means 'statements about physical laws'?), that mathematical procedures differ from scientific observation and experiment, and that kinds of proof and certainty[5] differ from field to field. But none of this proves that 'true' is systematically ambiguous, or indeed that 'verifiable' is so. Waismann has assumed that if the method of verification and the reasons for ascribing truth to propositions vary from case to case, then 'verifiable' and 'true' must be used in different senses. But this assumption, if carried to its logical conclusion, would mean that terms like 'accurate', 'probable', 'unlikely', and 'plausible' were systematically ambiguous too, since they are used of many different kinds of propositions which are established in different ways.

A second point against Waismann's conclusion is that, if it were correct, we would expect to find that no analysis of 'true' would fit all its uses when predicated of propositions. But in fact some analyses will fit the different cases which Waismann mentions. He says: 'a law of nature is never true in the same sense in which, say, "there is a fire burning in this room" is, nor in the sense in which "He is an amusing fellow" may be; and the two latter statements are not true in the same sense in which "I've got a headache" is' (p. 113). Now Tarski's semantic analysis 'X is true if, and only if p' (where X is the name of the sentence expressing p) fits all the four cases which Waismann mentions, e.g. 'I've got a headache' is true if and only if I've got a headache; 'He is an amusing fellow' is true if and only if he is an amusing fellow.

A similar analysis could be provided in terms of the 'Redundancy' or 'No truth' theory which reduces 'p is true' to an assertion of p (but perhaps Waismann would regard this as cheating) and also in terms of various versions of the Correspondence Theory, such as Austin's which I will discuss shortly. I do not think that Waismann's literary examples provide any special problem for the latter:[6] literature conveys general truths about human life and experience and uses a variety of genres to do so; it often expresses them very subtly so that great maturity, intelligence and sensitivity are required to appreciate them; moreover, it is often impossible to convey the complex psychological and sociological phenomena concerned in a more direct fashion. But none of this entails that 'true' is used in a special sense when predicated of literature. The fact that the situations described in it are fictional is neither here nor there, since a fictional example may convey a general truth about the world.[7]

Waismann seems to be on his strongest ground when dealing with mathematical examples: it does seem to be the case that we establish mathematical truths in a way vastly different from that in which we establish other truths, and that coherence is one of the criteria which we use. But here again, as Mellor points out, this does not prove that 'true' is used in a different sense, but only that the grounds for ascribing truth to a mathematical proposition are not observational and experimental evidence but its being deducible from certain axioms. Even here the analysis ' "p" is true if and only if p' still holds: for instance, 'There is no greatest cardinal number' is true if and only if it is a fact that there is no greatest cardinal number (Alan White, pp. 116–17). What is disputable here is the nature of the 'facts' in question: do mathematical objects exist independently of us, or are they mental constructions? Is the mathematician a discoverer or an inventor?

A further point to be noted now is one already made, that if we claim a special sense of 'true' here, to be consistent we shall have to claim a special sense of 'false', 'probable' and so forth. Moreover, all these special senses will need to be related to each other: as I said in the last chapter, it is insufficient to merely point out that a word is systematically ambiguous; we also need to interrelate the different senses, perhaps by using the theory of analogy. Waismann's claim, if valid, would need supplementing in some such way.

THE TWO SENSES OF TRUTH

Although I reject the view that 'true' has several different senses when applied to propositions, I think it is worthwhile pointing out that 'truth' does have two senses:

(1) Actual states of affairs, reality.
(2) True beliefs, judgements, propositions, etc.

The second usage is the most common, and requires no comment. But the first is philosophically important, because of its ancestry and because it takes us into the sphere of ontology. Plato and many other philosophers have often used 'truth' synonymously with 'what really exists', and something of this usage occurs in ordinary speech. We sometimes say 'truth' instead of 'what actually happened' or 'what actually is the case', as for example in statements like 'The truth is difficult to discover' or 'I would like to find out the truth about President Kennedy's assassination'. I do not think that 'truth' here means the same as 'true statement', since I may not actually want to hear or read something; it seems to mean rather 'real state of affairs' or 'actual sequence of events'.

The two meanings of 'truth' which I have just noted in ordinary language correspond to the two main meanings recorded by Liddell and Scott, who note that the first meaning, i.e. reality, is the opposite of appearance, while the second, i.e. true statement, is the opposite of lie. Heidegger (2) has noted that both concepts occur in Plato, but I think it is important to see that Greek 'ordinary language' contains them both, too. Tillich likewise has drawn attention to Plato's usage and has argued that truth is the essence of things as well as the cognitive act in which their essence is grasped, i.e. it is a matter of ontology as well as of language and epistemology (Tillich (1) p. 113). Recent English philosophers have tended to concentrate on the second sense because of their interest in language and epistemology. Aquinas would have agreed with them that this sense is primary, since he regarded truth as residing primarily in the intellect (*S.T.* 1a.xvi.1.). But he thought that truth exists secondarily in things, according as they express species in God's intellect and fulfil the purposes to which they have been ordained by Him: natural things are measured by the divine intellect in whom they are created, just as artifacts are designed in the mind of a craftsman (*De Ver.* I.2; *S.T.* 1a.xvi.6). So he too recognised two senses of truth.

Since 'truth' has these two different meanings, it fits into two families of concepts. The first family is an ontological one and includes concepts like 'real', 'actual', 'situation', 'event', 'state of affairs' and 'facts' — though this last raises some difficult problems, since there is some controversy about their status. The second includes epistemological concepts like 'evidence', 'knowledge', 'belief', 'learn' and 'communicate'. Each of these families of concepts raises its own theological problems: religious doctrines speak of special beings, events and situations, and these in turn raise epistemological problems. It seems that common terms like 'person', 'action', 'being' and 'reality' are not used in their ordinary sense in religious language and that they must be understood analogically. This is because God is not a material object or a human being, whose existence consists in being situated on a three-dimensional planet and moving around there. I discussed the analogy of being in the last chapter, so I will merely say here that I think that the mediaevals were right to stress different kinds of being rather than different kinds of truth, and that all the traditional problems about faith, revelation and so on stem from these ontological issues. It is because God is regarded as such an unusual kind of being that problems arise about how we get to know Him, whether we need a special ability or gift to do so, what the role of grace is and so on.

I think that the distinction between these two senses of 'truth' is very important for theology. Most theologians, at least until relatively recently, would have agreed that 'true' is not used in a special sense in theology, so that no special problem arises under this heading. Rather religion deals with special 'realities', so that there are corresponding problems about how we know these. Kierkegaard, for instance, describes God's truth as 'eternal' and 'objective'. But for him there is also the truth of man's subjectivity, of his inward relationship of unity with God in faith: 'An objective uncertainty held fast in an appropriation-process of the most passionate inwardness is the truth, the highest truth attainable for an existing individual' ((2) p. 182). The reason why it is an uncertainty is that God utterly transcends man, so that He cannot be known in the way that ordinary objects are known; moreover, He is a personal being who loves us, so that it would be inappropriate to try to approach Him through objective knowledge which 'rambles comfortably on by way of the long road of approximation without being impelled by the urge of passion' ((2) p. 179). Since we cannot prove God's reality, we can approach Him only through faith, and we are in the truth if our relationship is the authentic one of 'passionate inwardness'. Although Kierkegaard makes much of paradox in this connection, the paradox lies not in God's being but in our relationship to Him through Christ: 'The eternal essential truth is by no means in itself a paradox; but it becomes paradoxical by virtue of its relationship to an existing individual' ((2) p. 183).

I think that Kierkegaard's novelty lies more in his view of religious faith than in his account of truth. He owes much to Kant: the statement 'it is the duty of the human understanding to understand that there are things which it cannot understand, and what those things are' ((3) p. 117) might be taken as a summary of Kant's *Critique of Pure Reason*.[8] If my interpretation is correct, his contribution to the question of religious truth is more with reference to how we reach it rather than to what is actually believed. And indeed many theologians disagree with each other about the relative weight to be assigned to Natural Theology and religious experience, and about the nature and conditions of faith and revelation, without disagreeing about the content of what is believed. One might also adduce Newman's *Grammar of Assent* in evidence: its originality does not lie in its account of what is truth, but in its suggestion that the Illative Sense is the ultimate test of truth and error (p. 352); the book is mainly distinguished for its account of the psychology of belief.

TRUTH AND CORRESPONDENCE

If I am right in thinking that the so-called problem of religious truth is mainly a matter of ontology and epistemology, it will follow that much recent work by analytical philosophers on the question of truth will prove peripheral to our enquiry. There is no need for us to take sides between, say, G. E. Moore and Ramsey or Tarski, or between Austin and Strawson, because their disputes leave all our most serious problems still outstanding. Let us espouse Austin's version of the Correspondence Theory, according to which 'A statement is said to be true when the historic state of affairs to which it is correlated by the demonstrative conventions (the one to which it 'refers') is of a type with which the sentence used in making it is correlated by the descriptive conventions'.[9] Thus 'God sent His only-begotten son into the world' is true if it correctly describes a historic state of affairs. But what problems are opened up here, problems of a sort not discussed by Austin and Strawson! What sort of person is God, how is He related to His son, how did He send the latter into the world, and how do we know about all this? These are serious questions of ontology and epistemology, to which little is contributed by the assertion that our creeds and doctrines are true if they correspond to facts or describe actual states of affairs.

Perhaps we may be inclined to take Strawson's side of the controversy, viewing 'true' as the mark of an assertion or corroboration, or as abbreviatory. According to him, 'It is true that God sent His only-begotten son into the world' would merely assert or confirm the statement 'God sent His only-begotten son into the world'. Similarly 'That's true', functions like 'Yes' or 'ditto'; statements like 'Whatever the Pope says is true' (which are very awkward for those who would reduce 'p is true' to an assertion of p, as also are statements like 'If he testifies, what he says will be true' or 'Every statement is either true of false') are analysed by him as 'things are always as the Pope says they are' (Pitcher (1) p. 79). Again, exactly the same questions will arise as those mentioned in the previous paragraph, roughly: What do you mean? How do you know? If we say that 'The Athanasian Creed is true' means 'I agree with what the Athanasian Creed says' or 'Things are as the Athanasian Creed says they are', we are still faced with almost exactly the same questions as we are if instead we accept an Austinian analysis.

Strawson himself realised that this was so when he concluded one of his papers on the topic by saying that the differences between himself and Austin were not as great as they seemed and that perhaps the theory of truth should 'become, as it has shown so pronounced a historical tendency to become, part of some other theory: that of knowledge; or of mind; or of meaning' (Pitcher (1) p. 84). He suggested that the main difference between Austin and himself was that the former wished to construe 'p is true' as explicitly stating something about the relationship between language and the world; i.e. that the usual semantic conditions had been observed, whereas he himself took such conventions as being implicit in any use of descriptive language.

As it happens, I agree more with Austin than with Strawson on this issue, because I think that the latter has unwittingly embraced a version of the Correspondence Theory.[10] I think that 'p is true' may be analysed as 'things are as "p" says they are', and I regard this as a version of the Correspondence Theory, since we are asserting that 'p' correctly describes some actual state of affairs. I prefer this formulation to ones which speak of 'correspondence with the facts', since this may create difficulties with regard to the status of facts and what is meant by 'correspondence'.

I regard this analysis as applicable to religious contexts just as much as to others. Of course, it seems vacuous and unhelpful to say 'Religious doctrines are true if things are as they say they are'. A similar vacuity is found if we use Tarski's semantic definition and say ' "Allah is mighty" is true if and only if Allah is mighty' or ' "There are three persons in the Trinity" is true if and only if there are three persons in the Trinity'. Such formulae, while quite unexceptionable, seem disappointingly vacuous to the non-philosopher: they do not appear to offer any contribution towards the exciting and challenging question of religious truth. But this appearance of vacuity is, I think, caused by the fact that nearly all philosophical analyses of truth sidestep the ontological and epistemological issues which are the real problem at stake for those who feel troubled by the question of 'religious truth'. That is why I said that the Austin/Strawson controversy is of peripheral importance for the philosophy of religion.

DIFFERENT KINDS OF TRUTHS

We are now, I hope, in a position to clarify the matter by making a few distinctions. In general, I have rejected the view that religion has its own special sense of 'true' or 'truth'. It is true that the Bible does contain some unusual usages: *sometimes* 'faithfulness' is the best translation for *'emet*, e.g. in Isaiah 38.18 and Psalm 30.9 (see Kittel, pp. 233 ff. for other references); and St John does speak of doing what is true (3.21),[11] of Christ being the truth (14.6) and of the truth abiding in us (II John 2). But there are innumerable places in the Bible where 'true' and 'truth' have roughly the same connotations as in ordinary speech.[12] It would seem, therefore, fair to claim that the extraordinary usages are not the normative ones; rather they must be related to the ordinary uses and be regarded as analogical or 'stretched' meanings. For example, Christ's claim that He is the truth may be related to the other remarks in St John's Gospel about truth and knowledge, and to the *logos* doctrine, as I suggested in Chapter 2.

Likewise, I have rejected the view that different religions have different kinds of truth. In comparing the truth of various religions we need to be fairly specific about the kinds of question which they are trying to answer. Some differences between religions are matters of variety in rituals, moral codes, traditions and general styles of life; and differences in creeds are not always cases of direct contradiction: there is, for example, no *prima facie* contradiction between 'Jesus Christ was the Son of God' and 'Following the Noble Eightfold Path will lead to the cessation of suffering' because these statements are not speaking about the same thing. Hence there is no need to take refuge in 'different kinds of truth' or 'being true for me' here; and where there is a straight conflict, such as the one between Christians and Jews about, say, 'Jesus is the one whom God promised to send to redeem Israel', I fail to see how these subterfuges will remove the contradiction.[13]

Rather than talk about different kinds of truth, I would prefer to distinguish the different strata of religious beliefs. Ninian Smart has drawn attention to the fact that schemes of religious doctrine have several different 'logical strands': he argues that propositions about God the creator, mystical experiences or an incarnated god require different kinds of analysis (Smart (1) pp. 14 f.). I think that this difference is twofold: religious creeds describe different kinds of beings, actions and events (a question of ontology), and these descriptions may be expressed in different ways, e.g. through myths, parables or poetry.[14] These two aspects correspond to the two senses of 'truth' which I distinguished, i.e. 'actual state of affairs' and 'true judgement'. Religious 'truths' in the first sense include the existence and activity of transcendent beings, their relations to the world, historical events, facts about human spirituality (e.g. sin, holiness and prayer) and eschatological events. Religious 'truths' in the second sense include descriptions of the first, expressed in various literary genres. Since both categories of truths contain such a variety, it would after all be correct to say that religion has several different kinds of truth*s* (not truth), provided that all the distinctions and qualifications discussed in this chapter are kept in mind. Let me say a little more about this variety.

The Nicene Creed includes statements about God's creative action, the Trinity, Christ's Incarnation, Crucifixion and Resurrection, the Last Judgement and Future Life, and the remission of sins through baptism. When people raise the question of the truth of such statements, they are usually asking how anyone can rightly claim to be acquainted with certain facts, particularly those concerning transcendent beings and eschatology. Hence we get into all the familiar controversies about faith and reason, belief and knowledge, natural theology and revelation, and other such problems of religious epistemology. But before we embark upon such controversies we need to clear the ground by distinguishing the kinds of fact with which we are dealing. Many religious statements are straightforward reports about historical persons, e.g. Moses, Jesus or Muhammad. Such statements are logically no different from ones about Pericles or Napoleon. Of course, statements like 'Jesus fulfilled the prophecies of the Old Testament' are more difficult, but then there are different levels of complexity in ordinary historical judgements too.

Another category which we must consider is statements about what may be called 'moral psychology', e.g. Buddha's 'All suffering is due to attachment and ultimately to ignorance', the Old Testament's 'He that goes forth weeping, bearing the seed for sowing, shall come home with shouts of joy . . .' (Psalm 126.6) and Christ's 'He who finds his life will lose it, and he who loses his life for my sake will find it' (Matthew 10.39). These are in a sense moral principles, but they are also statements about the way things go in human life, and so they can be verified or falsified by experience. But the experience will not be that of a small number of observations or experiments, but that of living among people for several years. I take it that Tillich's notion of experiential verification is meant to apply particularly to such cases, which are not always specifically religious (Tillich (1) pp. 114–17).

An interesting transitional case is St James' remark that God opposes the proud (4.6). This might be classified as a statement about moral psychology, or as a metaphysical one, depending upon how one classifies 'spirituality': it describes a fact about pride which is recognisable to all, but does so in terms of the presence and absence of God. But, in any case, the category of the 'metaphysical' covers a variety of things. Statements like 'God created the world and is the ground of its being', 'God acts in history', 'Men's souls are immortal', 'God sent His only-begotten son into the world' and '*Ātman* and *Brahman* are one' might all be classified as metaphysical, as indeed might more purely philosophical statements about ontology or cosmology. The religious cases usually involve reference to the actions of spiritual, transcendent beings. But the difficulties which such statements raise do not, I think, justify a lapse into speaking of 'different kinds of truth', for this move will solve nothing: either statements of this type are compatible with each other, in which case there is no ·problem of conflict, or else they contradict each other, in which case they cannot all be true. There may, of course, be special kinds of *verification*: in the case of statements about spirituality, for instance, verification would presumably consist in showing that a possibility of spiritual transformation is realisable and that it is appropriately described in terms of a particular model (cf. what I have said in Chapters 5 and 6 about the parallel between scientific theories and systems of religious doctrine). Eschatological statements are presumably, by definition, verifiable only in the future — which is not to say that one may not enquire now about the grounds someone has for making such statements.

Systems of religious belief also contain ethical principles, and religions are generally judged by their success in transforming the moral character of their adherents. Christianity claims to be not only the truth, but the 'saving truth'. But again, I do not think this is a special kind of truth: rather, we are claiming two things for Christianity: (1) it is true; (2) its beliefs will lead men to salvation — 'You shall know the truth, and the truth shall set you free' (John 8.32). It only confuses the issue if one equates truth with 'authentic existence', since it is at least logically possible that a man might become 'true to himself' by holding some beliefs which were in fact false, in the ordinary sense of the word.

The second sense in which there are different kinds of religious truths is that religious ideas may be conveyed in various ways: in myths, parables, poetry and symbolic or analogical statements, as well as in straightforward descriptions.[15] The books of Job and Jonah, for example, use a narrative format to 'project' ideas about suffering, Providence, etc. But, again, I doubt whether anything is to be gained by speaking of special kinds of truth, for instance 'poetic truth': the facts which a poet is trying to convey, e.g. about the nature of love or suffering, are so elusive and intangible, that they can only be conveyed by means of suggestive images. Similarly with music: when listening to some of Beethoven's late piano sonatas and quartets I feel that I am learning something about the nature of suffering and resignation, and about the composer's own mental struggles, but I would be hard put to express this in words. It seems that music can succeed in conveying truths as well as feelings (which anyway covers a wide range of things), not because there is a special 'musical truth', but because such an infinitely delicate and suggestive medium is ideal for conveying very elusive thoughts about the nature of human life.[16]

Now religious truth is nothing if not elusive, so it too may need to be conveyed suggestively and indirectly.

These remarks may be connected with Wittgenstein's point, which we discussed in Chapter 1, about 'picturing', 'projection' and methods of representation. Wittgenstein mentioned the examples of portraits, genre pictures, machine drawings and maps: all of these attempt to picture something and all of them may be described as 'correct', but their correctness will depend on the kind of likeness which is intended (*P.I.* 291, 522). Moreover, there are many cases of correspondence which do not involve *any* relationship of picturing, for the relationship is one of correlation rather than congruity: for example, there is not necessarily any isomorphism between a signal and what it conveys (cf. Danto, p. 262, and Pitcher (1) pp. 9–14). This variety in the relationships of 'picturing' and 'projection' again confirms the inadequacy of simply defining 'truth' in terms of 'correspondence'. There are many different kinds of 'agreement with reality'.

Even in the case of apparently straightforward 'literal' doctrinal statements it is often difficult to see what they describe or depict, and how they do so: hence the difficulty of speaking of a 'correspondence' here, as Newman did, between a dogma and the 'inward idea' and 'impression' of God made on the recipient of a revelation.[17] It is hard to see how one could analyse theological concepts like 'redemption', 'grace' and 'salvation' in terms of Humean 'impressions' and 'ideas'. This is a particular case of the general difficulty of relating many traditional doctrines to our own lives and experience. I have already suggested that we learn the 'grammar' of such terms by studying their historical evolution and by seeing their place in a theological system, which in turn is to be related to a religious way of life, especially with regard to spirituality; and I will return to this topic in the next chapter. But as regards the question of truth, I think that the issue is resolved into the ontological, epistemological and linguistic problems which I mentioned at the beginning of this chapter. The burden of this chapter has been to show that when people are troubled by the issue of religious truth, it is nearly always issues of this kind which are at the back of their minds.

9 Conclusion: Concept Formation and Spirituality

TRUTH AND GENERALITY

If my argument in the last chapter is correct, then I have knocked the final nail in the coffin of some of the views considered in Chapter 2 by showing that there is no special kind of religious truth as such. I have not, of course, disposed of the claim that the language-games of religion are in some sense autonomous, nor have I wished to do so. But I have argued that this claim amounts to asserting that religion uses peculiar concepts and methods of representation to describe special beings or states of affairs, which may in turn call for some special knowledge or understanding. Now there are indeed such concepts in religion — though they constitute a relatively small part of 'religious language'. But when we employ them we must explain how they are formed, what role they play in our life and how they are to be related to other concepts: in other words, to use my own earlier terminology, they must be located and related. The upshot of the last chapter, and indeed of the last six chapters, then, is that philosophers of religion must proceed by carrying out in the case of *particular* concepts and language-games the procedure which I have sketched out in general terms. I do not think that any general account of religious truth can be given beyond the kind which I have provided: we can only look at each case on its merits, to see if a concept has application, a language-game has a point or a judgement is true.

I believe that this position is compatible with many of the conclusions which Wittgenstein reached by a different route.

For the later Wittgenstein there can be no *general* answer to the question of how language relates to the world. It is true that much of the *Tractatus* view remains in the later work, e.g. 'The agreement, the harmony, of thought and reality consists in this: if I say falsely that something is *red*, then, for all that, it isn't *red*. And when I want to explain the word "red" to someone, in the sentence "That is not red", I do it by pointing to something red' (*P.I.* 429). But Wittgenstein does not go on to simply repeat his earlier view that a proposition is a picture of reality (*T* 4.021) for, as we have seen, this would be to forget that there are many different kinds of 'pictures' and also many different ways of using one and the same picture. Wittgenstein expresses the latter point in terms of 'methods of projection': this suggestive phrase naturally invites exploitation by theologians, but Wittgenstein is more concerned with the relationship between, for example, a wish and its fulfilment or an order and its execution (which he takes to be analogous to the relationship between a proposition and a fact — cf. *P.G.* 112) rather than with the problems raised by mythological or symbolic modes of description.

As regards the actual concept of 'truth', the later Wittgenstein seems content to analyse ' "p" is true' as asserting 'p', and 'What he says is true' as equivalent to 'Things are as he says they are' (*P.G.* 79; *P.I.* 136; *R.F.M.* I, Appendix i.6). This is the same analysis as Strawson's, on which I have already commented, expressing some disagreement. But, like Strawson, Wittgenstein thinks that this question is relatively unimportant. He is much more concerned with he issue of what constitutes good grounds for asserting 'p'. This is most clearly brought out in *O.C.* 199–205, where Wittgenstein says that it is unilluminating to say that true statements tally or agree with the facts, for the real question is as to what constitutes this relationship: 'What does this agreement consist in if not in the fact that what is evidence in these language-games speaks for our proposition?' (203). This question leaves us, in turn, with the problem of deciding upon what constitutes appropriate grounds or evidence within a particular language-game. Now there can be no general answer to this question, because it will depend on what concepts are employed. The evidence for saying 'He is in pain', 'He intends to go away tomorrow', or 'He is expecting someone for tea' will differ, because the concepts of pain, intention and expectation each have their own grammar and criteria which we learn when we learn our language. It would be useless to say that these propositions picture states of affairs or agree with reality, because this simply means that they are supported by appropriate evidence, and what is appropriate depends on the language-game and the circumstances (*O.C.* 5, 82, 191, 197–200, 203). Of course, a man may be in doubt as to whether a concept is applicable in a particular case, e.g. if the evidence is unsatisfactory, but this does not mean that he is ignorant of the general conditions for its use (cf. *P.I.* 354–5 for Wittgenstein's distinguishing between general conditions of assertability and particular verifications).

These considerations perhaps explain why there is comparatively little about the question of truth and falsity in Wittgenstein's later work: he regards the question of concepts and their criteria of application as more fundamental. If there are general criteria for the use of terms and if the speaker knows them in virtue of his general mastery of language, then the question of the truth of a particular judgement is largely one of seeing whether the relevant criteria are satisfied on this occasion.[1]

Some commentators find this position unsatisfactory. James Bogen, for example, remarks on Wittgenstein's equation of conditions of truth with conditions for assertion and suggests, quite correctly, that he probably saw the various departments of ordinary language as too disparate to allow for any general account of such conditions; but he regrets the lack of any general theory of truth or evidence in the later Wittgenstein (Bogen, pp. 128–35, 206). Now I think that Bogen is right to fear the compartmentalisation of language-games which seems to follow from certain aspects of Wittgenstein's thought. But he has forgotten that Wittgenstein spends much time discussing the conditions for applying concepts like 'intention', 'expectation', 'pain' and 'hope'. Now in the nature of the case no *general* account of such conditions can be given. As it happens, I myself think that one can give a general account of *truth*: 'p' is true if things are as it says they are. But this is very empty for practical purposes: if the proposition in question was 'The devil tempted me', we would want to know what is the appropriate evidence in general for ascribing things to the devil, and whether it was found in this particular case. Hence I think that Wittgenstein is right in saying that the question of what constitutes grounds or evidence is paramount; and I do not see how there can be a comprehensive theory here.

If we are faced, then, with questions like 'What do religious doctrines picture, how do they do so, what is their method of representation?' or 'What grounds are there for asserting religious statements?' or 'What is the relationship between doctrines and our experience?', both Wittgenstein's analysis and my own account suggest that the truth of theological statements will depend on the concepts they employ and the relevant evidence. Again, to repeat something both obvious and disappointing, there can be no *general* answers here: we can only examine each case individually. Of course, the common use of analogical terms in religious language will prove to be important, in that our ordinary grounds for using the terms should enforce some control over their employment in religious contexts.

This brings us back to the point from which we started in Chapter 1. There we discussed Wittgenstein's own views about religious truth in his *Lectures* and found them wanting. Of course, these lectures preceded the writing of his last and most significant works, and so they may not be as important as some of his followers consider — I have tried to show, for instance, in Chapter 1 how Wittgenstein's views on 'picturing' underwent further development. But (the more's the pity) he never discussed the doctrine of God in his later works, or gave any detailed analysis of theological concepts (though he did throw out a number of interesting, if allusive, comments on religious matters). It would indeed have been interesting if Wittgenstein had discussed the question of what would constitute good grounds for believing in God's existence. Unfortunately, however, he did not do so (his few discussions on religious issues suggest that he thought it was improper to speak of 'evidence' in such cases, and that he would not have applied to religion the kind of approach used in the philosophy of mind). This means that there exists no specifically 'Wittgensteinian' philosophy of religion as such, treating of, for example, the grammar of the concept 'God' and the criteria for its application. His work needs to be supplemented if it is to make any really important contribution in this field — which is not to deny that he does offer great insight on the general philosophical problems which arise (e.g. with regard to inner processes and concept formation) and throws light on many points, as I have tried to show throughout this work, and that his basic categories offer us a starting point and a framework for a philosophy of religion.

My own answer to the question of religious truth is contained partly in the last chapter, where I specifically discuss the concept of truth. But probably Chapters 5 and 6 contribute much more to the question as it is generally conceived. There I tried to show how we proceed by investigating the logic of individual concepts and relating them to our lives and experience. If theology is indeed 'grammar', then it can only proceed through an examination of particular concepts. I have, therefore, provided a framework and a method for the student of comparative religion, and perhaps for the apologist.

RETROSPECT

It remains for me to put a little flesh on the skeleton of this conclusion and to point a few morals. The first thing which stands out is that I have eventually lined up with many of my opponents in stressing the importance of understanding religion (though I have tried to be more specific than they are about the nature of such understanding and the way in which it is reached). Questions of proof or verification are posterior to that of understanding, because we can only judge whether something is true or not after we have understood it (this does not amount to denying the obvious point that understanding a thing often involves seeing what would verify it). Of course, much of religion is very difficult to understand, and I think that this is the consideration which attracts people to the view that religion has its own special kind of truth, rationality or 'criteria of logic'. But I have argued that this fact can be explained otherwise, in terms of the relationship between understanding religious concepts and participating in a religious way of life with its attendant experiences and activities. In this connection D. Z. Phillips rightly stresses the importance of the community in controlling the way in which religious concepts are used and developed, whilst Paul Holmer draws attention to the inner conditions of the religious life.

I think, too, that such writers are right in querying both over-generalised questions about rationality and over-simple

patterns of justification in religion. It seems odd to ask, for
instance, whether it is rational to repent of one's misdeeds —
this is rather like asking if it is rational to love. It is odd, too, to
ask whether belief in transubstantiation is rational or whether it
is good to pray for the dead, but perhaps for a different reason:
these questions arise only within a certain framework. Similarly,
concepts like 'love of God' belong to a certain system of belief
and way of life, and so we run the risk of distorting them if we
discuss them without paying due attention to their context.
More generally, Phillips insists that the kind of 'existence' or
'reality' which is in question depends on the context, and that
this conditions the kind of 'agreement with reality' and descriptions which can be expected. This is not to say that questions of
evidence and proof can be dismissed: but before we ask them
we need to be clear as to *what would count as* evidence or
proof, and this again will depend on the context. In some cases
the questions may not be applicable or sensible, as Wittgenstein
showed that there is no point in asking what proof or evidence I
have that I am in pain. Thus Wittgenstein's philosophy shows up
misguided demands for proof or verification: and so, applied in
religious contexts, it can be used to counter crude scepticism,
facile scientism and bad apologetics. Of course, this still leaves
us with the crucial question of deciding just when questions of
proof and evidence are relevant — are they applicable in the case
of the existence of God or the divinity of Christ? It seems
sensible to ask, for instance, what would have to be the case for
us to be justified in surmising that a man was God.

These areas of agreement are offset, however, by several
fundamental disagreements. In Chapter 2 I discussed the difficulties involved in the 'autonomist' and 'no justification' theses,
e.g. with regard to conflicts between different religions, and my
later discussions on analogy and truth tried to meet these
difficulties to some extent. Great care is needed in handling
Wittgenstein's view, just mentioned, that what constitutes 'good
grounds' depends on the language-game in question. It is true
that within religion there are certain criteria of orthodoxy, just
as within chemistry experimentation is the method of discovery. Hence it is tempting to claim that as it makes no sense
to ask if chemistry is true or if its experiments discover facts
about reality, so it makes no sense to ask similar questions
about religion. But the existence of different and conflicting

religions, with their own sacred books, putative revelations and concepts of God breaks down the parallel. Similarly, it will not do to claim that belief in God is constitutive of the religious language-game, so that one cannot ask 'Does God *really* exist?' any more than a chemist can ask if the material world really exists. Again, there may be different and incompatible conceptions of God. Anyway, it is a fact that within religious language-games people *do* have doubts about God's existence, and wonder about the authority of the Bible or the Church's tradition. Or, to give an example at a different level, a Roman Catholic might accept that Anglican orders are 'invalid' and yet wonder whether it really mattered.

I also queried Phillips's and Holmer's distaste for metaphysics and natural theology. In the case of the former it leads, I think, to Reductionism and to a too-ready tendency to dismiss some religious beliefs and practices as superstition. It is not perhaps surprising that they should have taken the line which they have on these questions: in general, it seems that contemporary philosophers of religion, Wittgensteinian or otherwise, are unhappy in dealing with the cosmological and metaphysical strands in religious language. Their embarrassment is perhaps a more sophisticated form of the ordinary believer's puzzlement about many of the Church's traditional doctrines, e.g. the Nicene and Chalcedonian definitions on the Trinity and on the nature of Christ. But perhaps there are more specific reasons: in the first place, it is tempting to argue that Wittgenstein dissolved the branch of philosophy known as 'ontology' when he showed that we learn the nature of reality through language-games, e.g. when we learn what physical objects, pains and intentions are, and that we learn how to use the term 'God' in a similar way; secondly, there is Malcolm's interesting observation, mentioned in Chapter 3, that Wittgenstein could make sense of a judging and redeeming God, but not a cosmological one (Malcolm (1) p. 71). I shall go on to argue that the main value of Wittgenstein's work for religious belief is indeed with regard to spirituality. But the two factors I have just mentioned explain why so many of his followers side-step the doctrine of Creation and the ontological issues which it raises.

The problem is that God is regarded as transcendent and as governing nature and the cosmos: hence learning what He is cannot be like learning what, say, a pain or an intention is. I sympathise with the difficulties this raises, but I think it must be insisted that writers like Holmer who claim some Christian orthodoxy must eventually come to terms with this very tricky problem, since it is undeniable that the creeds and other traditional teachings of the Church do have a metaphysical strand, and that they relate God's sanctifying power to His creative and redemptive powers through the doctrine of the Trinity. It is perhaps natural that this should be the case: if men think that they can discern, say, the activity of the Holy Spirit, then they may wish to explain it in terms of an ontological model. For some the concept of Providence may act as a bridge: this concept arises in the religious life because one finds the ground prepared, as it were (cf. Romans 8.28 'to them that love God all things work together for good'), and indeed this may be evidence for Providence (what else would be?). But neither Wittgenstein nor his followers offer us much guidance on this point — little, I think is contributed by simply saying that there are different kinds of existence and evidence. Yet the philosophical problems raised are unavoidable, and perhaps more serious in the long run for philosophers of religion than those concerning verification (in any case I have already argued that much of the concern with the latter is really a concern about the meaning of the metaphysical strand in religious language and about how one would go about establishing the truth of metaphysical claims. There is much less worry about the historical claims or judgements of moral psychology involved in religion).

I also disagreed with the claim that philosophy can only describe religious beliefs, and I pointed out the importance of the way in which religious concepts and doctrines evolve in response to continuing discussions and to historical events. This complicates the issue of examining the 'grammar' of religious terms. I do not think that any of the writers in question even attempted to give an account of the processes of reasoning which occur in such discussions, and of the place of concept formation and analogy in them — even though these two topics are more obviously relevant to their own enterprises. Nor do I think that they have appreciated the way in which particular events (e.g. in the life of Christ) may be of great significance for the development of religious concepts, language-games and activities. These deficiencies are, I believe, the consequence of a lack of a sense of history. This lack is perhaps to be found in Wittgenstein himself. He compares language to an ancient city which has been gradually built up over the centuries, with houses, squares and streets in different styles (*P.I.* 18). This is a very apt comparison, both for languages and for systems of religious belief, but Wittgenstein says little about how this evolution has occurred and what the relationship is between the different strata. He also remarks that language-games come into being and pass away (*P.I.* 23), that they change with time and that this change involves a change in concepts and in the meaning of words (*O.C.* 65, 256). But, again, he does not stop to explain why these changes occur. And yet changes in concepts, beliefs, activities and forms of life are rarely an arbitrary matter.

In general, I think that it must be admitted that the applications made so far of Wittgenstein's philosophy to religious issues have been disappointing. This is partly perhaps because the models of 'form of life' and 'language-game' are too simple for a complex and continually developing system of beliefs like Christianity. But the main reason is, I believe, that his philosophy has tended to be used in an attempt to provide over-simple, evasive and question-begging solutions to very fundamental problems like the existence of God or the meaning of religious language, rather than as one contribution among others in a piece-meal approach. Hence in the last few chapters I have endeavoured to sketch out a way in which the work of Wittgenstein and his followers might be continued. If there are indeed religious language-games then we need to 'locate' and to 'relate' them, and to suggest how we might come to establish the truth of judgements made within them. I have used what Wittgenstein says about the variety of pictures to suggest that religious doctrines represent states of affairs, but often ones very different from objects in the world. The doctrine of the Holy Spirit, for example, represents in projection a possibility of spiritual renewal. There may be many such possibilities, and one may evaluate them on various grounds, e.g. moral ones.

PROSPECT: CONCEPT FORMATION AND SPIRITUALITY

My own discussions have, of course, been general in nature, since I have been trying to develop a framework within which further detailed studies might be fitted, rather than to establish any particular conclusions, e.g. by proving a particular religious doctrine. I am not doing apologetics, hence I wish whatever conclusions I have established to be compatible with several different religious and theological standpoints.

It would, however, be fitting to end by indicating the direction in which future work might profitably move. I think that what I have said about concept-formation, spirituality and religious understanding, especially in Chapters 5 and 6, indicates the way in which some of the ideas in this book might best be developed. The question of spirituality is extremely important in many different ways. It is intrinsically important, because it is a question of what we make of ourselves and of our lives, and of how we affect others: one can only help other people pastorally if one has something within oneself to give them. It is important in the present ecclesiastical situation: when I follow current controversies between religious 'progressives' and 'conservatives', I often feel like saying 'a plague on both your houses' because of the lack of real religious depth on both sides. It is also important ecumenically, both with regard to relations between different Christian denominations and, more widely, between different religions: although they may have varying spiritual ideals and use different concepts to describe these, all the major world religions have something to say about spirituality. It offers us, therefore, the possibility of understanding and comparing different religions. Questions about their truth or relative value will only come later. Finally, it has philosophical implications, which I have sought to bring out by linking the topic with the question of conceptual understanding. Many religious concepts are to be located in a way of life in which men seek spiritual transformation. It is in such contexts that people not only learn the 'grammar' of the term 'God' but, more importantly, feel that they experience His reality. Hence I think that an understanding of spirituality is one way of bringing religious concepts down to earth and showing how they 'latch on' to experience.

Towards the beginning of his *Philosophical Investigations* Wittgenstein remarked that 'to imagine a language means to imagine a form of life' (*P.I.* 19). I have observed that I do not think it appropriate to label religion as a 'form of life'; nevertheless, I think that the remark is of great significance for religion if it is connected with the question of spirituality. If a religion is a way of life (rather than a 'form of life') in which men attempt to achieve spiritual self-transformation by prayer, meditation and holy living, then we will come to understand the concepts, language-games, activities, institutions and so forth which constitute religion only by recognising the purpose which they serve.

Wittgenstein himself did not, of course, discuss this particular problem. My point is rather that a consideration of the way in which religious conceptual systems attempt to understand and explain possibilities of spiritual renewal would be the most profitable way of carrying on the task of applying his philosophy to religious issues. He offers us a number of important basic philosophical categories; and his insight into the connection between language-games and forms of life or activities, and between concepts and their surroundings, indicates the correct starting-point, for our initial problem is essentially one of showing what is the *Sitz im Leben* of a particular set of concepts, of understanding how a doctrinal system fits into a religious way of life, and of discerning the external facts which facilitate or influence that way of life.

The advantage of the approach which I have adumbrated is that it roots philosophy of religion in the actual practice of a deeply felt and deeply lived religion. Too many discussions in this field tend to treat questions like that of the existence of God in a vacuum; but, as a matter of fact, religious believers rarely talk about the 'existence' of God (which is not to say, of course, that questions about it are improper), though they may speak of His presence, distance, will, love and so on. The latter concepts are taught largely through the practice of religion, and the learning is often a very slow process: a significant fact which needs to be reckoned with is that many people who have been given a conventional religious education go through a period of luke-warmness, but come to gain a deeper understanding of their inherited beliefs as time goes on, a process which Newman described by contrasting notional and real assent. The change may, of course, be ascribed to incipient senility, but if there is an alteration in the style of life and a real growth in spirituality religious believers will be inclined to describe it as 'gradually finding God'.

Some of the writers whom we have considered were aware of

the importance of the topic, despite its comparative neglect by recent philosophers of religion. I have found Paul Holmer very suggestive in showing the direction in which we should move. H. H. Price explicitly raises the topic, and Diogenes Allen rightly draws attention to the nourishing and healing power of religion. But I think that some of these writers go too fast and make the wrong connections, particularly when they link the issue of spirituality to questions of verification and justification, and therefore ultimately to apologetics.[2] I argued that we need to proceed at a slower pace by first simply making a connection between man's spiritual transformation and the way of life in which he attempts to realise it, and many religious concepts, e.g. 'holiness', 'grace' and 'redemption'. Doctrinal statements containing these concepts are, partly at least, descriptions of possibilities of spiritual transformation and of the external facts which are considered to control such possibilities. They *may* be verifiable to some extent: for instance, in so far as the concept of 'redemption' describes such a possibility, the statement 'Jesus Christ is my redeemer' is partly verifiable — I say only 'partly', because the concept also refers back to Christ's atoning work and forward to the life after death, as well as to the present possibilities of spiritual renewal; and it is in any case part of a complex theological system in which different strands of religious language, e.g. the cosmological and the eschatological, are combined.

This last point shows that I am not claiming that the way of spirituality *exhausts* the meaning of religious concepts: if I were, I would be subject to criticisms similar to those which I have just directed at some followers of Wittgenstein (cf. my criticisms of Paul Holmer in Chapter 6 for his over-simple account of how we learn religious concepts). Possibilities of spiritual renewal are indeed expressed through religious language-games, hence this is one way of learning the 'grammar' of religious concepts. But we cannot leave it at that, for descriptions of spiritual transformation (like those of religious experience) are loaded with ontological implications — what William James called 'over-beliefs'. God is seen as the formal cause of spiritual renewal — we participate in His love and wisdom when we are transformed; and as the efficient cause — He precedes the change and effects it (whereas a formal cause need not precede its effects — unless you are a Platonist).

Moreover, the source of the transformation is not only hypo-statised but is related to the God of nature and cosmos.

The religious believer is perhaps not always greatly troubled by these issues: at times he feels that he is confronted by a power which is slowly changing his life. But I do not think that an appeal to religious experience can wholly evade questions of ontology and truth. That is why I have suggested that one might draw on discussions in recent philosophy of science about theoretical entities and models, in order to link the topic of spirituality with questions of ontology: the parallel shows that systems of belief need only 'touch down' in our experience at certain points. But this kind of theological investigation still forms part of an attempt by a religious believer to relate the concepts and doctrines of his religion to his life and experience. One cannot indeed use Wittgenstein's philosophy to escape from traditional theological problems: but it is important to see that these problems have arisen within a certain way of life, and that the urge to answer them is a religious urge.

My hope is that an understanding of 'lived spirituality' may serve as a stepping-stone to a wider understanding of religion, producing a fresh and clear picture of something which perhaps has been obscured by time. As Wittgenstein says in a somewhat different context, it is 'Not, however, as if to this end we had to hunt out new facts; it is, rather, of the essence of our investigation that we do not seek to learn anything *new* by it. We want to *understand* something that is already in plain view' (*P.I.* 89). Now the things which we are seeking to understand are the ways of life in which men seek spiritual renewal and the systems of belief which accompany them. These are not perhaps 'in plain view' today. But it is Wittgenstein's achievement to have provided our time with a means of beginning to recover some understanding of them.

Notes

Chapter 1

1. See Holmer (5) (6) (12) and (14) for one such application of Wittgenstein's philosophy to religion.

2. This example is suggested by Nédoncelle (1) p. 156, (2) p. 25, who points out, with reference to Newman's *University Sermons*, that the faith/reason antithesis covers: (a) assent in personal matters vs thinking about things and impersonal ideas; (b) unconscious, approximate or intimate knowledge vs explicit analysis in objective and communicable language; (c) grace vs nature; (d) Christian belief vs natural religion.

3. William James anticipated Wittgenstein's thought to some extent when he pointed out (with regard to definitions of religion) that 'the very fact that they are so many and so different from one another is enough to prove that the word "religion" cannot stand for any single principle or essence, but is rather a collective name' (James, p. 46), but the point has wider implications than he realised.

Wittgenstein's remarks form an interesting parallel with the Thomistic theory of analogy. Aquinas argued that many terms which we use in ordinary language are neither univocal nor simply equivocal, and he called these 'analogical'; one of the cases which he cites frequently is Aristotle's example of 'healthy', which can be used of a person, of food or medicine, and of urine or complexions. The first of these uses is the primary one, since only men and animals are intrinsically healthy; the other uses are derivative, since they are used with reference to the primary use, and denote causes or signs of this health in people or animals (see, for example, *S.T.* 1a.xiii.5). The relevance of this to theology is that many of the terms which we use in describing God, e.g. 'being', 'cause' and 'good', are, according to Aquinas, predicated analogically. Their theological uses are related to those in ordinary language, but they are not exactly the same. I shall return to this topic in Chapter 7.

4. Wittgenstein's views are also highly relevant to legal concepts since it is very often the circumstances which help us to determine whether an action is to be clarified in a particular way, e.g. as 'murder',

'fraud' or 'creating a public nuisance'.

5. It is interesting to note that Kierkegaard, though stressing the importance of 'subjectivity' in religion, attacked the view that the contemporary discipleship of Christ is a matter of mere 'inwardness'. He regarded Bishop Mynster's notion of 'hidden inwardness' as a gross confusion – as if holiness consisted in being silent about it – and as a dishonest attempt to evade the fact that the true disciples of Christ are marked by their courage, self-denial and renunciation of worldly things. He stigmatised Nicodemus as being, like Judas, an 'admirer' rather than a 'follower' of Christ, because he came to the Truth by night, so as not to be seen associating with it (Kierkegaard (1) pp. 208- 9, 214–17, 239–40).

6. See Phillips (1) ch. 7 for a development of this aspect of Wittgenstein's thought; and see High (1) pp. 182–3 for the accusation that Barth and Bultmann are in danger of making religious language a private language.

7. See Lewis (2) ch. 10 for one typical expression of this view and cf. more generally N. H. G. Robinson's contribution to Vesey. See also Foster, p. 185, for the comment that contemporary British philosophy concedes that ethical, aesthetic and theological statements are meaningful, but questions whether they can be true.

8. They are called this because they have the character of actions rather than that of descriptions. Thus, to give two other examples, the speaker of the words of the marriage service and of the consecration of Mass believes himself to be performing an action and actually bringing about a new state of affairs. See Evans (1) for a very thorough and interesting application of Austin's work to religious language. He points out that statements like 'God is my creator' are implicitly performative, because they involve the acknowledgement of a particular attitude and relationship towards God (pp. 158, 263).

9. Malcolm (1) p. 71. It could be replied, however, that Kierkegaard was giving a kind of argument (though perhaps not a 'proof') in that he was appealing to his experience, to his 'new life'.

10. See Smart (2) p. 177 for this point, and also Watt. Smart rightly goes on to accuse Wittgenstein of confusing myths with pictures (p. 181): the fact that we use mythological language when describing a future happening does not mean that we do not believe that it will, in some way, take place (see Webb (2) p. 167 for he view that myths take the place of history when a historical question is asked but the materials for a historical question are lacking, e.g. Creation or life after death. He cites *Rep*. ii. 382D, where Plato says that myths, though fictions, should be as like the truth as possible). W. D. Hudson traces Wittgenstein's error to an exclusive concentration on the 'commissive' force of religious beliefs, which led him to ignore the 'constative' force of statements like 'There will be a Judgement Day' (Hudson (2) pp. 43–4).

11. Wittgenstein also used the word 'projection' to describe the relationship between a command and its execution, an expectation and its object, a musical score and playing the piano, and automatic traffic signals and the movement of cars (*Moore/Lectures*, pp. 263–5; Z. 56,290). He came to realise that, because of the variety of 'methods of projection,' one

and the same picture can be intended or taken in many different ways: to convey orders, prohibitions, wishes and encouragement, or to depict historical facts. For instance, a picture of a boxer in a particular stance may be used to tell someone how he should hold himself, or how he should not hold himself, or how a particular man did stand (*P.I.* note on p. 11; cf. *P.R.* 24; *P.I.* 519,548, p. 205 and note on p. 54). Thus a picture does not, as it were, carry its meaning on its face.

12. In Wittgenstein's terminology 'grammar' includes the internal properties and relations of concepts, as well as the rules for their use: '*Essence* is expressed by grammar' (*P.I.* 371); 'Grammar tells us what kind of object anything is (Theology as grammar)' (*P.I.* 373). Thus the examples of grammatical propositions which Wittgenstein actually gives, e.g. 'Every rod has a length' or 'my images are private' (*P.I.* 251), specify what constitute essences. I shall say more about this concept and its relevance to theology in Chapter 6. For the moment it will be sufficient to note its connection with the concept of 'criterion': in both cases we are concerned with rules for the correct application of words. Thus in *P.I.* 572 Wittgenstein says that in order to understand the grammar of states like expecting, hoping and knowing we must ask 'What counts as a criterion for anyone's being in such a state?'

Chapter 2

1. As indeed have several other writers. Hudson (1) p. 69 speaks of 'The theistic language-game', while Hordern, p. 75, says that 'theology has its own language-game'. The latter speaks also of 'personal' and 'convictional' language-games (pp. 152, 180) and of the 'scientist's whole language-game' (p. 78).

2. In 470 he admits that we do *sometimes* think because it has been found to pay.

3. He heads off some possible misunderstandings when he points out that although calculating is part of a technique which is a fact of natural history, of course its rules are not propositions of natural history (*R.F.M.* V. 14–15).

4. Some critics have accused Wittgenstein of not doing justice to pure mathematics. G. Kreisel (p. 144) asks whether the classification of mathematics in terms of applications and intellectual institutions will help us with the traditional problems of the genesis of mathematical concepts or the justification of proofs.

5. It is important to realise that Malcolm is not bringing forward his 'this language-game is played' move as a proof of God's existence, since he thinks that this has already been provided by St Anselm in *Proslogion* II–III. He is merely trying to clear away a possible Humean objection that a logically necessary being is a contradiction in terms. (Presumably though if Malcolm's version of Anselm's argument were valid, this fact alone ought to be sufficient to clear away the objection. Moreover, if, as many philosophers have argued, by 'necessary being' St Anselm meant a being who is eternal, self-sufficient and indestructible, i.e. factually or ontologically necessary, rather than one whose existence is logically necessary, then both the Humean objection and Malcolm's reply become irrelevant.)

6. See Toulmin (1) pp. 99—101, 160—3 for the use of this parallel when discussing the question of whether we can justify our ultimate moral principles.

7. See J. O. Urmson, 'Some Questions concerning Validity', reprinted in Flew (3) pp. 120—33.

8. I think, however, that Toulmin is right to insist that not just any principle can be regarded as a moral principle, and that not just any argument constitutes a 'good reason' in ethics, because morality, by its very nature, has certain limits. Unfortunately, however, he goes beyond such a purely functional analysis and advocates a species of Rule Utilitarianism.

9. See Blank p. 170 for this neat suggestion. His article is very helpful in connecting St John's concept of truth with his ideas on revelation and the *logos* doctrine.

Chapter 3

1. It is, however, very similar to Tillich's view that 'Providence means that there is a creative and saving possibility implied in every situation, which cannot be destroyed by any event' (Tillich (2) p. 106).

2. It is worth noting that the arguments of natural theology are inverted forms of some of these doctrines. Thus, the doctrine of Creation says that God made the world and sustains it, while the cosmological arguments make an inference to a cause, mover or necessary being from the existence of the world; likewise, the doctrine of Providence says that God is actively working in the world for the good of his creatures, while the teleological argument claims to discern such working in the purposeful operations of nature.

3. Some other doctrines, e.g. those of Atonement and Redemption, involve causal notions, as also do the concepts of sacrament and miracle. In describing God as a 'cause' one is not necessarily viewing His relationship to the world on the lines of a mechanism: many personal relationships, e.g. asking or persuading, are causal but not mechanical.

4. A similar feeling is engendered by R. F. Holland's remark that 'God created the world' has religious truth when said by someone who is grateful for his existence and finds it good, and that it is not a question of some unique cosmological event (Holland, p. 163). But why should I be grateful unless God has, in some sense, given me my existence — or rather, *how* can I be grateful unless He has? Of course, it may be replied that contemporary philosophers of religion have a unitary view of what constitutes existence (that of what J. L. Austin called 'medium-sized dry goods') and that they therefore treat God's existence as analogous to that of ordinary objects in the world, losing sight of His eternity. But this reply is certainly not applicable to mediaeval theologians, who sought to evade such crudity by developing the 'analogy of being'. Wittgenstein himself found the concept of Creation difficult: he regarded the idea of Divine Judgement, forgiveness and redemption as intelligible, but had no sympathy with any cosmological conception of a Deity, according to Malcolm (1) p. 71. This may perhaps explain why so many of his followers seem to produce a purely spiritual God, not a God of nature or cosmology.

5. See further Hudson (2) p. 40; Bochenski (1) §§ 4, 14, 27.

6. Hick (1) p. 237 says that the 'autonomist' position derives both from Wittgenstein and from Barth.

7. R. F. Holland, p. 162, brushes aside this difficulty by saying that it is not clear what it means to say that God is a being, and asking what difference a 'special existent' makes to the practices of prayer and worship. One may admit his first point and yet still reply to his question 'A lot!' How will Holland distinguish superstition from true religion?

8. My hope is that philosophical theology will also be reinstated to a greater degree than it has been already.

9. See Foot for the relevant papers and bibliography.

10. See Hart, ch. IX. Hart's work on the philosophy of law is in general very relevant to my points about the necessity of relating different language-games to each other.

11. Again, see Foster p. 185, for the remark that contemporary British philosophers concede that ethical, aesthetic and religious statements are meaningful, but question whether they can be *true*.

12. A similar view is found, not surprisingly, in Phillips and Mounce.

Chapter 4

1. A difficult case is that of thanking God: D. Z. Phillips says that the religious believer responds to the whole of life and gives thanks, whatever occurs ((3) pp. 190, 209). In a sense this is true: even a person in a concentration camp could accept his lot and make the best of it by helping his fellow prisoners, loving his persecutors and perhaps dying heroically. But I wonder whether the term 'thanks' is always appropriate? Should we give thanks for Hitler's life and work?

2. I think that this distinction is facile and misleading in two ways: (a) 'cosmology' includes consideration both of the world as a whole and of purposive systems within it; (b) the Jews recognised that God could speak through a man's heart, e.g. a prophet's, as well as through historical events (see Barr (2) pp. 77—82).

3. This distinction is misleading because it is unclear whether it is supposed to be one of epistemology or of ontology: is 'revelation' a special faculty for getting to know things, or does it rather denote certain states of affairs, e.g. God's interventions in history? Likewise, are 'religious experiences' special states of mind in which we invest ordinary things with a special significance, or are they of extraordinary states of affairs?

4. Vaihinger regarded beliefs in immortality and the existence of God as fictions which have a regulative power in our lives. But if we know they are fictions, will they have this power? Kant never actually regarded them as fictions, even though he did consider them unprovable.

5. One difficult question which arises here is that of what sort of ontology, if any, is presupposed in Wittgenstein's later work. Fergus Kerr argues that in abandoning the picture theory of meaning Wittgenstein came to concentrate on the relationship between words and contexts rather than on that between words and things; hence Kerr concludes that our understanding of language must be orientated on situations rather than on things, since 'referring to objects' is only one of many possible

linguistic uses (see Kerr, pp. 508–12). Now this is true enough, but it will not enable us to evade questions of ontology – one cannot have 'situations' or 'contexts' without objects or people to constitute them.

E. K. Specht gives the most comprehensive treatment of the question, but seems to wobble somewhat as regards his own answer. He begins by noting (p. 25), like Kerr, that whereas the picture theory of language tends to Realism because it construes words as names, the language-game model seems to leave open the question of the nature of reality in itself. But he immediately goes on to say that 'our interpretation amounts to the view that in Wittgenstein we have to do with a linguistic "constitution theory"', in which language is not derived from the world of objects but is somehow involved in the construction of objects' (p. 25). This is to put Wittgenstein in the same camp as writers like Lichtenberg, Humboldt, Cassirer and Whorf, who claim that language determines our world view (cf. pp. 141–3), and thereby to raise questions about concept formation which I shall investigate in Chapter 5.

Specht goes on to claim that Wittgenstein's own ontological position is midway between Nominalism and Realism: he was opposed both to Reductionism and to the hypostatisation of entities. His acceptance of ordinary language (e.g. in *B.B.* p. 28 and *P.I.* p. 124, 654) marks his opposition to Reductionism, e.g. with regard to material objects (cf. *P.I.* 180 for his attack on Phenomenalism); while his realisation that not all referring is the simple naming of objects shows that he did not accept the hypostatisation of Realists (see Specht, pp. 84–7; the context shows that by 'Realism' Specht means the extreme position of those who seek entities corresponding to terms like 'pride' or 'purchasing power'; this explains how he can seek a middle position).

Not surprisingly (in view of the paucity of material dealing directly with the question) Specht finds it difficult to be more specific and he ends rather limply by saying that although Wittgenstein could have worked out a systematic ontology by thoroughly investigating various language-games, he never in fact attempted it since he was mainly concerned with particular problems, and anyway he considered that philosophy's task is merely to describe what we have always known. I think that this limp conclusion probably contains more truth than some of Specht's earlier claims: Wittgenstein was far more interested in the question of the connection between language and the world; and in his later work he came to believe that such connections are made through language-games. Because of the variety of the latter, there can be no *general* answer to the question of how language relates to reality. The 'grammar' of language tells us what kind of 'objects' are involved, e.g. pains, sensations and physical objects (*P.I.* 293, 304, 571, p. 200). I take it that the study of such grammar is regarded as superseding the traditional approach to 'ontology'.

The most serious question which all this raises for us is whether a philosopher of religion can use Wittgenstein's approach to 'dissolve' the ontological problems raised by religious belief. From what I have already said, I think it will be seen that I regard the attempt by his followers to do so as question-begging, since the claim that there exists a personal and transcendent God raises very special problems not covered in Wittgenstein's philosophy. But I will return to this issue in Chapter 5.

Chapter 5

1. It is noticeable that Alasdair MacIntyre provides few examples of obsolete religious concepts and practices to support his claim that religion has become unintelligible because social and cultural changes have rendered its concepts dispensable. He mentions only 'Prime Mover' and the practices of blessing and cursing. But these are poor examples, because the first is merely a case of a particular apologetic argument becoming invalidated, while the two practices mentioned are still current today (see his contribution to Hick (1), pp. 115—133 and the replies by Norris Clarke and R. Brandt; also Brown, Ch. V. § 16). In general I think that MacIntyre exaggerates the element of cultural change involved: these *were* religious sceptics in mediaeval times, just as there are still sincere and well-educated believers today.

2. See Evans-Pritchard for some amusing examples of difficulties in translating hymns for the Azande, who have none of the concepts mentioned above.

3. Cp. Charles Davis' view: 'Since it (revelation) is fundamentally an interpersonal communion, its formulation in concepts and words is not primary. But such a formulation is an essential moment in the appropriation of revelation by the community' (in Moran, p. 11).

4. A more sensible slogan might be 'this concept has application'.

5. It first appeared in a Latin translation of a selection of St Isidore's letters, but did not become common usage until the time of Aquinas and did not appear in ecclesiastical documents until the sixteenth century, according to de Lubac, p. 327. Part III of de Lubac's book gives a fascinating account of the word's evolution.

6. Hence I think it is incorrect to argue that even such facts as influence or limit our linguistic formations are themselves revealed only through language (see Specht, p. 181, and Hacker, pp. 162—4). For surely it is possible to *notice* something for which we have as yet no adequate linguistic expression? There is always the novel and unexpected.

7. Of course, the fact that a language does not contain a particular term does not entail that its speakers lack the concept in question, since they may use circumlocutions to express it. Hence we must be careful about claiming that a particular person or culture lacks a concept, e.g. that the Greeks had no concept of sin.

8. Wittgenstein seems to speak with a divided voice on the question of concept formation. Although he admits that something physical corresponds to concepts (e.g. colour concepts; cf. Z. 355) he toys with the idea that a different education from ours might be the foundation of quite different concepts because 'What interests us would not interest *them*'. (Z. 387 f.) Sometimes he takes a rather Kantian line: 'The limit of the empirical is concept-formation . . . our way of seeing is remodelled . . . it is as if the formation of a concept guided our experience into particular channels, so that one experience is now seen together with another in a new way' (*R.F.M.* III, 29—33; cf. *P.I.* 104: 'We predicate of the thing what lies in the method of representing it.')

In other places he takes a more empiricist or pragmatist approach: he speaks of the dependence of our concepts on certain general facts of nature (*P.I.* note on p. 56, p. 230), of 'the complex nature and variety of human contingencies' being the 'natural foundation' for the formation of a particular concept (*Z.* 439), of the *deep* need for a convention (*R.F.M.* I. 74), and of a concept forcing itself on one (*P.I.* p. 204). He asks 'Do we have the concepts we have, e.g. our psychological concepts, because it has proved advantageous?' and answers that we do, in certain cases (*Z.* 700; cf. *P.I* 480, where he says that past experience makes us play the game of induction). Although he specifies that the 'grammar' of our concepts is arbitrary in the sense that it cannot be verified, he allows that it may have a point and that it depends on certain facts about the world and human nature which place limits (*Z.* 331, 350; *R.F.M.* V.6: *Moore/Lectures*, pp. 277f; Specht, pp. 172–4). These passages show that it would be rash to follow those who present Wittgenstein as a kind of idealist, treating language as arbitrary conventions which we impose on a formless world (e.g. Hacker, p. 178).

These two different emphases in Wittgenstein's thought parallel what he says about 'forms of life': sometimes he merely accepts them as 'given', sometimes he connects them with facts about the world and human nature (see Sherry (1) pp. 164–6). As regards concept formation, both views have an element of truth in them: concepts are inherited through language and shape our experience; on the other hand, they do change, and new ones arise, not arbitrarily but because of specific factors (again, think of Freud: he introduced some new concepts into our culture, but did so because he wanted to describe or explain certain facts which he had noticed). Now this suggests a middle view such as I have recommended, and indeed it is possible to read such a view into Wittgenstein. He suggests that people might form concepts which cut across ours because some differences which do not seem important to us seemed so to them: they might want to pick out unusual deviations (*Z.* 376–9) or to introduce a new ground of classification (*R.F.M.* I. Appendix ii, 14). They could, for instance, have two different concepts of pain, the first where there is visible damage, the second when the source of pain is hidden, e.g. stomachache (*Z.* 380); or they might have no word for 'blue', but instead use 'Oxford' for dark blue and 'Cambridge' for light blue (*B.B.* pp. 134–5). These examples might be compared with the many interesting actual cases of different concept formation mentioned by Cassirer, pp. 288 ff.: some North American languages have thirteen words for 'to wash', according to whether it applies to washing the face, hands, clothes, eating utensils, etc.; some Arabic languages have a different name for every variety of camel. Such examples of different concept formations are based on observation, in that there *are* in nature fine distinctions between different shades of colour (or kinds of washing or camels). It is just that most of us cannot or need not discern them. K.-O. Apel has remarked in this context that Wittgenstein's work needs to be supplemented by some account of the relation between understanding and experience. He instances Dilthey's 'circulation' between our experience and understanding, and also the idea of the 'hermeneutic circle' (Apel (1) p. 52).

Thus I take it that whilst Wittgenstein denies that reality enforces one set of concepts and language-games on us, he allows for some human uniformity and he thinks that variations depend on our interests, education and purposes, and in some cases facts about the world, e.g. similarities and differences which we pick out as significant. The position with regard to mathematical concepts is somewhat more complicated.

9. See Clifford *passim* for an attempt to show that the Christian revelation makes intelligible and illuminates our experience; and Yandell, pp. 218—26, and Jeffner, Ch. V, for a discussion of this general line of thought.

10. Similarly, many critics of Freud have accused him (perhaps unfairly) of producing explanations which are vacuous because no observable state of affairs could falsify them. They ask, for example, what kind of behaviour a Freudian psychoanalyst would accept as evidence for a child's *not* having an Oedipus complex.

11. Elsewhere I have suggested that Prices' appeal to sanctification can be turned round to provide a *falsification* argument (see Sherry (5)).

12. See also *U.S.* V, §§ 27—35, where Newman speaks of holiness silencing scoffers by its beauty, inimitability and rareness, and of hidden saints carrying on God's work noiselessly, like a chain of beacons being lit.

13. See O. R. Jones, p. 89, for the point that 'holy', 'whole', and 'healthy' all derive from the same root 'hāl'. Similarly Burnaby, p. 145, argues that 'salvation' does not simply mean deliverance from evil: σωτηρία had positive connotations, being used in common speech for health or well-being. Oman, pp. 283—6, argues tha Otto's stress on the 'numinous' component of holiness led him to underestimate the importance of the ethical.

14. Evelyn Underhill suggests that terms like 'transcendent' and 'immanent' can be reinterpreted in terms of the life of prayer and the sense of God's presence achieved therein: 'The inner life means an ever-deepening awareness of all this: the slowly growing and concrete realisation of a life and spirit within us immeasurably exceeding our own, and absorbing, transmuting, supernaturalising our lives by all ways and at all times' (Underhill, p. 13).

15. Von Hügel seems to be doing this when he describes, very movingly, a young Irish girl offering her life to God and for other souls in her last agony: '. . . She died soon after in a perfect rapture of joy — in a joy overflowing, utterly sweetening all the mighty floods of her pain. Now *that* is supernatural' (von Hügel (2). pp. 223—4). A similar move is made by Wittgensteinian philosophers of religion like Paul Holmer who argue that one learns how to use concepts like 'God' and 'salvation' simply by living a religious life. I shall comment on their work in the next chapter: my fundamental criticism, again, is that they do not pay sufficient attention to God's transcendence and to the 'theory laden' character of religious concepts. If it is true that God is *shown* in spiritual transformation, it is only in certain of His attributes.

16. See de Lubac, p. 336, for the interesting observation that the early Christian Fathers introduced pagan cosmological terms as images of the states of the spiritual life. It is also worth noting that they applied

Plato's notion of 'participation' and Aristotle's 'formal causality' to the relationship between God and creatures (whereas Price's approach is limited to God's efficient causality), inspired perhaps by St Peter's remark about sharing in the divine nature. Such notions may perhaps be regarded as attempting to bridge God's immanence and transcendence.

Chapter 6

1. I owe this distinction (though not my development of it) to Brown, p. xvii.

2. Another factor which should be mentioned here is Plato's insistence that certain doctrines should not be committed to writing since their matter does not 'admit of verbal expression like other studies, but, as a result of continued application to the subject itself and communion therewith, it is brought to birth in the soul of a sudden, as a light that is kindled by a leaping spark, and thereafter it nourishes itself'; writing them down would only profit those few men able to discover the truth for themselves (*Letter* vii, 341, C—E; cf. *Symposium* 210E). This aspect of Plato's thought, allied to Gnosticism and Neo-Platonism, helped to produce a tradition of esoteric theology with an emphasis on the mysteries of the faith (see article 'Arcani Disciplina' in Hasting's *Encylopaedia of Religion and Ethics*).

3. Of course other religions besides Christianity have insisted that some holiness and spiritual insight are necessary in order to understand religious doctrines. See Smart (1) p. 112, and pp. 134—8 on mystical knowledge.

4. Bultmann (1) p. 243 compares such appreciation, along with the understanding of history and mathematics, to the hermeneutical understanding of Scripture.

5. I think that one could provide many other examples of a link between moral faults and intellectual perception or understanding, quite apart from the sphere of personal relations: laziness leads to a lack of concentration and observation, and thus to superficiality; pride leads to a depreciation of other people's ideas and to an overestimation of our own; cowardice may prevent a bold intellectual initiative through reluctance to challenge accepted ideas. It would be interesting to apply this line of thought to the appreciation of art: cf. Constable's remark 'No arrogant man was ever permitted to see nature in all her beauty'.

6. Newspaper interview, *The Guardian*, 5 July 1969.

7. An ethical relativist would object that the use of terms like 'sin' and 'holiness' presupposes certain ethical views which may be questioned. My reply is that I am mainly concerned at this stage with conceptual analysis, with explaining the meaning and background of certain religious concepts. Of course, the apologist will sooner or later have to defend his criteria of holiness, but this is a different question from the one which concerns us now. We shall see, however, later on that one's ethical views influence one's views about spirituality and indeed about religion generally.

8. Even within a single religion many different kinds of spirituality and saintliness may be recognised: compare, for instance, St Francis of

Assisi and St Jerome, or St Francis of Sales with St Bernard. It would seem, therefore, that they are 'polymorphous' concepts, i.e. they have many different embodiments. On the other hand, there may be some features which we must exclude in every case, e.g. gross lack of charity. And it may be that there are *some* features which a Christian should insist upon in every case: it is worth noting that when Pope Benedict XIV laid down the conditions for canonisation, he stipulated that there must be a note of joy in the life and influence of the saint. See further Sherry (5).

9. William James argues that our ethical views affect our concept of God: 'When we cease to admire or approve what the definition of a deity implies, we end by deeming that deity incredible' (James, pp. 323—4).

10. Diogenes Allen argues that biographical reasons are a proper basis for the affirmation of Christian beliefs, i.e. that our being 'nourished' by prayer, reading the Scriptures and associating with other Christians, and thereby finding a 'new life' is a sufficient ground for adhering to religious beliefs as true, provided that nothing else counts against them (Allen (1) pp. 111—13). There is a logical gap in his argument, in that he does not deal satisfactorily with the objection that a person may be 'nourished' by a false belief. He merely says that of course we cannot assent to 'any kind of fanciful conviction' (p. 116): Christian teaching and practices are evaluated by the Christian community and continually reformulated. Yes, but what were the grounds for their formulation in the first place?

11. See Moltmann, I. 5, III. 7, V. 2, for the comment that Bultmann and other existentialists are in danger of confining God to man's subjectivity. My own approach does, of course, have much in common with Bultmann. But I have little sympathy with the programme of demythologising; and I wish to avoid his tendencies towards subjectivism and Reductionism.

12. I suspect that the doctrine of the Holy Spirit is the natural starting-point today both for considering how people gain some sense of God's power and for seeing how ontological models are formulated to cover such experience.

13. This is not to say that God's actions must be totally unpredictable. Presumably the ascription to Him of attributes like 'justice', 'mercy' and 'goodness' must at least exclude certain eventualities; and that of 'fidelity' entails that He must keep His promises (assuming that these can be identified).

14. He may perhaps be regarded as giving a modern version of Calvin's view of religious understanding.

15. Incidentally, there seems to be an inconsistency in claiming that understanding and belief go hand in hand and yet admitting that a man may reject religious beliefs because he finds them sufficiently intelligible to know what it would be for them to be false (pp. 142—4).

Chapter 7

1. See Brown, pp. 66—8, 131, for the charge of 'isolationism' often made against Barth. Earlier on I suggested that those followers of Wittgenstein who adopt the 'autonomist' position, i.e. the view that each department of human thought has its own standards of rationality, may

incur a similar charge.

2. Bochenski (2) p. 104 points out that this term, coined by Russell and Whitehead, is an exact translation of the mediaeval *aequivocatio a consilio*.

3. It should be noted that Duns Scotus agreed with Aquinas on many of these points and yet regarded our predications of God as univocal. He thought that 'being' must be a univocal concept, for in all cases it is opposed to 'nothingness'; and if it were not univocal, God could not be known naturally (*Op. Ox.* I iii. 3.9 ff.). Likewise, although he accepted Aquinas's view that in predicating perfections like 'goodness' and 'wisdom' of God we take human concepts, purge them of their limitations and imperfections and then project them, he nevertheless denied that this amounts to making them non-univocal (*Op. Ox.* I. iii. 2.10: viii. 3.8).

I think that the issue between them is to a large extent a linguistic dispute about what it is to be 'univocal'. Scotus adopts a simple logical approach, designating a univocal concept as one which has sufficient unity in itself that it can serve as a middle term of a valid syllogism and that it cannot be affirmed and denied of the same thing without contradiction (*Op. Ox.* I. iii. 2. 5–6). By contrast, Aquinas's definition of 'univocal' is far more complex and, as can be seen from what I have said above, involves many metaphysical issues (see Sherry (4) for a full list of his criteria of univocity). Scotus does not regard such issues as relevant to the linguistic question of univocity: for instance, he agrees with Aquinas that being is not a genus, but he does not think that this makes 'being' non-univocal (Lect. I. iii. p. 1. q. 2 – Vat. ed. XVI, pp. 272 f.). I am inclined to the view that 'univocal' and 'equivocal' are opposites; yet I think that it is worth keeping the term 'analogical' for the middle ground, for concepts which do not fit easily into either grouping, because they are systematically equivocal or because, though univocal, they have different shades of meaning or cover things in a wide number of categories.

4. Of course many Scriptural analogies presuppose Analogy of Attribution: the Good Shepherd is regarded as *loving* and *caring for* his flock.

5. Hepburn has a second and more serious objection, that if we employ the term 'cause' analogically, we rob the cosmological argument for God's existence of its empirical base (Hepburn (2) p. 236). But Farrer ((1) p. 7) admits that he does not want to make a straight causal inference to God's existence.

6. Aquinas gives such an analogy in *De Ver.* xxiii. 7 ad 9: after mentioning the example prince : state :: captain : ship, he says 'as He [God] is related to the things which belong to Him, so the creature is related to what is proper to it'. This is perhaps a good example of a vacuous use of analogy.

7. Cf. Waismann (1), p. 69, for Wittgenstein's saying that man has a tendency 'to run against the boundaries of language'.

8. G.E.L. Owen mentions these passages but goes on to argue that Aristotle's examples do not show that 'exist' has several senses, any more than the difference between the work of a banker and a hangman shows that 'work' has different senses (in Bambrough (1) pp. 76, 93). Duns

Scotus would have agreed. But again, we are faced with the problem of defining univocity: if indeed 'exist' is univocal, then it is not so in the straightforward way that 'octagonal' or 'emerald-green' are. The parallel of 'work' is not a happy one for Owen's case: we also speak of machines and theories 'working', and the latter at least is surely an analogical use (a theory's working cannot be timed, paid, etc.). Aristotle's point of view is worth comparing with what Heidegger says about the differences between *Dasein, Leben, Bestehen, Anwesenheit, Vorhandenheit, Zuhandenheit*, etc. (Heidegger (1) pp. H. 7, 25, 104—6, 194).

9. Strawson's claim that 'material bodies' and 'persons' are 'basic particulars' has much in common with part of Aristotle's argument (see *Individuals*, ch. I, § § 6—7). Strawson argues that they are 'ontologically prior' (pp. 17, 59), since we cannot identify or re-identify other particulars like colours, sounds, and mental states without first identifying material objects or persons. Both he and Aristotle may be contrasted with Quine who describes the concept of a physical object as a 'convenient myth' ((1) p. 18).

10. The term '*analogia entis*', popularised by Suarez, is not found in Aquinas. But he does say '*ens analogice dicitur*' (see Bouillard, pp. 104—5).

11. One might insist that 'to be' is univocal and yet still want to engage in ontological analysis, as Duns Scotus did.

12. That is why I reject Fr McCabe's view, quoted earlier, that Aquinas's use of analogy is merely a linguistic matter. L. J. O'Donovan similarly rejects McInerny's view that for St Thomas the analogy of names is a logical doctrine based on the systematic ambiguity of certain words, on the grounds that McInerny has ignored ontology (O'Donovan, pp. 69—71).

13. Actually, there is a third argument, that of the *Quarta Via*, where Aquinas argues both that there is something truest, best and noblest, and that this Being is the cause of all perfections in creatures, because 'the maximum in any order is the cause of all the other realities of that order' (*S.T.* 1a.ii.3).

14. An obvious alternative lies in the work of Ian Ramsey: he claims that 'models' like 'cause', 'wise' and 'good' (which are modified by qualifiers like 'First' or 'infinitely') serve to give an empirical anchorage to religious language by grounding it in familiar situations (Ramsey (1) p. 61). Yet I think that Ramsey's work lies closer to the traditional doctrine of analogy than he realised: although he presented his treatment of models as an alternative to the Scholastic doctrine he also described his work as a 'possible generalisation of Thomism' (cf. (3) p. 7; (1) p. 185).

Chapter 8

1. Again, I must stress that I am not trying to prove that any particular religious claim is true, but merely to consider what kind of truth we should expect to find within the language-games of religion.

2. Robert Holcot, a disciple of Occam, adopted a 'double truth' theory when he said that 'A proposition may be false in theology and true in philosophy, and *vice versa*' (Gerrish, p. 52; cf. pp. 53—4 for a comparison with Luther).

3. It is worth noting here that the moral sense of 'untrue' or 'false', i.e. 'treacherous', often depends on the ordinary cognitive sense, for betrayal usually involves telling lies and making false promises, that is, saying things which are not true.

4. Jung, p. 129. He is arguing that religious teaching about a life hereafter is consonant with psychological health, because the shrinking away from death is something unhealthy and abnormal which robs the second half of life of its purpose. In general, he seems to evaluate religions as 'psycho-therapeutic systems'.

5. Cf. *P.I.* p. 224: 'The kind of certainty is the kind of language-game." Wittgenstein is making the point that there is a logical difference between mathematical certainty and our sureness about, say, our age or other people's feelings. Cf. *B.B.* p. 28 for different kinds of proof.

6. Laws of nature are a more tricky case: it would depend on whether we were considering experimental or theoretical laws. I think that the former can certainly be handled along the lines of Tarski's or Austin's analysis. The latter are usually evaluated for their predictive and explanatory value and for their fruitfulness in increasing our understanding by simplifying and connecting. The difficulty with ascribing truth to them is not so much that they call for a special definition of truth as that we often cannot, strictly speaking, verify them.

7. See further Mellor on the nature of fiction and literary truth. I agree with his general comment (p. 157) that there are 'different kinds of truth' only in the sense that statements may be classified into kinds according to the grounds of their truth, e.g. scientific observation or mathematical deduction, and that this does not mean that there are two or more *senses* of truth.

8. There is some parallelism between Kierkegaard's rejection of Hegel and his emphasis on the infinite qualitative distance between God and Man, Kant's criticisms of Wolff, and Barth's condemnation of nineteenth century Liberal Protestantism, in that all three are emphasizing God's transcendence.

9. Austin's and Strawson's controversy has been conveniently reprinted along with some other papers, in G. Pitcher's anthology *Truth*. See p. 22 for this quotation.

10. This is suggested by Strawson's analysis of statements like 'What the Pope says is always true'. Surely the analysis 'things are always as the Pope says they are' is very similar to the analysis 'the Pope's statements always correspond to the facts'? And surely it is very different from Strawson's analysis in his earlier paper, where he equated 'It is true that . . .' with phrases like 'How often shall I have to tell you that . . .' and 'It is indisputable that . . .' (Pitcher (1) p. 45) and suggested that it is used to express emphasis or agreement? The fact is that saying 'I agree with what he says' is *not* the same as saying 'Things are as he says they are'. Moreover, if 'What he said is true' meant 'I agree with what he said', then we could not answer the question 'Why do you agree with what he said?' with the reply 'Because it's true', since this would presumably be a tautology. Likewise, it would be inappropriate to answer the statement 'What he said is true' with the question 'How do you know?' if the former

was merely an expression of agreement. These points are brought out by the following dialogue:

A. I agree with what that witness said.
B. Why?
A. Because what he said is true.
B. How do you mean?
A. Well, things were as he said they were.
B. How do you know?
A. Because I was at the scene of the crime and saw what happened.

The essential point is that Strawson confuses the issue by his apparent failure to see that A's first and third statements are not equivalent to each other.

    11. A Hebraism, according to Dodd, p. 174, meaning to practice fidelity or act honourably.

    12. For example, Deuteronomy 13.14, Romans 9.1. See Kittel for numerous other references, and Barr (1), pp. 195 ff., for a discussion of their interpretation.

    13. See further W. Christian, Chapter II, for a discussion of the ways in which religions may conflict with each other. He makes a distinction between 'doctrinal proposals', where different predicates are assigned to the same subject, and 'basic religious proposals', where the same predicates, e.g. 'holy' or 'most important', are assigned to different subjects.

    14. Smart's discussion raises a third issue, that of the epistemological status of 'revelation', mysticism, numinous experience, etc. But I would prefer to make such contrasts a consequence of the different kinds of 'states of affairs' concerned. If there are indeed special modes of religious knowledge, this may be because the beings and events known are of a very special kind.

    15. Creeds may also contain 'performative' utterances, but I shall not consider these since I am mainly concerned here with the 'fact stating' uses of language. In any case, writers like Donald Evans have dealt very fully with this feature of religious language. It needs to be noted that such utterances, like orders and questions, may use special religious concepts, and thus raise problems similar to those raised by indicative sentences. Moreover, performatives and imperatives can conflict with one another.

    16. Cp. Mendelssohn's remark that 'the thoughts expressed to me by a piece of music which I love are not too indefinite to put into words, but too definite'.

    17. *U.S.* XV, § 18. He did, however, realise that it is often difficult to see whether a dogma is a true representation of our meaning, because for instance it is the representation of an 'idea in a medium not native to it, not as originally conceived, but, as it were, in projection' (§ 16). The use of the term 'projection' is striking, reminding one of Wittgenstein but also of writers (e.g. Antonia White) who see religious doctrines as maps of the spiritual life or, to use George Tyrrell's phrase, 'representations in another mode'.

Chapter 9

1. Wittgenstein's views on 'criteria' have aroused a vast amount of comment (see Lycan for a bibliography). Much of this centres round his treatment of pain and sensation, perhaps because his position is least convincing in these cases — whereas he seems to be clearly right about concepts like 'ambition' or 'over-scrupulousness' where the behavioural criteria are uncontroversial. The extent of the application of his views is as yet unclear, though they obviously have great epistemological importance: for, if Wittgenstein is right, in the criterial relationship we have an example of a connection which is logical and yet looser than that of entailment.

I pointed out the difficulties involved in applying his views to theological concepts in Chapter 1: religions conflict in their views of what constitutes salvation, revelation, etc. and indeed about God's attributes; moreover, many religious terms introduce an ontology involving reference to a transcendent being.

2. W. Cantwell Smith, whose views we considered in the last chapter makes a similar mistake, though he is not concerned with verification. He short-circuits the argument, as it were, by jumping from the question of spiritual renewal to that of the truth of a whole system of belief. I have argued that we must consider the individual concepts and judgements of such systems.

Bibliography

Allen, Diogenes
    (1) 'Motives, Rationales and Religious Beliefs', *American Philosophical Quarterly* (1966) 111–27.
    (2) 'Christianity's Stake in Metaphysics', *Theology Today* (July 1967) 185–202.
Allen, R. T.
    'On not Understanding Prayer', *Sophia* (Oct. 1971) 1–7.
Alston, William
    'The Elucidation of Religious Statements', in W. L. Reese and E. Freeman (eds.), *Process and Divinity* (La Salle, 1964) pp. 429–43.
Ambrose, Alice and Lazerowitz, Morris
    Ludwig Wittgenstein: Philosophy and Language (London, 1972).
Anscombe, G. E. M., and Geach, Peter
    Three Philosophers (Oxford, 1961).
Apel, K.-O.
    (1) *Analytic Philosophy of Language and the Geisteswissenschaften*, Foundations of Language, Supplementary Series, vol. 4 (Dordrecht, 1967).
    (2) 'Wittgenstein und das Problem des Hermeneutischen Verstehens', *Zeitschrift für Theologie und Kirche* (1966) pp. 49–87.
Aquinas, St Thomas
    Summa contra Gentiles, Book I (trans. English Dominican Fathers), (London, 1924).
    Summa Theologica, Prima Pars, trans. English Dominican Fathers (London, 1911–).
    Philosophical Texts, ed. and trans. Thomas Gilby (London, 1951).
Aristotle
    Metaphysics, Loeb ed., trans. H. Tredennick (Harvard, 1936).
Armstrong, A. H. and Markus, R. A.
    God and Greek Philosophy (London, 1960).
Austin, J. L.
    (1) *Philosophical Papers* (Oxford, 1961).

(2) *How to do Things with Words* (Oxford, 1962).
Ayer, Sir A. J.
  (1) *Language, Truth and Logic*, 2nd ed. (London, 1946).
  (2) *The Concept of a Person and Other Essays* (London, 1963).
Bambrough, J. R.
  (1) (ed.) *New Essays on Plato and Aristotle* (London, 1965).
  (2) *Reason, Truth and God* (London, 1969).
Barr, James
  (1) *The Semantics of Biblical Language* (London, 1961).
  (2) *Old and New in Interpretation: a study of the Two Testaments* (London, 1966).
Barth, Karl
  Church Dogmatics, vol. II: *The Doctrine of God*, pt 1, English trans. (Edinburgh, 1957).
Bartsch, H. (ed.)
  Kerygma and Myth, trans. R. H. Fuller (London, vol. 1. 1953, vol. 2. 1962).
Bell, D. R.
  'The Idea of Social Science', *Supplementary Proceedings of the Aristotelian Society* (1967) 115–32.
Bell, Richard H.
  (1) *Theology as Grammar: Uses of Linguistic Philosophy for the Study of Theology* (Ph.D. thesis, Yale University, 1968; published by University Microfilms Inc., Ann Arbor, U.S.A.).
  (2) 'Wittgenstein and Descriptive Theology', *Religious Studies* (Oct. 1969) 1–18.
Bennett, Jonathan
  Kant's Analytic (Cambridge, 1966).
Black, Max
  Models and Metaphors (Ithaca, New York, 1962).
Blank, Josef
  'Der johanneische Wahrheits-Begriff', *Biblische Zeitschrift* (1963) 163–73.
Bochenski, I. M.
  (1) *The Logic of Religion* (New York, 1965).
  (2) 'On Analogy', in A. Menne: *Logico-Philosophical Studies* (Dordrecht, 1962) pp. 97–117.
Bogen, James
  Wittgenstein's Philosophy of Language–Some Aspects of its Development (London, 1972).
Bonhoeffer, Dietrich
  Letters and Papers from Prison, Fontana ed. (London, 1959).
Bouillard, Henri
  The Knowledge of God, trans. S. D. Femiano (London, 1969).
Braithwaite, Richard
  An Empiricist's View of the Nature of Religious Belief (Cambridge, 1955).
Brown, Stuart C.
  Do Religious Claims Make Sense? (London, 1969).

Brunton, Alan
  'A Model for the Religious Philosophy of D. Z. Phillips', *Analysis* (Dec. 1970) 43—8.
Bultmann, Rudolf
  (1) *Essays Philosophical and Theological*, trans. James C. G. Greig (London, 1955).
  (2) *Existence and Faith*, ed. and trans. S. Ogden (London, 1961).
van Buren, Paul
  The Secular Meaning of the Gospel (London, 1963).
Burnaby, John
  Christian Words and Christian Meanings (London, 1955).
Burrell, David
  Analogy and Philosophical Language (London and New Haven, 1973).
Burrhenn, H.
  'Religious Beliefs as Pictures', *Journal of The American Academy of Religion* (1974), pp. 326—35.
Butler, R. J.
  (1) *Analytic Philosophy*, Series I (Oxford, 1962).
  (2) *Analytic Philosophy*, Series II (Oxford, 1965).
Cajetan, Thomas de Vio, Cardinal
  De Analogia Nominum, ed. Bushinski and Koren (Pittsburgh, 1953).
Cameron, J. M.
  (1) *The Night Battle* (London, 1962).
  (2) 'R. F. Holland on "Religious Discourse and Theological Discourse" ', *Australasian Journal of Philosophy* (1956) 203—7.
  (3) 'Newman and the Empiricist Tradition', in John Coulson and A. M. Allchin (eds) *The Rediscovery of Newman, an Oxford Symposium* (London, 1967) pp. 76—96.
Carnap, Rudolf
  (1) 'The Development of my Thinking', in P. Schilpp (ed.) *The Philosophy of Rudolf Carnap* (London and La Salle, 1963) pp. 3—43.
  (2) *The Logical Structure of the World*, trans. Rolf A. George (London, 1967).
  (3) *Pseudo-problems in Philosophy*, trans. Rolf A. George (in the same volume as (2) above).
Carse, James P.
  'Wittgenstein's Lion and Christology', *Theology Today* (July 1967) 148—59.
Cassirer, E.
  The Philosophy of Symbolic Forms, vol. I, trans. R. Manheim (New Haven, 1953).
Chavchavadze, M. (ed.)
  Man's Concern with Holiness (London, 1970).
Christian, William
  Meaning and Truth in Religion (Princeton, 1964).
Clifford, Paul R.

Interpreting Human Experience (London, 1971).

Coburn, Robert
'The Concept of God', *Religious Studies* (Oct. 1966) 61–74.

Collingwood, R. G.
(1) *Essay on Metaphysics* (Oxford, 1940).
(2) *The Idea of History*, ed. T. M. Knox (Oxford, 1946).

Copleston F. C.
Aquinas (Harmondsworth, 1955).

Daly, C. B.
'New Light on Wittgenstein', *Philosophical Studies* (Ireland), (1960) 5–49; (1961–2) 28–62.

Danto, Arthur
An Analytical Philosophy of Knowledge (Cambridge, 1968).

D'Arcy, Eric
Human Acts (Oxford, 1963).

D'hert, Ignace
Wittgenstein's Relevance for Theology (Berne and Frankfurt/M. 1975).

Dilthey Wilhelm
Gesammelte Schriften, vol. VII (Leipzig, 1927).

Dodd, C. H.
The Interpretation of the Fourth Gospel (Cambridge, 1953).

Downing, F. G.
(1) *Has Christianity a Revelation?* (London, 1964).
(2) 'Games, Families, the Public and Religion', *Philosophy* (1972) 38–54.

Drury, M. O'C.
The Danger of Words (London, 1973).

Edwards, Paul
'A Critical Examination of "Subjective Christianity" ', *Question*, 4 (1971) 93–110.

Eliade, Mircea
(1) *The Sacred and the Profane: the Nature of Religion* (New York, 1959).
(2) *Myths, Dreams and Mysteries*, Fontana ed. (London, 1968).

Ellis, A.
'An Operational Reformulation of some of the Basic Principles of Psycho-analysis' in *Minnesota Studies in the Philosophy of Science*, vol. I (Minneapolis, 1956), pp. 131–54.

Elton, William (ed.)
Aesthetics and Language (Oxford, 1954).

Engelmann, Paul
Letters from Ludwig Wittgenstein, with a Memoir, trans. L. Furtmüller, ed. B. F. McGuinness (Oxford, 1967).

Evans, Donald
(1) *The Logic of Self-Involvement: A Philosophical Study of Everyday Language with Special Reference to the Christian Use of Language about God as Creator* (London, 1963).
(2) 'Ian Ramsey on Talk about God', *Religious Studies* (1971)

125—40, 213—26.

Evans-Pritchard, E. E.
   'The Perils of Translation', *New Blackfriars* (1969) 813—15.

Evdokimov, Paul
   L'Esprit Saint dans la Tradition Orthodoxe (Paris, 1969).

Fann, K. T.
   (1) (ed.) *Ludwig Wittgenstein: the Man and his Philosophy* (New York, 1967).
   (2) *Wittgenstein's Conception of Philosophy* (Oxford, 1969).

Farrer, Austin
   (1) *Finite and Infinite*, 2nd ed. (Westminster, 1959).
   (2) *A Science of God?* (London, 1966).

Ferré, Frederick
   (1) 'Analogy', in Paul Edwards (ed.) *Encyclopedia of Philosophy* (New York, 1967) vol. I, pp. 94—7.
   (2) 'Mapping the Logic of Models in Science and Theology', in High (2) pp. 54—96.

Flew, Anthony
   (1) (ed.) *Logic and Language*, First Series (Oxford, 1951).
   (2) (ed.) *Logic and Language*, Second Series (Oxford, 1953).
   (3) *Essays in Conceptual Analysis* (London, 1956).

Flew, Anthony and MacIntyre, Alasdair (eds)
   New Essays in Philosophical Theology (London, 1955).

Foot, Philippa (ed.)
   Theories of Ethics (London, 1967).

Foster, Michael
   'Contemporary British Philosophy and Christian Belief', *Christian Scholar* (1960) 185—98.

Freud, Sigmund
   An Outline of Psycho-analysis, revised ed. trans. James Strachey (London, 1969).

Gahringer, Robert E.
   'Can Games Explain Language?' *Journal of Philosophy* (1959) 661—7.

Geach, Peter
   Mental Acts (London, 1957).

Gealy, W. L.
   The Religious Conception of Truth (unpublished B. Litt. thesis, Oxford University, 1966).

Gerrish, Brian
   Grace and Reason (Oxford, 1962).

Gewirth, Alan
   (1) 'Political Justice', in R. B. Brandt (ed.) *Social Justice* (Englewood Cliffs, New Jersey, 1962).
   (2) 'Categorical Consistency in Ethics', *Philosophical Quarterly* (1967) 289—99.

Gilkey, Langdon
   'Trends in Protestant Apologetics', *Concilium* (June, 1969) 59—72.

Gill, Jerry H.

'Wittgenstein and Religious Language', *Theology Today* (April 1964) 59—72.

Glenn, A. A.
The Relationship between Theology as a Special Science and Analytic Philosophy, with Special Reference to the Theology of Karl Barth (Ph.D. thesis, Northwestern University, 1967; published by University Microfilms Inc., Ann Arbor, U.S.A.).

Grant, C. K.
'From World to God?' *Supplementary Proceedings of the Aristotelian Society* (1967) 153—62.

Hacker, P. M. S.
Insight and Illusion (Oxford, 1972).

Hallie, P.
'Wittgenstein's Grammatical—Empirical Distinction', *Journal of Philosophy* (1963) 565—78.

Hamlyn, D. W.
'The Correspondence Theory of Truth', *Philosophical Quarterly* (1962) 193—205.

Hare, R. M.
(1) *The Language of Morals* (Oxford, 1952).
(2) *Freedom and Reason* (Oxford, 1963).

Hart, H. L. A.
The Concept of Law (Oxford, 1961).

Heidegger, Martin
(1) *Being and Time*, trans. J. MacQuarrie and E. Robinson (London, 1962).
(2) *Platon's Lehre von der Wahrheit* (Berne, 1954).

Helm, Paul
The Varieties of Belief (London, 1973).

Hempel, Carl G.
(1) *Fundamentals of Concept Formation in Empirical Science*, International Encyclopedia of Unified Science, vol. II, no. 7 (Chicago, 1952).
(2) *Aspects of Scientific Explanation, and Other Essays in the Philosophy of Science* (New York, 1965)

Henze, Donald F.
'Language-games and the Ontological Argument', *Religious Studies* (Oct. 1968) 147—52.

Hepburn, Ronald
(1) *Christianity and Paradox* (London, 1958).
(2) 'Cosmological Arguments for the Existence of God', in Paul Edwards (ed.) *Encyclopedia of Philosophy* (New York, 1967) vol. II, pp. 232—7.

Hick, John
(1) (ed.) *Faith and the Philosophers* (London, 1964).
(2) (ed.) *The Existence of God* (New York, 1964).
(3) *Faith and Knowledge*, 2nd ed. (London, 1967).
(4) *Christianity at the Centre* (London, 1968).
(5) 'Necessary Being', *Scottish Journal of Theology* (1961) 353—69.

(6) 'The Justification of Religious Belief', *Theology* (1968) 100–7.
Hick, John and McGill, Arthur C. (eds.)
    The Many-faced Argument (London, 1968).
High, Dallas M.
  (1) *Language, Persons and Belief* (New York, 1967).
  (2) (ed.) *New Essays in Religious Language* (New York, 1969).
Holland, R. F.
    'Religious Discourse and Theological Discourse', *Australasian Journal of Philosophy* (1956) 147–63.
Holmer, Paul
  (1) *Theology and the Scientific Study of Religion* (Minneapolis, 1961).
  (2) 'The Nature of Religious Propositions', reprinted in Santoni, pp. 233–47.
  (3) 'Kierkegaard and Theology', *Union Seminary Quarterly Review* (1957) 23–31.
  (4) 'Christianity and the Truth', *Lutheran Quarterly* (1957) 33–41.
  (5) 'Language and Theology: some Critical Notes', *Harvard Theological Review* (July 1965) 241–61.
  (6) 'Theology and Belief' *Theology Today* (Oct. 1965) 358–71.
  (7) 'Metaphysics and Theology; the Foundations of Theology', *Lutheran Quarterly* (1965) 291–315.
  (8) 'The Logic of Preaching', *Dialogue* (1965) 291–315.
  (9) 'Paul Tillich and Language about God', *Journal of Religious Thought* (1965–6) 35–50.
 (10) 'Paul Tillich: Language and Meaning', *Journal of Religious Thought* (1965–6) 85–106.
 (11) 'Atheism and Theism, a Comment on an Academic Prejudice', *Lutheran World* (1966) 14–25.
 (12) 'History and Understanding', *Hibbert Journal* (spring 1966) 114–18.
 (13) 'Kierkegaard and Philosophy', in R. McInerny (ed.) *New Themes in Christian Philosophy* (Notre Dame, 1968) pp. 13–33.
 (14) 'Wittgenstein and Theology', in High (2) pp. 25–35.
 (15) 'Contra the New Theologies', in J. L. Ice and J. J. Carey (eds) *The Death of God Debate* (Philadelphia, 1967) pp. 133–42.
Hook, Sidney (ed.)
    Religious Experience and Truth (London and Edinburgh, 1962).
Hordern, William
    Speaking of God (New York, 1964).
Hudson, Donald
  (1) *Ludwig Wittgenstein: The Bearing of his Philosophy upon Religious Belief* (London, 1968).
  (2) *Wittgenstein and Religious Belief* (London, 1975).
  (3) 'Some remarks on Wittgenstein's Account of Religious Belief' in Vesey, pp. 36–51.
  (4) 'On Two Points against Wittgensteinian Fideism', *Philosophy* (1968) 269–73.
Hügel, Baron F. von
  (1) *Eternal Life*, 2nd ed. (London, 1913).

(2) *Essays and Addresses on the Philosophy of Religion*, First Series (London, 1921).

Hunter, J. F. M.
' "Forms of Life" in Wittgenstein's "Philosophical Investigations" ', *American Philosophical Quarterly* (1968) pp. 233—43.

James, William
The Varieties of Religious Experience, Fontana ed. (London, 1960).

Jeffner, Anders
The Study of Religious Language (London, 1971).

Jones, O. R.
The Concept of Holiness (London 1961).

Jung, C. G.
Modern Man in Search of a Soul, trans. W. S. Dell and F. C. Bayne (London, 1933).

Kant, Immanuel
(1) *Critique of Pure Reason*, trans. Norman Kemp Smith (London, 1933).
(2) *Prolegomena to any Future Metaphysics*, trans. Peter G. Lucas (Manchester, 1953).
(3) *Religion within the Bounds of Reason Alone*, trans. T. M. Greene and H. H. Hudson (La Salle, 1960).

Kasachkoff, Tziporah
'Talk about God's Existence', *Philosophical Studies* (Ireland), (1970) 181—92.

Kellenberger, James
'The Language-game View of Religion and Religious Certainty', *Canadian Journal of Philosophy* (1972) 255—75.

Kennick, W.
'The Language of Religion', *Philosophical Review* (1956) 56—71.

Kenny, Anthony
(1) *The Five Ways* (London, 1969).
(2) (ed.) *Aquinas: a Collection of Critical Essays* (London, 1970).
(3) *Wittgenstein* (London, 1973).
(4) 'Aquinas and Wittgenstein', *Downside Review* (summer/autumn 1959) 217—35.

Kerr, Fergus
'Language as Hermeneutic in the Later Wittgenstein', *Tijdschrift voor Filosofie* (1965) 491—520.

Kierkegaard, Soren
(1) *Training in Christianity*, trans. W. Lowrie (Princeton, 1941).
(2) *Concluding Unscientific Postcript*, trans. D. Swenson and W. Lowrie (Princeton, 1941).
(3) *Journals 1834—54*, ed. and trans. Alexander Dru, Fontana ed. (London, 1958).
(4) *Works of Love*, trans. H. and E. Hong (London, 1962).

King, R.
'Models of God's Transcendence', *Theology Today* (1966) 200—9.

Kittel, Gerhard (with R. Bultmann and G. Quell)

Article on αλήθεια (truth) and its cognates in G. Kittel (ed.)
Theological Dictionary of the New Testament, vol. I, trans. G. W.
Bromiley (Grand Rapids, 1964) pp. 232–51.

Klemke, E. D. (ed.)
    Essays on Wittgenstein, Urbana, Ill. (1971).

Klinefelter, Donald
    'D. Z. Phillips as a Philosopher of Religion' *Journal of the
    American Academy of Religion* (1974) pp. 307–25.

Klubertanz, George
    St Thomas Aquinas on Analogy (Chicago, 1960).

Kreisel, G.
    'Wittgenstein's Remarks on the Foundations of Mathematics',
    British Journal of the Philosophy of Science (1958) 135–58.

Kuhn, Thomas S.
    The Structure of Scientific Revolutions (Chicago, 1962).

Lessing, G.
    Theological Writings, ed. H. Chadwick (London, 1956).

Lewis, H. D.
    (1) *Our Experience of God* (London, 1959).
    (2) *Philosophy of Religion* (London, 1965).

Locke, John
    An Essay Concerning Human Understanding, ed. John W. Yolton,
    two vols (London, 1964–5).

Loretz, Oswald
    The Truth of the Bible, trans. D. J. Bourke (London, 1968).

Lossky, Vladimir
    The Mystical Theology of the Eastern Church (London, 1957).

Lubac, Henri de
    Surnaturel: Études Historiques (Paris, 1946).

Lycan, W. Gregory
    'Noninductive Evidence: Recent Work on Wittgenstein's "Cri-
    teria" ', *American Philosophical Quarterly* (1971) 109–25.

Lyttkens, Hampus
    The Analogy between God and the World (Uppsala University
    Arsskrift, 1953:5).

McCabe, Herbert
    Note on 'Analogy', in Aquinas: *Summa Theologiae*, Blackfriars ed.
    (London, 1964) vol. III, pp. 106–7.

McGuinness, B. F.
    'The Mysticism of the Tractatus', *Philosophical Review* (1966) pp.
    305– 28.

McInerny, Ralph M.
    The Logic of Analogy: An Interpretation of St Thomas (The
    Hague, 1961).

MacIntyre, Alasdair
    (1) *A Short History of Ethics* (London, 1967).
    (2) 'The Logical Status of Religious Beliefs', in A. MacIntyre, R.
        Hepburn and S. Toulmin *Metaphysical Beliefs* (London, 1957).
    (3) 'A Mistake about Causality in Social Science' in P. Laslett and W.

C. Runciman (eds.) *Philosophy, Politics and Society*, First Series (Oxford, 1962) pp. 48–70.
(4) 'Is Understanding Religion Compatible with Believing?', in Hick (1) pp. 115–33.
(5) 'The Idea of a Social Science', *Supplementary Proceedings of the Aristotelian Society* (1967) 95–114.

MacIntyre, John
'Analogy', *Scottish Journal of Theology* (1959) 1–20.

MacKinnon, D. M.
(1) *The Borderlands of Theology* (London, 1968).
(2) 'Le Problème du "Système de Projection" approprié aux affirmations Théologiques Chrétiennes', in Enrico Castelli (ed.) *L'analyse du Langage Théologique, Le Nom de Dieu* (Paris, 1969).

McLain, F. M.
'Analysis, Metaphysics and Belief', *Religious Studies* (Oct. 1969) 29–39.

Malcolm, Norman
(1) *Ludwig Wittgenstein, a Memoir* (London, 1958).
(2) 'Anselm's Ontological Arguments', *Philosophical Review* (1960) 41–62.
(3) 'Is it a Religious Belief that God exists?' in Hick (1) pp. 103–10.

Martin, J. A.
The New Dialogue between Philosophy and Theology (London, 1966).

Mascall, E. L.
(1) *He Who is* (London, 1943).
(2) *Existence and Analogy* (London, 1949).

Mehta, Ved
The New Theologian (London, 1968).

Mellor, D. H.
'On Literary Truth', *Ratio* (1968) pp. 150–68.

Meynell, Hugo
(1) *Sense, Nonsense and Christianity* (London, 1964).
(2) *Grace versus Nature* (London, 1965).
(3) *God and the World* (London, 1971).
(4) 'Truth, Witchcraft and Professor Winch', *Heythrop Journal* (1972) pp. 162–72.

Mill, John Stuart
An Examination of Sir William Hamilton's Philosophy, 3rd ed. (London, 1867).

Mitchell, Basil (ed.)
Faith and Logic (London, 1957).

Moltmann, Jürgen
Theology of Hope: on the Grounds and Implications of Christian Eschatology, trans. J. W. Leitch (London, 1967).

Montagnes, Bernard
La Doctrine de l'analogie de l'être d'après St. Thomas d'Aquin (Louvain, 1963).

Moore, G. E.

(1) *Some Main Problems of Philosophy* (London, 1953).
(2) *Philosophical Papers* (London, 1959).
Moran, Gabriel
    Theology of Revelation (London, 1967).
Mundle, C. W. K.
    A Critique of Linguistic Philosophy (Oxford, 1970).
Murdoch, Iris
(1) 'Vision and Choice in Morality', *Supplementary Proceedings of the Aristotelian Society* (1956) 32—58.
(2) 'Metaphysics and Ethics', in Pears (1) pp. 99—123.
(3) 'Against Dryness', *Encounter* (Jan. 1961) 16—20.
Nédoncelle, Maurice
(1) *La Philosophie Religieuse de J. H. Newman* (Strasbourg, 1946).
(2) Introduction to Newman's University sermons, in the series '*Textes Newmaniens*' (Paris, 1954).
Newman, John Henry, Cardinal
(1) *Fifteen Sermons preached before the University of Oxford*, 3rd ed. (London, 1872).
(2) *An Essay in Aid of a Grammar of Assent* (London, 1870).
(3) *Essay on the Development of Christian Doctrine*, 2nd ed. (London, 1878).
Nielsen, Kai
(1) *Contemporary Critiques of Religion* (London, 1971).
(2) *Scepticism* (London, 1973).
(3) 'On speaking of God', *Theoria* (1962) 110—37.
(4) 'Wittgensteinian Fideism', *Philosophy* (1967) 191—209.
(5) 'Wittgensteinian Fideism Again: a reply to Hudson', *Philosophy* (1969) 63—5.
(6) 'Language and the Concept of God', *Question* 2 (1969) 34—52.
(7) 'The Coherence of Wittgensteinian Fideism', *Sophia* (Oct. 1972) 4—12.
(8) 'Empiricism, Theoretical Constructs and God', *Journal of Religion* (1974) 199—217.
O'Donovan, L. J.
    'Methodology in some Recent Studies of Analogy', *Philosophical Studies* (Ireland, 1967) 63—81.
Oman, John
    'The Idea of the Holy', *Journal of Theological Studies* (1924) 275—86.
Otto, Rudolf
    The Idea of the Holy (Harmondsworth, 1959).
Palmer, Humphrey
(1) *Analogy* (London, 1973).
(2) 'Understanding First', *Theology* (1968) 107—14.
Passmore, John
    The Perfectability of Man (London, 1970).
Pears, D. F. (ed.)
(1) *The Nature of Metaphysics* (London, 1957).
(2) *Wittgenstein* (London, 1971).

Penido, M. T.-L.
   Le Rôle de l'Analogie en Théologie Dogmatique (Paris, 1931).
van Peursen, C. A.
   Ludwig Wittgenstein: an Introduction to his Philosophy trans. R.
   Ambler (London, 1969).
Phillips, D. Z.
   (1) *The Concept of Prayer* (London, 1965).
   (2) (ed.) *Religion and Understanding* (Oxford, 1967).
   (3) *Faith and Philosophical Enquiry* (London, 1970).
   (4) *Death and Immortality* (London, 1970).
Phillips, D. Z. and Mounce, H. O.
   Moral Practices (London, 1970).
Pitcher, George
   (1) (ed.) *Truth* (Englewood Cliffs, New Jersey, 1964).
   (2) *The Philosophy of Wittgenstein* (Englewood Cliffs, New Jersey,
   1964).
   (3) (ed.) *Wittgenstein, the Philosophical Investigations: a Collection of
   Critical Essays* (London, 1968).
Pole, David
   The Later Philosophy of Wittgenstein (London, 1958).
Popper, Karl R.
   (1) *The Logic of Scientific Discovery* (London, 1959).
   (2) 'Philosophy of Science: a Personal Report', in C. A. Mace (ed.)
   British Philosophy in the Mid-Century (London, 1957) pp.
   153–91.
Price, H. H.
   (1) *Thinking and Experience* (London, 1953).
   (2) *Belief* (London, 1969).
   (3) *Essays on Philosophy of Religion* (London, 1972).
Prior, Arthur N.
   'Correspondence Theory of Truth' in Paul Edwards (ed.) *Encyclo-
   pedia of Philosophy* (New York, 1967) vol. II, pp. 223–32.
Quine, W. V. O.
   (1) *From a Logical Point of View* (Harvard, 1953).
   (2) 'On What There is', *Supplementary Proceedings of the Aristotelian
   Society* (1951) 149–60.
Rahner, Karl
   *Theological Investigations vol. 3: The Theology of the Spiritual
   Life*, trans. K.-H. and B. Kruger (London, 1967).
Ramsey, Ian
   (1) *Religious Language* (London, 1957).
   (2) (ed.) *Prospect for Metaphysics* (London, 1961).
Rawls, John
   A Theory of Justice (Oxford, 1972).
Rhees, Rush
   (1) *Without Answers* (London, 1969).
   (2) *Discussions of Wittgenstein* (London, 1970).
Ross, J. F.
   (1) 'Analogy as a Rule of Meaning for Religious Language', in Kenny

(2) pp. 93—138.
(2) 'Analogy and the Resolution of some Cognitivity Problems', *Journal of Philosophy* (1970) 725—46.
Santoni, Ronald E. (ed.)
   Religious Language and the Problem of Religious Knowledge (Bloomington and London, 1968).
Schneider, Erwin E.
   'Die Wahrheit als Zentralbegriff der Theologie, *Theologische Zeitschrift* (1967) 257—66.
Schon, Donald
   The Displacement of Concepts (London, 1963).
Scotus, Duns
   Philosophical Writings: a Selection, ed. A. Wolter (Edinburgh, 1962).
Seeley, J. R.
   Natural Religion, 3rd ed. (London, 1891).
Sherry, Patrick
   (1) 'Truth and the "Religious Language-game" ' *Philosophy* (1972) 18—37.
   (2) 'Is Religion a "Form of Life"?', *American Philosophical Quarterly* (1972) 159—67.
   (3) 'Learning how to be Religious: the Work of Paul Holmer', *Theology* (1974) 81—90.
   (4) 'Analogy Today', *Philosophy* (1976) 431—46.
   (5) 'Philosophy and the Saints', *Heythrop Journal* (1977).
Shwayder, D. S.
   'Wittgenstein on Mathematics', in Winch (2) pp. 66—116.
Singer, M.
   Generalization in Ethics (New York, 1961).
Smart, Ninian
   (1) *Reasons and Faiths: an Investigation of Religious Discourse, Christian and non-Christian* (London, 1958).
   (2) *Philosophers and Religious Truth*, 2nd ed. (London, 1969).
   (3) 'Interpretation and Mystical Experience', *Religious Studies* (Oct. 1965) 75—87.
   (4) 'Myth and Transcendence', *The Monist* (1966) 475—87.
Smith, Wilfrid Cantwell
   (1) *The Meaning and End of Religion*, Mentor ed. (New York, 1964).
   (2) *Questions of Religious Truth* (London, 1967).
Specht, E. K.
   The Foundations of Wittgenstein's Late Philosophy, trans. D. E. Walford (Manchester, 1969).
Strawson, Peter
   Individuals (London, 1959).
Sutherland, Stewart
   'On the Idea of a Form of Life', *Religious Studies* (1975) 293—306.
Tarski, Alfred
   'The Semantic Conception of Truth', reprinted in Herbert Feigl

and Wilfrid Sellars (eds.) *Readings in Philosophical Analysis* (New York, 1949) pp. 52—84.

Thornton, T. C.
　'Religious Belief and "Reductionism" ', *Sophia* (Oct. 1966) 3—16.

Tillich, Paul
　(1) *Systematic Theology*, vol. I, (London, 1953).
　(2) *The Shaking of the Foundations* (London, 1949).

Toulmin, Stephen
　(1) *An Examination of the Place of Reason in Ethics* (Cambridge, 1950).
　(2) *Human Understanding*, vol. I (Oxford, 1972).
　(3) 'Ludwig Wittgenstein', *Encounter* (Jan. 1969) 58—71.

Trigg, Roger
　Reason and Commitment (Cambridge, 1973).

Underhill, Evelyn
　Concerning the Inner Life; the House of the Soul (London, 1947).

Vesey, G. N. A. (ed.)
　Talk of God, Royal Institute of Philosophy Lectures, vol.II, 1967—8 (London, 1969).

Waismann, Friedrich
　(1) *Ludwig Wittgenstein und der Wiener Kreis* (Oxford, 1967).
　(2) *How I see Philosophy*, ed. R. Harré (London, 1968).

Ward, J. S. K.
　'Existence, Transcendence and God', *Religious Studies* (April 1968) 461—76.

Watson, Philip S.
　The Concept of Grace (London, 1959).

Watt, A. J.
　'Religious Beliefs and Pictures', *Sophia* (Oct. 1970) pp. 1—7.

Webb, C. C. J.
　(1) *Problems in the Relations of God and Man* (London, 1911).
　(2) *God and Personality*, Gifford Lectures, Series I (London, 1918).

Weber, Max
　The Theory of Social and Economic Organization, trans. A. M. Henderson and T. Parsons (Glencoe, Illinois, 1947).

White, Alan R.
　Truth (London, 1971).

White, Antonia
　The Hound and the Falcon (London, 1965).

Wicker, Brian
　Culture and Theology (London, 1966).

Wilson, Bryan (ed.)
　Rationality (Oxford, 1970).

Winch, Peter
　(1) *The Idea of a Social Science* (London, 1958).
　(2) (ed.) *Studies in the Philosophy of Wittgenstein* (London, 1969).
　(3) 'Understanding a Primitive Society', reprinted in Phillips (2) pp. 9—42.
　(4) 'Comment', in R. Borger and F. Cioffi (eds.) *Explanation in the*

Behavioural Sciences (Cambridge, 1970), pp. 249—59.
Wittgenstein, Ludwig
   Notebooks 1914—16, ed. G. H. von Wright and G. E. M. Anscombe, trans. G. E. M. Anscombe (Oxford, 1961).
   Tractatus Logico-Philosophicus, trans. D. F. Pears and B. F. McGuinness (London, 1961).
   Philosophical Remarks, ed. R. Rhees, trans. R. Hargreaves and R. White (Oxford, 1975).
   Philosophical Grammar, ed. R. Rhees, trans. A. Kenny (Oxford, 1974).
   Blue and Brown Books, ed. R. Rhees, 2nd ed. (Oxford, 1966).
   Lectures and Conversations on Aesthetics, Psychology and Religious Belief, ed. C. K. Barrett (Oxford, 1966).
   Remarks on the Foundations of Mathematics, ed. G. H. von Wright, R. Rhees and G. E. M. Anscombe, trans. G. E. M. Anscombe (Oxford, 1956).
   Philosophical Investigations, trans. G. E. M. Anscombe, 2nd ed. (Oxford, 1963).
   Zettel, ed. G. E. M. Anscombe and G. H. von Wright, trans. G. E. M. Anscombe (Oxford, 1967).
   On Certainty, ed. G. E. M. Anscombe and G. H. von Wright, trans. G. E. M. Anscombe and Denis Paul (Oxford, 1969).
   Lectures in 1930—3 (reprinted in G. E. Moore (2) pp. 252—324).
   'A Lecture on Ethics', *Philosophical Review* (1965) 3—12.
   'Bemerkungen über Frazer's "Golden Bough" ', *Synthese* (1967) pp. 233—53. (Parts of this have been translated by A. C. Miles and Rush Rhees in *The Human World*, May 1971, 28—41).
   'Notes for Lectures on Private Experience and Sense Data', *Philosophical Review* (1968) pp. 271—320.
Wollheim, Richard
   Art and its Objects (New York, 1968).
Woods, G. F.
   Theological Explanation (Welwyn, 1958).
Yandell, Keith E.
   Basic Issues in the Philosophy of Religion (Boston, 1971).
Zaehner, R. C.
   (1) *Mysticism, Sacred and Profane* (Oxford, 1957).
   (2) *At Sundry Times* (London, 1958).

Index